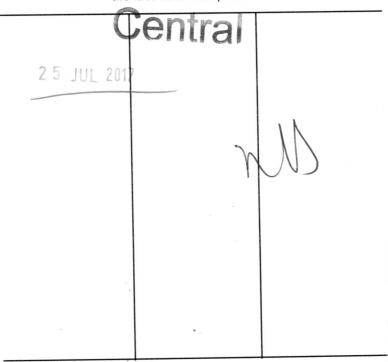

GARY

Also by Sean Smith

Alesha

Tulisa

Kate

Robbie

Cheryl

Victoria

Kylie: The Biography

Justin: The Biography

Britney: The Biography

J. K. Rowling: A Biography

Jennifer: The Unauthorized Biography

Royal Racing

The Union Game

Sophie's Kiss (*with Garth Gibbs*)

Stone Me! (*with Dale Lawrence*)

GARY

Sean Smith

**SIMON &
SCHUSTER**

London · New York · Sydney · Toronto · New Delhi

A CBS COMPANY

First published in Great Britain by Simon & Schuster UK Ltd, 2013
A CBS COMPANY

Copyright © 2013 by Sean Smith

3 5 7 9 10 8 6 4 2

Simon & Schuster UK Ltd
1st Floor
222 Gray's Inn Road
London WC1X 8HB

www.simonandschuster.co.uk

Simon & Schuster Australia, Sydney
Simon & Schuster India, New Delhi

A CIP catalogue record for this book is available from the British Library

ISBN: 978-1-47110-221-9
eBook ISBN: 978-1-47110-224-0

Typeset in the UK by M Rules
Printed and bound by

To Little Bee

Contents

Contents

Introduction:
Gary's Farewell

Halton Royal British Legion Club,
Runcorn, 25 June 1989

It may have been his last night at the club but some things never change. At 8p.m. sharp, Gary Barlow strode on to the stage and played the national anthem. Everyone stood up respectfully as they always did. Some of them sang. Then it was eyes down for three-quarters of an hour of bingo with popular compère Chris Harrison calling the numbers. Every few minutes there were excited shouts of 'line' or 'house' when one of the members had won. Their numbers had to be checked out loud before a new game could start and eyes were firmly down again.

There was a big crowd in and all the tables were taken because Gary was playing solo for the first time in the four years he had been the resident organist at the club. Backstage in his dressing room he had made last checks so that everything would run smoothly. He had prepared all the backing tracks in his bedroom at the family bungalow in Frodsham and had rehearsed patiently and methodically until he knew all the material inside out. He didn't suffer from nerves, or at least he didn't let them show. Chris recalls, 'I've never seen any nerves. I have got to say that was one thing that amazed me about him.'

When he had started playing at the club, aged fourteen, Gary wasn't too bothered about style. He used to wear bits of his navy

1

school uniform on stage. For this big night, however, he looked like a fully fledged eighties pop star – a cross between Nik Kershaw and Simon Le Bon – in a bright white shirt with large black stars splattered all over it, black baggy trousers and a fashionable eighties mullet. He was a non-smoker then, and looked fit and healthy and not like a teenager who spent most of his time playing smoky clubs or shut away in his bedroom.

From the very first minute of the opening number, Michael Jackson's 'The Way You Make Me Feel', two of Gary's qualities were obvious: first, he had a very clear vocal style with just a light vibrato; secondly, he had natural rhythm and moved easily around the stage with some fancy footwork. He may not have had the dance training of his future bandmates in Take That but he clearly didn't have the two left feet hinted at by the pop columns. This wasn't an ordinary performance: it was a one-man tour de force.

Gary's mate Neil Oldfield was off to the side sorting out the sound. Neil, also a talented musician, would later play guitar on the Take That albums. The regulars loved their Gary and he was clearly going to show them what they had been missing during all those nights when he had merely backed some mediocre singers and comedians. It wasn't the usual elderly crowd on a Sunday night but a lively 300-strong audience, ranging in age from those not long out of school to their grandparents. They pushed their bingo cards to one side of the polished wooden tables and settled into the red banquettes to give Gary their undivided attention.

After Michael Jackson, Gary went straight into five songs by Andrew Lloyd Webber, beginning with 'Love Changes Everything' from *Aspects of Love* and ending with 'The Phantom Of The Opera'. The movement from song to song was completely seamless, with pure and precise vocals punctuated by nimble breaks on the keyboard.

It was fifteen years before *The X Factor* would begin on television but if there had been judges rating Gary's performance, their remarks would have been all too familiar: 'There were no tuning issues', 'You smashed it', 'You made the songs your own', 'You could win this competition'.

There's no denying that this was a very middle-of-the-road segment of the performance, and there was a hint of a teenage Michael Ball about his vocal delivery, but it was what the audience wanted. They lapped it up. Next he introduced Neil, 'a great friend of mine', on to the stage to accompany him on electric guitar. Gary sang 'The Power Of Love', the Jennifer Rush classic, with no earpiece, no whinging about noise and no nonsense. It was quite beautiful and, yes, Louis Walsh, he might well have won *The X Factor* with this one song. The big last note he completely 'nailed'.

The audience knew Gary, so good-natured banter came easily. He then launched into a fifties and sixties medley. It was a triumph to remember the running order, as songs slipped from one into the next, let alone the lyrics. He sped through twelve songs, using all his own backing tracks, which he had adapted to his key. It was Gary's own version of a Jive Bunny collection. Songs like 'Be My Baby' by The Ronettes and Neil Sedaka's 'Happy Birthday, Sweet Sixteen' had been hits long before he was born. He ended with 'Sailing', the Rod Stewart classic that was released in 1975, when Gary was four.

As the final chorus finished, Chris Harrison strolled on stage in a casual shirt and white jeans, sporting the sort of Freddie Mercury moustache that was fashionable then. Chris had become one of Gary's closest friends despite a twenty-year age gap and their last number together was a poignant farewell – 'Somewhere Out There', originally a Grammy Award-winner for Linda Ronstadt and James Ingram. In the best showbiz tradition, they pretended it was a spur of the moment duet and not something they had been practising that afternoon at Gary's home. The teenager hadn't mastered falsetto yet, so Chris sang the higher harmonies, while Gary, clutching the mic in his left hand, would pick out a melody on the keyboard with his right. They sang the last line with their arms around each other's shoulders like two old soldiers enjoying a chorus of 'Auld Lang Syne'.

At the end of the song, Gary said, 'Stay here, Chris,' and went to the back of the stage to fetch a gift. This was something they hadn't rehearsed and Chris was completely taken aback when Gary presented him with a framed photograph of the two of them on a January visit to Aber Falls, a tourist favourite in North Wales. Chris was genuinely moved when Gary said, 'Thanks very much, mate.' The picture still has pride of place in his house.

Gary wasn't one to get oversentimental, so it was back to business, informing the audience that they could buy a tape of the songs he was performing for £3. It was an idea that would prove to be quite a money-spinner as he performed more gigs around the working men's clubs in the Northwest. He lightened the mood by announcing, 'It's awfully weird thinking I won't be coming back next week. I'll have to go up Mecca for bingo now,' before launching into a big ballad, 'One Moment In Time' by Whitney Houston.

That ended the first set. Twenty different songs had been tackled. Chris bounced back on stage: 'Mr Gary Barlow – one more bow before you go. Mr Gary Barlow – star of the future.'

Then it was time for another three-quarters of an hour of bingo. Gary didn't call any numbers himself on this particular night but he had been happy to host a session when required during the previous four years and he had always enjoyed it. He never lost the knack: twenty-one years later he brought 'Barlow's Bingo' to the Mandarin Oriental Hotel in Knightsbridge when he hosted a party full of celebrity friends to mark his tenth wedding anniversary. Guests including Cheryl Cole, Alesha Dixon and Mark Owen happily crossed off their numbers as Gary shouted out 'clickety click' (sixty-six) and 'Burlington Bertie' (number thirty).

His final set at the Halton Legion began with Gary trying out some of his disco moves on Gloria Estefan's dance hit '1-2-3'. The first set had been full of power ballads while the audience relaxed with some food. Now his job was to get them up dancing.

Gary was in full wedding singer mode as he moved effortlessly from 'The Only Way Is Up', the feel-good number one for Yazz in 1988, 'You To Me Are Everything', the classic disco hit by The Real Thing, and on to the timeless 'I'll Be There' by The Jackson 5. He clearly had a prodigious ability to learn song after song. He must have got the balance right because the dance floor was heaving all night, whether he was performing a smoochy ballad like 'A World Without Love', one of the biggest hits of the sixties for Peter and Gordon from his mum's record collection, or the singalong Beatles' classic 'With A Little Help From My Friends'.

It was time for another medley that included 'Here Comes The Sun' from The Beatles, which he sang with The Commonwealth Band for the Jubilee album *Sing* in 2012. Finally, he told his audience it was time to say good night – except it wasn't really. 'Do you want a fast one or a slow one?' he asked, before inviting everyone to 'swing their hips' to a string of Bee Gees hits that began with 'Stayin' Alive' and 'Night Fever'. He included 'Woman In Love', which had been written by Robin and Barry Gibb for Barbra Streisand and was a slightly unusual song for a teenage boy to sing. The highlight, however, was 'How Deep Is Your Love', which he could sing in his sleep long before it was the final single when Take That split in 1996.

Perhaps it summed up the audience and the night that he ended with a Chris de Burgh song, inviting everyone to 'Grab a partner for this one' before giving a perfect rendition of 'Lady In Red'. Yes, this may have been a cabaret performance but as a showcase for an accomplished entertainer it could scarcely have been bettered. The audience loved it – and him.

It was time for Bernie Collings, the club secretary, to saunter on to the stage. The enthusiastic crowd on the dance floor was already shouting, 'We want more!' Bernie told them, 'One more we are going to have from the great man,' before standing patiently in the wings while Gary sang 'New York, New York' in the style of a teenage Frank Sinatra. Everyone held hands as he hit every powerful note.

And finally that really was farewell for Gary at the Halton Royal British Legion Club. Incredibly, at the age of eighteen, on his last night there he had performed fifty numbers. Bernie came back to the microphone and wished him well: 'Four years ago this lad came in the club for an audition. He told me he was seventeen. Then his mother rang me and said, "Bernie, I have got to come and talk to you. Gary's been telling you lies." She came in on a Saturday afternoon and said, "Gary's only fourteen." I said, "Oh shit!" So we had to take out a special licence for him to play on Friday and Saturday. He couldn't play Sundays then because he had school the next day.

'Let's wish him all the best. He has got everything ahead of him.'

The Set List

| The Way You Make Me Feel | Michael Jackson |

Andrew Lloyd Webber segment

Love Changes Everything	*Aspects of Love*
The Phantom Of The Opera	*The Phantom of the Opera*
The Music Of The Night	*The Phantom of the Opera*
Jesus Christ Superstar	*Jesus Christ Superstar*
Memory	*Cats*
The Phantom Of The Opera (reprise)	*The Phantom of the Opera*

| The Power Of Love | Jennifer Rush |

Medley

I Only Want To Be With You	Dusty Springfield
Be My Baby	The Ronettes
Take Good Care Of My Baby	Bobby Vee
Dream Lover	Bobby Darin
Happy Birthday, Sweet Sixteen	Neil Sedaka

A Teenager In Love	Dion and The Belmonts
Why Do Fools Fall In Love	Frankie Lymon and The Teenagers
Bye Bye Love	The Everly Brothers
All I Have To Do Is Dream	The Everly Brothers
There Goes My First Love	The Drifters
Sailing	Rod Stewart
Somewhere Out There	Linda Ronstadt and James Ingram
One Moment In Time	Whitney Houston

Interval and Bingo

1-2-3	Gloria Estefan
The Only Way Is Up	Yazz
Can't Get By Without You	The Real Thing
You To Me Are Everything	The Real Thing
The Power Of Love	Huey Lewis and the News
Get Outta My Dreams, Get Into My Car	Billy Ocean
Tragedy	Bee Gees
I'll Be There	The Jackson 5
Can't Give You Anything (But My Love)	The Stylistics
A World Without Love	Peter and Gordon
Stuck With You	Huey Lewis and the News
With A Little Help From My Friends	The Beatles

Medley

Don't You Want Me	The Human League
Here Comes That Rainy Day Feeling Again	The Fortunes
Do You Want To Know A Secret	The Beatles

Gary

Eight Days A Week	The Beatles
Here Comes The Sun	The Beatles
Let's Hang On	The Four Seasons
Got My Mind Set On You	George Harrison

Bee Gees Medley

Stayin' Alive
Night Fever
More Than A Woman
How Deep Is Your Love
Woman In Love
Too Much Heaven
You Should Be Dancing
Jive Talkin'

Lady In Red	Chris de Burgh
New York, New York	Frank Sinatra

PART ONE

The Mozart of Frodsham

1

Lighting the Fire

Gary Barlow wasn't making it up when he told his much-maligned *X Factor* finalist Christopher Maloney that he was his mum's favourite. He admitted, 'My mum and all her friends are voting for Chris.' Coincidentally, Chris is from Kirkdale, a traditionally working-class area of Liverpool down the road from Walton, the old stamping ground of Marjorie Cowan, Gary's mother.

Chris was the second Liverpool lad that Gary guided to the final. In his first year as an *X Factor* judge, he was mentor to runner-up Marcus Collins, who was born and raised in Crosby, five miles to the north of Walton. It really is a small world.

Marj, as everyone calls Gary's mum, is proud of her heritage. If the cards had fallen differently, Gary too might have been a 'proud Scouser'. Although Walton is home to the Everton football ground Goodison Park, Marj grew up supporting Liverpool, whose Anfield Stadium is a mile to the south, and she is still a season ticket holder. It was a golden age for the club, the era of Bill Shankly, and she never tired of telling her youngest son all about those glory days. While Gary could never be described as football mad, he loved to join his family for a game and still enjoys going to a match when he is visiting his mum.

Gary has never played up his Liverpool connection, however. He could have been the next songwriting great in a tradition begun by John Lennon and Paul McCartney, who had been born in Walton Hospital. Instead, Gary became the most famous son of Frodsham, a large village in Cheshire, where Marj and Colin Barlow settled after marrying in Liverpool in early 1967.

Gary was born on the wrong side of the tracks – not literally, of course, but Frodsham is split east to west by the High Street. To the south are the homes of generally middle-class Cheshire folk. To the north lie the council estates where Gary spent the first ten years of his life.

Although his family jokingly referred to the area where they lived in those days as 'The Bronx', it wasn't as bad as the grim urban sink estates and high-rise blocks in the cities. Cheryl Cole, for instance, was brought up in an area of Newcastle where there were a dozen crack dens within a half-mile radius of her home.

Frodsham is nothing like that. It's a bustling, friendly place, the shopping centre for a network of picturesque Cheshire villages. It's also an easy commute to both Manchester and Liverpool and a host of thriving towns like Warrington, Runcorn, Chester and Wigan – all of which Gary would get to know well when he was a young musician playing local gigs.

The place was expanding so rapidly when Gary was growing up that it was upgraded from a village to a town in 1992 and could choose a mayor for the first time. It can now boast much of the window dressing that small English towns possess: a Costa coffee house, WH Smith and Boots, and a Morrisons supermarket on the High Street. There are still independent stores that give the town individuality, as well as quirky tea rooms with an ageing but loyal clientele.

You can't pop out to buy a morning paper in Frodsham without stopping to chat to someone you know. The main part of the town lies at the foot of Overton Hill, known locally as Frodsham Hill. At the top, dog walkers and ramblers can enjoy views right across the

Mersey to Liverpool. The Mersey View Hotel commanded the best position. An adjoining nightclub used to host under-21 discos, as well as popular singles' nights known locally as 'no knickers Fridays'. The Beatles once performed there before they were famous and Gary too played at 'the View' when he was a teenager. These days the site is occupied by a Best Western hotel.

On the way to the View there is a 400-year-old traditional pub in Bellemonte Road called the Ring o'Bells, which is best known as the childhood home of Daniel Craig. The James Bond actor lived there when his father was the landlord in the late sixties and early seventies. Sadly, there is no record of Gary and Daniel ever bumping into each other as toddlers.

Gary was born on 20 January 1971 at 13 Ashton Drive, his parents' first family home. Colin's mum and dad lived around the corner in Clifton Crescent. Ashton Drive is one of those streets that never changes, the sort of road where people pop in and out of each other's houses for a cup of tea. Number 13 was a red brick three-bedroom semi with just enough space for Gary, his parents and his brother Ian, who was three when Gary was born. Ashton Drive wasn't the most attractive street in the world but the houses were neat and tidy and Gary's dad, who loved the outdoors, made sure he kept the back garden looking spruce.

All the neighbours piled into the garden to celebrate the Queen's Silver Jubilee when Gary was six. He recalled, 'There were lots of sandwiches and sausage rolls. It brought everyone together. We watched it on TV and all the mums and dads crowded round getting all emotional.'

Colin kept pigeons, a pursuit as northern as a Lowry painting or a rugby league game on a muddy December afternoon. Gary recalls in his memoir, *My Take*, that his mother Marj hated the birds. The weekly evening meeting of the local pigeon-fancying society was the highlight of Colin's week. Sometimes he would take his younger son along and Gary would entertain Colin's mates with an impression of someone off the television or a magic trick he had painstakingly learned.

Gary's upbringing was unusual for a modern-day superstar in that his parents were happily married for more than forty years. They lived a simple life, socializing with their friends, working hard and looking after the pennies to provide their children with the best possible life they could afford. Colin was employed as a warehouseman at United Kingdom Fertilisers at Helsby Marshes when Gary was born but soon worked his way up to become a project manager.

Gary has never shown anything but honest appreciation of his mum and dad and the efforts they made on his behalf. In an early Take That interview he said, 'I couldn't have wished for a better mother and father really. They never had a cross word to say to each other. Their relationship has made me look forward to the day when I can get married and have kids.'

Like most couples, the Barlows missed the wife's wages while the children were small but as soon as Gary was old enough to start at Frodsham Weaver Vale Primary School, Marj was back out to work. She began as a lab technician at a hospital in Chester before taking a similar job as a classroom assistant in the science block at Frodsham High School. She continued to work there even after Gary became a multimillionaire, right up until she retired at the age of sixty.

Colin did shift work, so he wasn't on hand to help look after the boys during the day. Marj would generally take them to school in the morning but in the afternoon Gary would walk back with Elizabeth and Rod Maddock, who lived across the road at number 20, and play there until his mum got back from work.

It wasn't ideal but it did mean there was extra money for a decent television, as well as holidays to Ibiza and Butlin's in Skegness. The trip to Ibiza when he was seven was the first time Gary travelled abroad and was most memorable for his faltering efforts to attract the attention of a young girl. He recalled the embarrassment: 'I saw this girl I really liked the look of at the side of the swimming pool.

So I decided to dive into the pool, which I'd never done before, and I nearly broke my neck. It was pretty ridiculous.'

Young Gary's love life perked up the following year when he tried his first kiss with his steady girlfriend at the time, Melanie Garnett. It was at dark-haired Melanie's seventh birthday party and Gary revealed his early passion in a book about Take That: 'I was totally in love and we taught each other how to kiss.'

All the time, Colin and Marj were saving hard to achieve their aim of moving their family across the High Street in Frodsham. Gary has always been very close to his mother, referring to her on more than one occasion as 'the boss'. She clearly has a strong personality and, while not a traditional pushy showbiz mum, she was protective of her youngest son and encouraged his single-minded approach to ful-filling his ambitions.

She was very popular around the town. She was always quick to put the kettle on if someone called round and would have a home-made cake or scone ready to go with it. Chris Harrison, who would get to know her well when Gary was playing at the Halton Legion, observes, 'She was very homely, genuine and sincere.'

His metalwork teacher at senior school, Dave Mort, added, 'With Colin and Marj what you saw was what you got. There was no side to them at all. They were very down-to-earth, very local.' Musician John Tedford, who played drums for the teenage Gary, agrees. 'They were fantastic to get on with. If you did anything for them, they always wanted to return the favour.'

The young Gary looked almost cherubic with his pudding basin haircut and a fringe that hung down to his eyebrows. He did have a tough streak, however – perhaps a reaction to growing up in the shadow of a boisterous older brother. Gary was not, according to a former teacher, 'much of a team player'. Instead, even as a young-ster, he preferred pursuits in which he could excel as an individual – none more so than karate, which he took up when he was six and practised tirelessly twice a week.

He proved to be a natural in martial arts, even as a young boy displaying the complete focus and determination you need to succeed. The classes helped him develop two key aspects of his character: perseverance and leadership.

Students begin with a plain white belt and then move through the grades, obtaining different-coloured belts as they improve. Eventually they become a black belt, the ultimate achievement in karate. It's a steady progression – becoming a black belt doesn't happen overnight. Although these days children as young as six or seven have achieved that standard, generally it takes about five years. Gary reached his target when he was eleven, and was proud to learn that he was then the second-youngest black belt in the country. Once you reach black belt status, there are another ten grades or *Dans* to go.

One of the unspoken laws of martial arts is that one should never use one's expertise and training in an aggressive manner. The nearest Gary ever came was when he sorted out the school bully. He told *Smash Hits* that this boy 'was trouble'. He bullied Gary's friends and was generally a pain: 'I thought, "One day I'm going to teach this guy a lesson." He threw a punch, I blocked it with a karate move and broke his arm. I remember the sheer horror on everyone's face. I got suspended for two weeks, so that put an end to that. I was never violent . . . just protective.'

Gary's other passion as a young boy was magic. When he was at primary school he didn't entertain ambitions to be the new Elton John; instead he wanted to be the next Paul Daniels. The magician's corny catchphrases and toe-curling patter may seem hugely dated these days, but in the eighties he was one of the biggest names in British entertainment. *The Paul Daniels Magic Show*, which began on a Saturday night in 1979, was required viewing in the Barlow household.

Gary showed the same single-mindedness in mastering difficult tricks that he brought to learning karate, and it would serve him well when he later turned his attention to music. He never lost his love of magic though.

Dave Mort recalls the day in 1989 when he got married in Chester. It was at the start of Take That and Gary's world was rapidly changing but he didn't want to let down Dave or his bride Sue. 'He had bleached blond hair and was wearing the braces he often wore with his trousers then. I remember that he sat with all the young nephews and nieces and did magic tricks for them. He didn't sing, just did magic.'

While he was at Weaver Vale, Gary didn't show much enthusiasm for music – that would come later. He did, however, appear on stage for the first time in his last year there, playing the title role in the school's production of *Joseph and the Amazing Technicolor Dreamcoat*, the famous Andrew Lloyd Webber and Tim Rice musical. Dressed in a brightly coloured silk robe, he belted out the most famous number from the show, 'Any Dream Will Do', as Colin and Marj looked on proudly. In subsequent years his parents would have to get used to watching their son lap up the applause.

This was the start of Gary's lifelong love of Lloyd Webber's music, and he would later become a great friend and collaborator of the composer. Gary has never lost his affection for *Joseph* and went to see the revival starring Lee Mead in 2007. It resulted in a song called 'When I Need You The Most', which was the stand-out track on Lee's first solo album.

Despite loving his initial taste of performing, Gary didn't see a future on the West End stage. Instead, he wanted to be a pop star, inspired, as so many were, by tuning in on a Thursday night to watch *Top of the Pops*.

He was sitting in front of the TV to watch a particular edition in October 1981 because his childhood hero Adam Ant was number one with 'Prince Charming'. He so admired the flamboyant and colourful singer with the trademark warpaint that he even had a poster of him on his bedroom wall. It was the very first act of the night, that grabbed his attention however, and would have a lasting effect on his musical life.

Depeche Mode were a bunch of very cool guys from Basildon in Essex and were, it seemed, a million miles away from the quiet world of Frodsham. The charismatic lead singer Dave Gahan, for instance, had a chequered upbringing that featured juvenile court for criminal damage and joyriding in stolen cars. His rich baritone vocal was to the fore on their second single, 'Just Can't Get Enough', which was climbing the charts. But it was the synthesizers behind him that had young Gary transfixed. It was the first time he was exposed to this kind of electronic wizardry, known, in those days, as 'synthpop'.

While the swashbuckling Adam Ant's time at the top of the pop tree was short, Depeche Mode went on to become what *Q* magazine described as 'the most popular electronic band the world has ever known'. They have had forty-eight UK hit singles and twelve top ten albums, and featured in VH1's list of the 100 Greatest Artists of All Time with worldwide record sales of 100 million. Their many years of sustained success is a wonderful example for any budding musician to follow.

Adam Ant may have been a poster on Gary's wall but the rest of his bedroom became a shrine to the latest electronic equipment. The difficulty for Gary was that he came from a non-musical family. Marj could play piano a little but they didn't own one. His brother Ian took after his father and was happiest outdoors, not hunched over scales before tea. While his parents may not have been able to offer Gary experience or expertise, they were able to give him encouragement to follow his new interest. They couldn't have guessed at this point that music would become an obsession.

Gary's parents had been planning to buy him a BMX bike for Christmas that year but it was no contest when they offered him the option of a keyboard instead. For the first time the Barlow household was woken to the sound of Gary plugging in his Yamaha PS-2 and firing up the drum machine.

The old cliché about being a natural barely does Gary justice. He was one of those gifted musicians whose left hand could work independently from his right practically the first time he placed them on the keys. He told Piers Morgan, 'Within about two weeks I'd done everything this keyboard could do.'

Gary was ready for an upgrade by the time he reached his eleventh birthday at the end of January 1982. The only problem was the organ he had seen in a music store in Chester cost £600 – a considerable sum for the Barlow family even though both Marj and Colin were in full-time employment. They saw something special in their son, however. His application to karate from an early age was evidence that he wasn't prone to starting something on a whim. 'My dad said I obviously had a bit of talent for playing it, and he sold all his days off at work to buy me the new keyboard.' Colin actually did more than sell his holiday back to the company; he took on extra shifts ploughing for a local farm. His ambition had always been to have his own farm, so it was extra work that he enjoyed.

The past few months had been important for the Barlow family as a whole and not just for Gary's musical development. They finally left 'The Bronx' for the more appealing surroundings of 'Manhattan' or, more precisely, a pleasant bungalow called Ravenscroft in London Road, Frodsham.

Gary left his initials behind, carved into the floorboards of his bedroom at Ashton Drive for the new tenants to discover. He was sorry to move away from his childhood pal Graham Hitchen, who lived a couple of streets away in Hayes Crescent, but on the bright side it was only about a mile to London Road and Graham would be joining him at Frodsham High School the following September.

Their new home, the first the Barlows owned, was on the right side of the High Street. These were the Thatcher years in government, when home ownership was vigorously pursued. The Barlows were an archetypal 'aspirational' family more than thirty years before

David Cameron's speechwriters thought up the phrase 'aspiration nation'.

Ravenscroft wasn't particularly large but it was a lovely, old-style three-bedroom, brown brick bungalow with a kitchen-diner and a good-sized garden begging for Colin and Marjorie's attention. There was enough land out the back to build a conservatory when they could afford it. Estate agents would no doubt have said that it was 'located handily for Frodsham town centre', which was a couple of hundred yards away. It would take Gary five minutes to walk to school when he started at Frodsham High.

Shortly before he left primary school, Gary went for an audition with Frodsham Panto Group, which needed local children to take part in *Jack and the Beanstalk*. Gary didn't get the part of Jack but was signed up for the chorus. There he met a local girl called Emma Cunniffe who wanted to be on stage when she grew up. She is now an award-winning actress and a familiar face in the West End and in television dramas, including *The Lakes*, *Clocking Off* and *Doctor Who*.

Weekly rehearsals were at the Frodsham Community Centre in Fluin Lane, which was practically the next street to London Road. Gary would drag himself away from his new keyboard to join the other children watching the panto take shape. He loved it. When the group celebrated its twenty-fifth anniversary in 2000, he sent them a signed message for the programme of *Mother Goose*: 'Frodsham Panto was my starting block. I look back on those days of auditions, rehearsals and then ultimately the pantomime with pleasure. I loved it all… Good luck to you all for the Millennium panto *Mother Goose*… Love Gary Barlow xxxx'.

While the panto was undoubtedly useful in helping Gary become accustomed to performing on stage and in front of an enthusiastic audience, the most significant thing about it was that he was introduced to the wonderfully named Christopher Greenleaves, who was the musical director and played an all-singing, all-dancing Wersi organ. Gary was spellbound.

Chris recalls, 'Gary and my son Paul were friends and Gary lived just around the corner. He turned up out of the blue for auditions at the pantomime group one year. I hardly knew him but I was struck by how full of confidence he was. Most children are quaking at the knees but Gary sort of bounded onto the stage and did his little audition piece and had everybody laughing.

'He was one year ahead of my son in school and would come round to visit. I had the Wersi organ set up in the house. It was quite a sophisticated one and I could take it apart and put it in the back of the car to take to venues. Gary was fascinated by it and he would have a go playing it. He clearly had some talent.

'At the time I think he had a single keyboard but his mum and dad soon bought him an actual organ, one with two keyboards and pedals, and that extended his horizons a bit. His family are very lovely, ordinary people but he just got this passion for music and it set him on fire with everything he did.'

Many appraisals of Gary's musical life say he was entirely self-taught, which isn't true. Chris was hugely influential. Modestly he observes, 'I'm not a qualified teacher in any sense of the word, so to say I gave him lessons would be overstating it. He would come down to the house for some encouragement and he was such a likeable lad it was good fun for everybody.

'To start with, I would just show him some technique. He wasn't very interested in reading music, but I encouraged him to do that, which he did. I would give him bits of an exercise and say, "Off you pop and go and see what you can do with that." I was expecting it to be perhaps the next day or the day after but, as often as not, he would be back within an hour or two, having mastered whatever it was I was telling him.'

One of the first songs Chris took Gary through was the iconic 'A Whiter Shade Of Pale' by Procol Harum. It has a descending bass line and is the perfect song for a novice to learn how to use the bass pedals. Chris recalls, 'When it came out, it aroused a lot of interest in organs as part of popular music. The organ suddenly took the stage amongst everything else going on in the music scene at that time.'

The Wersi boasted a complicated array of pedals, buttons, stops and drawbars, and the rest of the extras that make an organ such a unique instrument to play. Gary wasn't the least overawed. Chris recalls, 'He made light work of anything like that. He just dealt with all the technology on the organ as easily as anything.'

Most days, Gary would pop in and see Chris after school. At first he was learning and repeating what Chris had shown him but that soon changed: 'He moved away from repeating stuff and he would come back with ideas of his own.'

Gary has never forgotten how important these first musical steps were to him. When he compiled a double CD entitled *Milestones: The Songs That Inspired Gary Barlow* to mark his MITS (Music Industry Trusts) Award in November 2012, 'A Whiter Shade Of Pale' was there – as the very first track.

2

Always Look on the Bright Side

Gary must have been extremely irritating to sit beside in class. He was constantly singing 'Always Look On The Bright Side Of Life', the cult Monty Python song from their acclaimed religious parody *Life of Brian*. If he wasn't singing 'Life's a piece of shit, when you look at it', he would be whistling it.

The song, written by Eric Idle for the closing scenes of the film, is one of those that never goes away – and when it gets inside your head, it stays there. The peerless Harry Nilsson included it in his last studio album, *Flash Harry*, in 1980. Jack Nicholson sang it repeatedly during the Oscar-winning *As Good As It Gets* in 1997. It was a chart hit in the early nineties, when it was sung on the terraces by football fans whose team was getting a sound thrashing. Eric Idle even sang it at the Opening Ceremony of the London 2012 Olympic Games.

Gary Barlow sang it in maths lessons when everyone was grappling with a particularly thorny equation. Giselle Cropper had to suffer it when the teacher decided to arrange the classroom boy/girl, boy/girl: 'He thought we would work better if we weren't sat next to our best friends. It didn't work, as we all just turned round to talk. Gary was definitely better than me at maths and soon got moved up to the top group.'

Giselle didn't really mind Gary singing a happy tune. He fitted in

23

easily at school, and was described by another classmate as a 'proper nice kid'. It helped having a popular older brother. 'Dinky' Barlow, as Ian was nicknamed, was definitely 'one of the boys' at school, a Jack the Lad character who could always be found behind the bike sheds enjoying a sneaky cigarette with his long-term girlfriend, Carol. Frodsham High was one of the rare schools where the old cliché of 'behind the bike sheds' was actually true.

Gary, who, for reasons nobody remembers, was called 'Goose' at school, didn't smoke as a boy or as a teenager, so he didn't join in. In his early years at secondary school, he didn't have a steady girlfriend either, so he didn't wander over to the park after lessons as most of the couples at school tended to do. It was the place to be seen.

Gary wasn't slow or particularly bashful where the other sex was concerned. He took one classmate to see *The Karate Kid* when it came out in 1984. The cinema in Frodsham had closed in 1961 to make way for Morrisons, so they had to catch a bus into nearby Warrington. His date recalled, 'At the end of the film he tried to kiss me but I said I had to go to the loo and ran away.'

Gary's luck would change when he was fourteen. In the meantime, after school he would either be on his way to a karate class with his mate Ian Shepherd or dashing home to practise his music. He wasn't unsociable but he was beginning to lead a double life.

At Frodsham High he was an ordinary schoolboy who kept out of trouble, mostly because his mum was a well-liked member of the staff and there was always the threat 'I'll tell your mother' lurking in the background. Outside of school, Marj, encouraged by the progress he was making, was keen to see just how good her musical son was.

Gary was never reserved when it came to performing. When he was twelve, he appeared at the Overton primary school (Daniel Craig's old school) fair, singing the country and western standard 'One Day At A Time', which had been a number one hit for the

Glaswegian singer Lena Martell four years before. It went down well with the mums and dads, but Gary was about to move up a division.

The small North Wales town of Connah's Quay is one of those grey places where it always seems to be drizzling. It took Marj forty-five minutes to drive Gary there for his first talent contest in the spring of 1984 after he had turned thirteen. In the best showbusiness tradition, they had spotted an advertisement in a local paper, the *Chester Observer*.

The evening was held at the town's Labour Club in Fron Road, an old-fashioned-looking brown building that had been opened in 1968 by the then Labour Minister of Housing and Local Government, Anthony Greenwood. Inside, the club was a thriving social centre for local factory workers, who could enjoy cheap drinks and good old-fashioned entertainment. Nothing much has changed over the years – except there are far fewer factories.

When Gary arrived, he was greeted by Norman Hill, a popular figure who was also the club chairman and doorman. He told Gary that he would be performing fourth on the list. Norman noticed the confidence the young teenager displayed as he settled down to play an unfamiliar keyboard and chatted to the club's drummer, whom he had never set eyes on before.

Gary played 'A Whiter Shade Of Pale' and Norman was instantly impressed. He didn't place him first in the competition, but Gary apparently was 'elated' at coming third. Norman was quick to seize the moment and made sure he spoke to Marj before they left, promising he would be in touch.

Norman also told people at the club that he had spotted a lad with the talent to go a long way in music. One of the bar staff, Vicky Mason, recalled, 'Right from the start Norman said Gary would be famous, but I don't think anyone could have realized how famous – I certainly didn't.'

True to his word, Norman rang the Barlow home and, without any hesitation, offered Gary a job as the resident Saturday night organist in the bar. It was quite a gamble for Norman, who had seen him play only once. Gary had been a teenager for just two months and already he would be earning £18 a week doing something he absolutely loved.

Every Saturday his mother and father would take him to the club and cheer him on. Sometimes it seemed like they were the only ones there but on karaoke nights the place was packed. Gary would cheerfully play standards for the assortment of pub singers, like 'All I Have To Do Is Dream' by The Everly Brothers and 'Feelings', the classic seventies ballad that received a revival when it featured on the soundtrack of *An Officer and a Gentleman* in 1982. These were the sort of songs that would form part of his act for years to come. He had to play two 45-minute sets, starting at 8p.m., with a break in the middle and finishing when last orders were called at 10.30. These nights proved to be so popular that Norman, whose judgement was properly vindicated, graciously gave him a raise of £2.

Vicky soon found herself agreeing with Norman that Gary was very talented. 'Gary looked so angelic then. He would drink juice or Coke on draught and when he wasn't playing he would hardly say a word.' His months at Connah's Quay helped toughen him up for his years as a teenage performer. Gary was never exactly shy but he was a schoolboy in an adult environment.

On weekdays he was still putting on his uniform and going to school, where he studied music just like any other youngster in Frodsham. His first music teacher was the popular and eccentric Norman Davies. One of Gary's fellow students at the time, Emma Stokes, recalls, 'Norman was an inspirational teacher who left at the end of our third year. He was completely bonkers but amazing. He was responsible for making music "cool" in the school. We brought in posters of our favourite bands and he would put them up around the room – often upside down if he didn't like them. He used to make predictions about which bands he thought would go the distance and why.'

Norman would usually begin his lessons with the call, 'Name that tune in three.' It worked a lot better than 'Shut up and pay attention.' It would invariably be a few notes from *The Black Adder* theme tune, which everyone was able to guess because they had heard him play it so often. Norman's offbeat approach might have shocked a few of the more conservative teachers, especially when he got the choir to sing the Easter hymn 'Thine Be The Glory' and then spliced it with 'Sweet Dreams (Are Made Of This)', the Eurythmics' hit from 1983. It was a far more imaginative mash-up than anything *The X Factor* can come up with.

Even more fun than this, Norman started up a gamelan orchestra at Frodsham High, one of only two gamelans in the country at the time – the other was at York University. A gamelan is a set of musical instruments that provide the distinctive sound of Indonesian music, most notably from the island of Java.

It was a masterstroke from Norman, who was able to include many more pupils in this musical endeavour than might have been the case in a small school chamber orchestra. Everybody could have a go on one of the weird and wonderful instruments. There were all manner of gongs, kendang (drums), bamboo flutes, unusual stringed instruments that you plucked and others that you struck with hammers like a bonang, a form of xylophone or glockenspiel.

The class loved it and quickly named it the school 'gammy leg orchestra'. York University, which had much more money, had all the authentic instruments; Mr Davies and his pupils had to set about making theirs. Emma recalls, 'We had some genuine ones but the made ones were pretty cool.' Nothing was safe in the school if it wasn't nailed down: if the canteen staff ran short of a frying pan or two, they might have found them in the gamelan orchestra doubling as cymbals.

Fellow teacher Martin Smiddy remembers watching them play: 'The kids loved it because they were making a noise. It was like the end bit of the *1812 Overture* with all the pans clattering and everything. It really was great. Norman dressed the whole orchestra in Javanese costumes.'

Surprisingly, perhaps, Gary wasn't one of the musicians in the Frodsham Gamelan Orchestra, as they were known; he was a dancer. When the school travelled down to London to perform at the tenth anniversary Schools Prom at the Royal Albert Hall in November 1984, Gary donned what can only be described as a Javanese sarong. Bare-chested, along with his mate Ian, he performed a traditional sword dance in front of the musicians to add an air of authenticity. The dancing looked suspiciously like Gary's karate kata movements.

Apart from Ian and Gary, there were three girl dancers and five singers, including Sara Jones, who was fifteen and sang solo. She had a superb low and husky voice and was considered the best singer in the school at the time. Finally, the orchestra itself was made up of fifteen musicians. The music they played was called *Gending Awan Mas*, which was a suite of traditional and newly composed pieces played without a break.

The introduction in the official programme for the event hoped that the young people taking part would learn 'there is much more to music than four beats to a bar and *Top of the Pops*'. Ironically, Gary's principal ambition at the age of thirteen was to appear on the famous TV show. Still, the Schools Prom was the first time Gary had a mention in the programme for such a big and prestigious occasion, even if it was as a dancer.

Two months before the Schools Prom, Gary had popped along to watch the Frodsham Carnival, one of the big events of the year locally, and bumped into a girl from school called Heather Woodall. She was in the year below him, so their paths seldom crossed although they knew each other to say hello to, especially as Heather's parents lived just a few streets away.

They met up again at an under-14s disco after the carnival and decided there and then to become boyfriend and girlfriend. From then on every morning Gary would finish his music practice and go round to Heather's so they could walk to school together. Heather was twelve and Gary was thirteen. Heather would later describe them as being 'like Romeo and Juliet'. It was young love and they became inseparable – so much so that Heather's mum and dad jokingly used to call her Heather Barlow.

Heather was popular, quiet, pretty and the sort of girl next door nobody has a bad word to say about. Glyn Haslam, a schoolmate, observes, 'She was a proper beauty.' Dave Mort confirms, 'She was a very quiet, unassuming girl. She wasn't exactly in the background but she wasn't in your face at all. She was a lovely girl.'

Heather soon became swept along by Gary's passion for music. She would go around to his house for tea before listening patiently, perched on the bed, while he practised the exercises Chris Greenleaves had suggested or learned a new song for Connah's Quay. Sometimes Heather would join in and they would sing duets together.

Eventually Gary suggested that they should become a singing duo and earn some extra money. At first they were billed as 'Gary Barlow and Heather', which sounded as if they were either a magic act or an animal act. They started off very locally, playing events such as the Harvest Supper at the Union Church in Frodsham. They were the entertainment and tickets cost a pound. Those attending were advised to bring their own knife, fork and spoon. They then decided to call themselves Karisma, which sounded very eighties disco but at least gave Heather equal billing.

Six months after they started going out, Gary and Heather were ready to enter their first talent contest, a local one called Starmaker '85. They wore matching outfits that made them look more like fledgling snooker players than budding pop stars. Gary had a red shirt with a black bow tie and trousers, while Heather was literally the 'lady in red' in a scarlet dress and matching shoes.

Although they didn't make the final with their medley of

Carpenters hits, they still won a £100 prize for being the act with the most potential. Gary had already been saving the cash he earned from playing at Connah's Quay Labour Club, and put his share towards new equipment. Throughout his teenage years he would continue to spend most of his money on his home studio.

The contest did at least get Karisma noticed. Subsequently Gary and Heather played regular gigs all over the area, including Frenchies in Widnes, where you had to be over twenty-one and 'neat and tidy dress' was essential. They had business cards drawn up with little stars around their name 'Karisma' and Gary's home phone number.

Gary and Heather had a rather strange relationship. In Piers Morgan's official book about Take That, written when the group was only just finding fame, Gary is quite gushing about Heather, describing her as the 'love of my life'. He recalls giving her a huge box of presents, including a gold chain, a watch with her name engraved on it and a cuddly bear. He described it self-assuredly as 'everything a girl could possibly dream of from a boyfriend'.

Thirteen years later and she is not spoken of with such fondness. In his autobiography he observed that she had a 'reasonably nice voice', which wasn't exactly praising her to the rafters. He also mentions that some evenings he was so absorbed in his music that he didn't say two words to her before it was time for her to go home.

Perhaps Gary's distinctly unromantic recollection of their time together has something to do with Heather subsequently talking to the *News of the World* about their relationship. She certainly describes him as being 'super romantic' at first, buying her little gifts like a gold bracelet or giving her a tape of his latest home-recorded song.

All the time Gary was getting more serious about his music and, as Heather later admitted, less serious about his girlfriend. He dreamed of owning a Yamaha DX7 like Depeche Mode and Phil Collins but that cost more than £1,000. His mother went ahead and bought it for him anyway on the understanding that he had to pay her back – which he did by taking every gig he could find for the next thirteen months.

He told *Sight & Sound* magazine, 'It was worth it. I used to get in at two in the morning after a gig and then put on my headphones and play until four... I was mad. That was another good thing about the DX7, though: I could play with headphones and not disturb anyone.'

Twenty-eight years later, in 2013, Gary tweeted a picture of the same, much-loved DX7 with the message that he had spent a whole afternoon cleaning up the 'old girl'. The keyboard certainly received more attention over the years than Heather did.

3

The Legion

Gary's musical ability was developing rapidly. Chris Greenleaves was no longer his local mentor: 'He'd quite quickly grown out of any tuition that I could help him with. He was better than me in quite a short space of time.' Chris was able to give Gary a helping hand in another way, however: 'I was the resident organist at the Halton Legion and I wanted to move on from there. They asked me if I knew anybody. I said I did but he was still at school and I didn't know if it was going to be permissible.'

Gary had to go along and play in front of some of the club's committee, including Bernie Collings and concert secretary Jimmy Gill. It was the latter's job to make sure everything at the club was top notch so that his members had an entertaining evening. The post of resident organist was therefore an important one.

Gary arrived after school with his father. The club's drummer, John Tedford, was already there, although he thought it was Colin who had come to audition: 'I was up on stage tuning my kit up when Gary got up and started playing the Hammond organ we had there at the time. I turned around and said, "Don't touch that, son! It's a dear piece of equipment." He must have been fourteen. And then Jimmy came up and said the lad had come for an audition, so I just looked and thought, "Oh . . . right."

'So he got his music out and started playing. He said to me, "Is there anything you want me to play?" And I said, "No, just play what you know." And he did and we seemed to gel instantly. He was very, very good. He knew exactly what he was doing. Then we started throwing different songs into the mix, seeing how far we could push each other, so instead of it being a twenty-minute audition, it ended up being about one and a half hours! Jimmy, who was a happy-go-lucky lad, just looked at me and we didn't have to come off and have a discussion about it. I gave him a wink as if to say "this is the one".'

John, who was always smartly turned out, was in his thirties at the time and had twenty years' experience in the local music scene, playing in bands like The Lonely Hearts Duo and The Little Men. He was more like a well-nourished Ringo Starr than a wild man of the drums like Keith Moon. John knew all the popular old songs that the Legion's members wanted to hear; Gary needed to learn them but that was no problem. 'He was like a sponge,' recalls John. 'He just soaked everything up that was there.'

During the day, John worked for a car dealership in Runcorn, where he lived with his wife Linda and their family. He never sold Gary a car but he did sell Colin and Marj a new Ford Escort. On Wednesdays after work he would drive over to the club for a practice session with Gary. One of the reasons they were so accomplished at the weekends was they put the hours in rehearsing during the week. Sometimes they had musical evenings at John's house but usually they had the stage to themselves at the Halton Legion when Gary finished school.

Anyone popping into the club for a drink after work on a Wednesday could have enjoyed hearing Gary Barlow running through his collection of classics. Gary loved to learn new songs and was addicted to buying songbooks. John recalls, 'He'd see a song-book and he would buy it. He would go, "Do you know this one?" and I'd say, "Yeah, I know that one." And he would say, "Well, let me try it." And he would just do it. He was so enthusiastic.

'He used to play all the Barry Manilow songs. He enjoyed playing those because his voice was suited to them. But he used to play more modern stuff as well – like the Pet Shop Boys.'

If anyone asked Gary for a particular song after they had finished their set, he would make a note and tell John, 'We will learn that one.' And they did. At their rehearsals he would produce a list and make sure they could play all the songs the following weekend. John observes, 'That's the reason he was so well liked there.'

The club was a step up from Connah's Quay in that it was much bigger and had a large stage with proper lighting and plush red seats. The crowds at weekends when Gary was hired to play could be five times those at the Labour Club – 300 or so on a Sunday evening. One of the first things Gary did was persuade them that Karisma should have a spot when the night's headliner, usually a comedian, was taking a break. Chris went to see how he was getting on and was impressed: 'His singing had improved spectacularly.'

Gary was intent on forging ahead, fuelled with an ambition to be a famous musician. Heather didn't share that dream. She later explained, 'One night I said I didn't want to keep singing. I didn't like that kind of life. He was very angry and said he intended to continue alone whether I liked it or not. I realized that music was the most important thing for Gary – even more than me.'

The situation was made more complicated by the concerns of Heather's mum and dad. In the beginning, the youngsters' devotion to one another was sweet, young love but it became increasingly clear that she was besotted with him and her parents were worried it was harming her future.

The teenagers agreed to see less of one another, although Heather still went to many of Gary's gigs, especially the ones after school. He admitted that things were never the same between them after the age of fifteen. Heather will always be Gary's 'first love', however.

★

Halton Legion was, as John Tedford puts it, 'the smokiest club going'. He and Gary hated that but it was good money and they both loved performing. Each of them could pick up as much as £120 a night for playing Friday, Saturday and Sunday. The routine was that either Colin or Marj would take Gary to the club and John would give him a lift home. It was only an extra ten minutes out of his way: 'We used to get out of the club and sit in the car and say, "Ugh, we stink of smoke."'

Whenever there was a break during the evening, they would step outside for some fresh air. John would have a pint of bitter and some bacon fries. Gary would sip a Ribena or orange juice, which he preferred to Coke at the time, and eat a packet of bacon fries. He would often take a notebook out with him to jot down ideas and would ask the drummer's opinion of any new melody he was working on.

John was like another big brother to Gary then. He could appreciate Gary's talent and would advise him about the pitfalls of the music business: 'I always told him to get it written down and never to go on a handshake – and to be very wary. There are a lot of sharks out there.' It was good advice that Gary wouldn't always follow.

The two musketeers became three when Chris Harrison joined the Halton Legion. The first time Chris set eyes on Gary all he could see was a little head poking out from above a giant organ. It was June 1986. Gary was now fifteen and, relatively speaking, an old hand at the club. Chris had heard there was a job going as resident compère. One of the committee members had heard him singing with his group The Christopher Three in Liverpool and suggested he pop down to the club to take a look at the set-up.

'It wasn't that much money but the girl I was living with said I might as well go. I saw this brilliant keyboard player, who turned out to be Gary, and the drummer, John. I was told that the guys rehearsed on a Wednesday night and that, if I was interested, I should come down and bring some music. I remember introducing

Gary

myself to them both, handing them some music and Gary just started playing. He was quite happy.'

Between songs, Gary turned to Chris and asked, 'Are you going to start?'

Chris replied, 'They want me to start Friday if everything goes OK tonight.'

Gary, in his customary direct manner, said, 'Oh, we're going to be great together.'

'I was in my thirties at the time, about the same age as John, which was relatively young compared to what had gone before at the club, but Gary was ahead of his time for a fifteen-year-old. His voice was very mature for someone of that age, but I remember that it was his musical knowledge that was so impressive. My music had been written by a proficient music writer for me to use as a solo performer. Gary unfolded it and said, "Hey, this is great," and started using musical terms at fifteen that I didn't know.'

Chris had stipulated when he was hired that he wasn't going to call any bingo but that was soon ignored – they both had to do it. Gary didn't mind. He had been working at the club for more than a year and was entirely comfortable in the setting. He wasn't hesitant about telling the older men exactly what they needed to do on stage.

The following Sunday, Chris was given an insight into the level of commitment Gary had. One of the club members came up to Gary after lunch and asked him if he knew 'In Your Eyes', a romantic hit for George Benson. 'All Gary said was "I like that song". He went home at about 2.45. By the time he came back at 7.30 he had learned the song, written it out in his own key and he sang it that night . . . perfectly. It was amazing he could learn stuff so quickly.'

Gary and Chris began to build up a store of club favourites that they would dip into, depending on how much time there was between bingo and the visiting comedy acts. Chris always liked their versions of 'I Can See Clearly Now', the much-covered Johnny Nash

hit of the seventies, and 'I'm A Song' by Neil Sedaka. They also used
to do a rock and roll medley that began with 'Roll Over Beethoven'
and ended with 'I Saw Her Standing There'.

Chris was a big hit at the club. The regulars loved his mischievous
good humour and he had the knack of making Gary smile. John
observes, 'He was a very colourful person in both character and
dress. All of a sudden he would come out of the dressing room in
bright yellow trousers. Gary and I used to chuckle. He gave us a
good tickle.'

Besides his flamboyance, Chris was also a natural entertainer and
started to introduce some comedy into their spots. While Gary sang
'Eye Of The Tiger', the theme from *Rocky III*, Chris would run
round the stage taking his shirt off. When Chris was crooning
'Singin' In The Rain', someone would sneak onto the stage and
throw a bucket of water over him.

These hijinks reveal the point of the Halton Legion and many
other clubs in the Northwest where Gary would perform as a
teenager: they were places for family entertainment, for men and
women old and young, who could enjoy bingo, comedy, some good
value drinks and wholesome grub. Then there was time for a bit of
a dance before heading home.

Gary enjoyed the comedy and since the early days at Connah's
Quay had worked hard on his banter with the audience. At the club,
he provided the musical accompaniment for many household
names, including Russ Abbot, Jim Davidson and Bob Monkhouse,
but he particularly admired the best local acts, like Jackie Hamilton,
the legendary Liverpool stand-up who had made his name on the
ITV show *The Comedians* in the seventies.

Jackie had been born in Scotland Road, Liverpool, a couple of
miles from where Marj Barlow grew up in Walton. He was the quint-
essential Scouse comic, a revered figure until his death, aged
sixty-five, in 2003. One of his old comic partners, Micky Finn, who
was also born in Scotland Road, was another favourite of Gary's. A

third was the late Eddie Flanagan, a master of his craft. 'He could take fifteen minutes to tell one joke and you wouldn't be able to stop laughing for that fifteen minutes,' said actor Ricky Tomlinson, who was a good friend.

Occasionally, Gary would record these greats while he sat on stage, patiently waiting in case he was needed for some musical accompaniment. Then he could play the tape back in the comfort of his bedroom and laugh again.

It's often been mistakenly written that Gary began his career in Ken Dodd's band. The king of Liverpool comedy for half a century did play Halton Legion occasionally. He is one of the very few that Gary does not remember with much affection, though, because looking after Ken was hard work. He would meander from his script for up to an hour at a time and Gary and John would be poised, hanging on the master entertainer's every word for fear they might miss the cue to go into the next song.

Gary was so immersed in his life at the Legion that it's easy to forget how young he was. He spent more time with Chris and John than anyone of his own age and that probably included Heather. John says simply, 'She wasn't around a lot.'

Chris Harrison observes, 'Socially he was a normal fifteen-year-old. We used to go walking up Frodsham Hill looking for squirrels or driving off to hunt for a McDonald's – there wasn't one in Frodsham – and things like that. But on stage, when he got behind the keyboard, he could be very authoritative – shouting to the drummer, "One, two, three, four."

'I always felt he was in charge on stage even at that age. I think the karate had a lot to do with it. It had given him an assurance. In some ways on stage he was sort of expressing his prowess as a karate expert.'

Gary finally gave up karate in favour of badminton and squash after he broke his finger. He didn't want to threaten his musical future with another injury. He already had a scar on his left cheek from demonstrating a karate move and forgetting he was holding a knife in his hand.

He could now devote even more time to his passion. Occasionally he would take in a song for Chris Harrison to listen to. 'One time he came out on stage clutching a piece of paper and he said, "Chris, I've just written this song. Any chance of singing it?" And I said, "Yes, no problem." So I got on the mic and I said, "Ladies and gentlemen, can you please be quiet. Gary has written this song and I want you all to listen to him while he sings it and plays it and directly after that I want a massive applause." So he puts the paper up and I remember he blew on the mic, which he always did, and he started to sing, "Put your head against my life, what do you hear . . ."'

It was the first public performance of 'A Million Love Songs' and the Halton Legion did indeed give it a massive round of genuine applause.

4

Batch 13

Gary was never reluctant to share his earliest compositions. Heather had a selection. His form teacher Martin Smiddy has a pile of old cassette tapes tucked away safely in the study of his house in Frodsham that contain more than one hundred original Gary Barlow compositions. Just four of them have ever been released for the ears of the general public but they are four of his finest and most famous songs. He was only fifteen when he wrote 'Babe', 'Open Road', 'Why Can't I Wake Up With You' and the evergreen 'A Million Love Songs'. When Gary originally wrote the song in his bedroom in the bungalow in London Road, he called it '1 Million Love Songs Later' and included it on a tape which, in his no-nonsense way, he called 'Batch 13'.

Martin is very proud of his contribution to that classic. At the time he and his wife Kate were living close to the Ring o'Bells pub. When Gary had written some new songs, he would walk up with Heather, pop into the newsagents to buy some of his favourite Coconut Boost bars for everyone and ring Martin's doorbell. 'We would put the tape on, listen to it and pass opinions on things,' recalls Martin. 'And I would always say, "Well, it could do with a bit of a sax break on here" and I would get my Isaac Hayes LP out and play him this one track all the time, which had a brilliant sax break on it . . . and he would roll his eyes. So when some years later I heard it on the radio with the saxophone intro, I went, "Yeah!"'

The same year he wrote 'A Million Love Songs', Gary wrote another song, which, at the time, was much better known and also employed a saxophone for the introduction. 'Let's Pray For Christmas' was his entry for an annual BBC *Pebble Mill* competition to find a new seasonal song for 1986.

Norman Davies had left Frodsham High School by this stage and been succeeded by Val Mason, who made an immediate impression by the individual way she dressed for school. Emma Stokes recalls, 'I loved her dress style. She would wear a cerise blouse with cerise tights or jade shirts with jade tights. I had tights envy!

'She was a very encouraging and warm teacher who took a real interest in all pupils who demonstrated any talent. She encouraged Gary to enter *A Song For Christmas*.'

Val had already identified Gary as having an extraordinary gift for music: 'The moment he put his hands on the piano and started singing there was something special. I could tell that what I had in front of me wasn't an ordinary pupil; this was somebody who did have an incredible talent.'

Gary had to compose at school as part of his music O level. Emma confirms, 'He was the best composer in our music class by a long chalk – although we all gave it a go. He had an amazing natural talent and just sat down and composed effortlessly. The rest of us took hours over it.'

Gary threw himself into the task of writing a song that Cliff Richard would be proud of. He made several attempts, including 'Christmas Everywhere', 'He Was Jesus Christ', which had the flavour of 'A Whiter Shade Of Pale' about it, and 'It's Christmas Today'. He eventually settled on a ballad, the simply titled 'Let's Pray For Christmas', even though Marj thought it was far too miserable for Christmas. His music teacher loved it, however, and sent it straight off to the judges.

Gary

Marj may not have been keen but the competition judges liked it enough to invite Gary down to the Pebble Mill Studios in Birmingham to sing it in the semi-final of the competition. First of all, though, he had to go to the producer's studio in London, West Heath Studios in West Hampstead, to make a recording of the song that he could then mime to on television. It was the first time he experienced the thrill of being in a studio and hearing one of his songs become a record. He loved it.

The producer, Bob Howes, was always there to give him advice in the early days of his music career. Twenty years after they first met, they formed BHK Media, along with the renowned Sheffield-based songwriter Eliot Kennedy, writer of many Spice Girls hits and one of Gary's longest-standing friends and collaborators.

The semi-final was a fun day out. The first thing Gary did was go to the canteen and grab a handful of paper cups with 'BBC' written on the side so he could take them back to school to prove to his class-mates he had really been there.

Martin Smiddy and Dave Mort were among the teachers who went to support him. Martin recalls, 'Marj said, "Oh, he's down at Pebble Mill." So a bunch of us went down to support him in the semi-final. And then he made it through to the final and we went down again the next day. So that made us all pretty close – the fact that we had made the effort to go down twice. Marj always appreci-ated that.'

The final was introduced by Phillip Schofield, who looked about twelve and had dark hair. Gary, wearing a fluffy pink sweater and a New Romantic-style white scarf, had to stand in front of a giant Christmas tree complete with fake snow and sing to a studio audi-ence and a panel of judges. Gary was now a practised performer and there was no sign of a shaky microphone as he smiled and looked sincere. At the end, he beamed, knowing he had delivered a faultless performance. Phillip was impressed: 'Well done, Gary. Fifteen years old – what a stunning voice.'

The judges agreed and called 'Let's Pray For Christmas' a first-rate song: 'Gary's delivery of it was tremendous and he is a very good singer.' The competition was about finding a new Christmas song. If it had been about the performance, then Gary might well have won; instead he came second. 'Let's Pray For Christmas' is a song that deserves a big production and the Military Wives would have a number one single if they recorded it now – and so would Cliff.

Gary's performance was dusted off during the 2012 series of *The Xtra Factor* to raise a few chuckles. It's not a song that features in his repertoire these days. He did sing it a few times at school assemblies but never at the Halton Legion. At the Christmas assembly, he also brought along a pile of cassette tapes featuring the recording from West Heath Studios and invited his fellow pupils to purchase one for 50p.

Martin and his gang of supporters thought it counted against Gary that a young male soloist had won the previous year's competition. He observed, 'The cards were stacked against him.' Val Mason, who had married and become Mrs Nelson, remembered that he didn't seem at all upset about not winning.

Meeting Bob Howes and visiting his studio had a much longer-lasting effect on Gary than the competition itself. Chris Greenleaves, who still took a keen interest in the career of his young protégé, observed, 'The competition got him in contact with some big names and some big talents. Gary was good at getting people to encourage him. He had got his foot in the door now with the professional music scene.'

In his last year at school Gary was doing more gigs than ever, building his playlist of songs as well as writing his own. At weekends his mum and dad would usually drive him but during the week he often relied on Dave Mort.

The pair had become friends when Gary worked on a metalwork project: 'He had built a stand for his keyboard and also his computer, which was new technology at the time. I helped him carry it across the road to his home about half a mile away. We set it up and he gave me instructions on how to use all the stuff he had there.

'It was all musical equipment that I certainly didn't expect to see. He gave me a demonstration of computerized music, which I didn't know about them. He said, "Say hello into this, Dave, and I can make you sing" – which he did.'

Dave was very impressed and, later, when he heard Gary play at a friend's birthday party, he offered to help fix him up with a few local gigs and act as his driver. As a result, Gary played some weekday nights in popular pubs like the Boot Inn and the Royal Oak in Kelsall, and the Abbey Arms in Delamere. Dave's parents lived in Kelsall, which is about ten miles from Frodsham, so he was able to call on local support, especially when Gary played the Village Institute.

Heather would usually come as well and she and Dave would dance in front of Gary to try to get everybody in a fun mood. He observes, 'I would say that 25 per cent listened and 75 per cent carried on drinking because it was the village pub. They were there to go out for a pint and maybe have a meal and Gary was the music in the background. Sometimes it would be: "Can you turn the music down, Gary? It's a bit loud."'

Gary would usually pick up about £30 for the evening and, as part of the deal, he would go to the back door of the metalwork room and slip Dave forty John Player Specials for driving him. Gary still wasn't smoking but he was a thrifty lad and had probably worked out where he could get the best deal on cigarettes.

Even his sceptical classmates were beginning to realize that Gary was going places, although most of them thought he would end up a crooner like Barry Manilow. Emma Stokes recalls he was by far the best musician of his year. She shared the music prize with him in Year 10: 'They couldn't have Gary winning everything – they needed to enthuse the rest of us a little.' Needless to say, Gary sailed through his O-level music.

Martin Smiddy was Gary's form tutor during his fifth year at

Frodsham High. Each week he would have an hour with the pupils to discuss current affairs or personal and social development skills. He still chuckles at the occasion he decided to talk about pocket money: 'I was going round the class, as you do, asking the kids what they did for it. So it was walk the dog, wash the car, clean the dishes, keep their bedroom tidy – all that sort of stuff for a quid or two. When we got to Gary, he said he had to earn his but he got £200 from the Linnets Club, which is Runcorn FC's social club, when he used to play his organ down there. And that's what he did. It was quite funny at the time.'

Gary was also earning as much as £120 a night for three nights a week at the Halton Legion, as well as the various gigs he would do with Dave Mort and others during the week. He was earning more than his young music teacher, Val Nelson. He wasn't completely mercenary, however. He sang at a birthday party for Martin Smiddy's mother at the Frodsham Conservative Club. Martin's father also fixed it for him to perform at the Frodsham Golf Club. At this stage, Gary saw himself as some sort of all-round entertainer and, rather than just play and sing, he would try to engage the audience with some banter and a few jokes. After a particularly ill-judged joke about Chanel perfume, the general consensus at the golf club was that he should stick to the music.

Gary's bank balance was about to become even healthier. He and John were leafing through the local paper, the *Runcorn & Widnes Weekly News*, during a break at the Halton Legion, when they noticed an advertisement to find the new Club Act of the Year. The competition was sponsored jointly by the paper and the Greenall Whitley brewery, which was based in nearby Warrington. The first prize was a more than attractive £500. 'Do you fancy it?' asked John. 'No, no,' came the less than enthusiastic reply from the keyboard player.

John decided to ignore Gary and sent off the application forms anyway. He received a favourable reply: they were in. Gary had forgotten all about it when a few weeks later he was told to keep

Tuesday night free. He agreed, 'if you think we can do it'. John was confident: 'We can do it, mate, no problem.'

John had entered them as Stax, which was a name he had used often. Many years before, he had been putting a band together with his cousin, Arthur Kerrivan, who was a hugely respected lead guitarist in Liverpool from the sixties onwards in a band called Cy Tucker and the Friars. They were discussing what to call themselves one evening when they were stacking up equipment before a gig. 'I just went, "What are we doing now? We're stacking. Let's call ourselves Stax."' At least it was a better name than Karisma.

The competition was a bit like *The X Factor* in that Stax had to battle through six rounds before they reached the grand final at the Ball O'Ditton Royal British Legion Club in Widnes. Gary had swapped the black bow tie he wore in Karisma in favour of a white one with a turquoise silk shirt. John wore the same. They weren't the favourites; another local group, Fizzy Drinks, was expected to win.

This wasn't a contest in which you sang one song and hoped for the best: the contestants had to perform for half an hour. Stax began with the rock anthem 'The Final Countdown' before moving on to The Commodores' romantic ballad 'Three Times A Lady', one of Gary's tunes called 'So Hard Being Alone', 'My Life' by Billy Joel, 'Suddenly', which had been a hit for Olivia Newton-John and Cliff Richard, before closing with Barry Manilow's party favourite 'Copacabana'. It went well but they didn't know they were the winners until the announcer called out that Fizzy Drinks had finished second – Stax had won by a single point. John recalls, 'Everyone thought they had won but when we all realized it was Stax, the roof was lifted off the place.'

They picked up the trophy, which John still has, and then had to go back on to perform a rockin' version of 'Eye Of The Tiger' and a reprise of 'My Life'. John recalls, 'They were all shouting for that one.' It was a great night and the first time Gary had ever won a competition.

He didn't have long to wait for the second success. He wrote a song called 'Now We're Gone' for the National Schools Make Music Competition, sponsored by EMI. He came first out of thousands of entries and, besides winning a lot of musical equipment for his school, was invited to the world famous Abbey Road Studios in St John's Wood where The Beatles had recorded many of their songs. The prize was to watch as the single was recorded.

The headmaster of Frodsham High, Robin Browne, couldn't go, so he asked Martin Smiddy to stand in for him. Martin travelled down on the train with Colin and Marj and Gary's beloved grandmother Nan Bo, who lived in Widnes. She was a wonderful lady, a real character, who would have been waiting in the wings to give her grandson a big hug if he had been a contestant on *The X Factor* or *Britain's Got Talent*. Gary adored her and dedicated his autobiography to her. Martin took loads of pictures and remembers how much fun they all had, although Gary was most interested in helping with the production for the first time rather than just watching.

Gary's home studio was not yet of Abbey Road proportions, but it was forever growing larger. Martin Smiddy joked, 'He used to invite me round to see some new piece of equipment he had bought. His single bed was in the middle of the room, which wasn't a particularly big one, but all the floor space was taken up by drum machines and keyboards. He didn't have just one keyboard but three or four, as well as a couple of drum machines that made slightly different noises. I stood in the doorway and said, "How do you get into bed, Gary, this is ridiculous."

'If you put the scene in a sitcom and said, "This is Gary Barlow's bedroom", then people would just laugh. It was that full of electronic stuff. You would say that nobody could live like that but he did. He must have got dressed and changed in the bathroom because there was nowhere for him to stand in the bedroom. He could have had an idea in his sleep and sat up and played it in bed.'

★

The younger girls at Frodsham High School fancied Gary. He became a bit of a heart-throb after appearing on television and singing in assembly. The girls in his year were not so star-struck. Gary was quite trendy, could afford to buy nice clothes and was not at all standoffish. Giselle Cropper recalls, 'He was always performing at school concerts and was great even then. I think some of the younger girls probably had a crush on him when he did the competition – he made tapes of the song and they wanted him to sign them. At the time we thought it was funny and laughed about it, but if they kept the signed tapes they're the ones laughing now!'

Gary had a great opportunity to meet girls if he had chosen to do anything about it. The O-level pupils at the school needed to make a recording of an original composition, so he would invite them back to his bedroom to record their music. Gary, however, was more interested in showing them his computerized equipment than making a move on a pretty classmate.

Throughout his school days Gary stayed with Heather, perhaps not out of devotion but because he was too busy and too ambitious to have time for dating. Heather and Gary may have been thought of as boyfriend and girlfriend, and they were both well liked, but there wasn't much of the couple about them. They were seldom seen holding hands.

Martin Smiddy would often end up having to drive Heather home after an evening listening to Gary's songs at his house: 'I would look at the clock and it's 10p.m., 10.30p.m., 11p.m. and I would end up saying, "It's about time you were getting home." But he would stay there with his cup of tea and I'd run Heather home.' Gary would still be on the sofa when Martin got back.

By his own admission, Gary didn't treat Heather very well. She stayed with him out of loyalty and love. He reveals in the few lines he devotes to her in his autobiography that he wasn't very nice to her, never took her out for dinner and never told her he loved her, despite a five-year relationship.

Heather's own account is similar but she gave the *News of the World* more details. She claimed their relationship went sharply downhill after Gary left school and was spending even more time composing and travelling to gigs. He had passed his driving test when he was seventeen and was now the proud owner of a red Ford Orion. Having his own transport and not relying on friends and his parents meant he could take on more gigs and travel further afield.

He had little time for Heather, who said, 'He could be nasty. He would say I was fat and had a big bum even though there was no way I was overweight. He made me believe I was ugly and horrible. He was saying I wasn't good enough for him. He made me feel I was worth nothing and I allowed myself to be downtrodden because I loved him so much.'

Heather's recollection is different to Gary's about one key element of their relationship. She maintains that he did say he loved her but not in a way she liked: 'What made it worse was that he was horrible one minute, and then the next he would say he loved me.'

Heather's mum and dad may well have been right to worry about their daughter's relationship with the budding pop star. She sacrificed her teenage years, not socializing or partying with her friends, in order to spend all her time with Gary. They were both too young.

His split with Heather motivated him to change other things in his life. Now was the right time to give up his regular gigs at the Halton Legion. John Tedford had already left and moved to Spain with his family to open a restaurant called Memories in Benalmádena on the Costa del Sol. Gary used to ring up his old friend to find out how it was going. On one occasion John said, 'I'll tell you what I could do with: write me an opening theme tune with a voiceover welcoming people in to the restaurant or the bar.' Gary didn't need a second invitation and within a few days he had sent over an original Barlow composition. John would play it every evening when he opened up.

Gary also liked to pop over for a visit. It was a chance to get away from it all during the early mad days of Take That. He would quietly fly into Gibraltar, where there was much less fuss than nearby Málaga airport. John would drive over to pick him up and Gary would recharge his batteries in the Spanish sun. John had started a new band over there, another version of Stax, but he was never able to persuade Gary to come out and join them permanently.

Back at the Halton Legion, Gary performed his farewell concert in June 1989. It was a triumph. Gary was sorry to leave behind a place that had been so important to him. In particular, he would miss his friend Chris Harrison, who observes, 'The time had come for him to move on. It had served its purpose and he wanted to advance and go and do his own thing.'

They kept in close contact, however, and Chris would go to hear Gary play when he could. He travelled up with Gary's family to see him perform at The Viking, his first gig in Blackpool, and was struck by how much he was improving: 'I always say he had crotchets and quavers through his veins. You could tell he had the aura of potential greatness.'

When he left the club, Gary had given Chris a photo of them together. Chris returned the compliment by handing Gary a poem he had written that began: 'You were like a mountain stream, flowing quickly towards your dream'. It would have made a sincere and sweet song lyric.

5

Every Part of Me

A new girl was about to come into Gary's life. She was slim, blonde and a knockout. Nicky Ladanowski was fifteen and still at Frodsham High but she was definitely on Gary's radar. He would see her from time to time around the town and always smiled and said hello but nothing more. One afternoon, however, he was in his car when he saw her walking down the street with a friend. He decided to seize the moment. The only problem was that Heather was in the car with him.

He zoomed off to Heather's house, told her he wasn't feeling well and dropped her off as quickly as he could before whizzing back to where he had spotted Nicky. He then drove by again as if this were the first time he had seen her, pulled over and said nonchalantly, 'Do you want a lift?' Nicky had no idea he had engineered the 'casual' meeting and was delighted to be offered a ride because it was a bit of a walk to her house. Gary politely dropped her off and drove away. Nicky just thought he was being nice and he was a lovely guy. She didn't know that he was in the habit of driving up and down Frodsham High Street in the hope that he would catch sight of her.

She saw him again a while later at a disco at the Mersey View when she was with a gang of young friends. Gary was taking great care in his personal appearance at this stage. Since he had left school he had invested in a sunbed, which he spent a lot of time on, and so had what he imagined was the hippest tan in Frodsham. He had also invested in a new haircut that required a lot of spray to hold the spikiness in place. One of Nicky's pals recalls, 'He was wearing a pink fluorescent T-shirt and I remember thinking he looked ridiculous. But he came over and said to Nicky, "Would you like a drink?" But one of our friends, another boy, was already getting us one, so she said, "It's OK, thanks. Someone's buying me one," so he sort of skulked off and looked really disappointed. I suppose that's when I realized he was interested in her.'

Gary must have thought Nicky was the coolest fifteen-year-old in town because of the way she seemed completely oblivious to his charms. She had never had a serious boyfriend, though, and was a teenager who wasn't that into boys. She had no idea that her apparent indifference was making Gary keener. She was quite shy beneath a lively exterior and thought he was too old for her; she wasn't being cool at all. She thought he was just being polite when he asked, 'Do you want a drink?' Her friend may have clocked what was going on but she didn't. It obviously meant something to Gary because he didn't give up.

The next time Nicky came across Gary, he was in his car again and he was bolder than before. He stopped to chat and told Nicky that he was playing a gig down the road in Warrington that night and afterwards there would be a disco. He casually asked her if she wanted to go with him and made a joke. She still thought he was just being nice and replied in the time-honoured fashion that can dash any young man's hopes: 'OK – if I can bring a friend.'

When she reached home, Nicky asked her friend if she wanted to go and, when she agreed, insisted, 'If you leave me on my own with him, you are in big trouble! Even if you are going to the bathroom, let me know first. Don't just go!'

It was a brilliant night. Gary finished his gig and drove back to Frodsham to pick the girls up from Nicky's house. He was at his funniest in the car, cracking jokes as if he were the stand-up comic at the Halton Legion. The two girls laughed the whole way there and were delighted when they arrived at the club and found the DJ playing all the songs they liked. Gary dragged them onto the dance floor and they were dancing happily when Nicky realized her friend had slipped off to the ladies without telling her. Typical! Nicky was stranded with Gary when the next song started up – it was a slow one. Gary, understandably, was keen to carry on. When her friend returned, they were smooching away and gazing into each other's eyes.

It was Nicky's first slow dance and she later confided that it was then that she realized she was a little in love. The feeling was clearly mutual. Their first kiss on the dance floor of a small nightclub in Warrington was the start of a four-year relationship.

It was common knowledge in and around Frodsham that Gary and Heather had split for good a few months before, so Gary was free and single for the first time in more than five years. Heather, it seems, did not quite see it that way.

Nicky was over at his home less than two weeks after their first kiss when there was a knock at the back door – everyone always came round the back at Ravenscroft. Gary went to see who it was, as his parents were out. It was Heather and they started having strong words. At this point, Nicky didn't know who was there because she didn't really know Heather, having only said the occasional hello to her in the past, but she could hear a raised voice and someone sounding a 'bit stroppy'. As she went to the door to find out what was going on, she saw Heather striding away angrily.

Understandably, Nicky wondered what the problem had been between Gary and his ex-girlfriend. It was clear from the scene that Heather was upset. Nicky's friend observes, 'Heather always seemed like a nice girl and I think Nicky felt sorry for her because it was clear that Heather still had feelings for Gary. Unfortunately, they weren't mutual. Nicky tried to get Gary to go after her but he said it would be best to leave her.'

Gary

Afterwards, Gary tried to explain that he hadn't seen Heather for months and hadn't spoken to her and that they had a bit of a 'weird' relationship. He told Nicky that he had ignored her most of the time and didn't understand what she saw in him – all of which rang true, affirming the general view that it was a relationship that lacked the spark of romance.

Heather's version of events is that she had been told about Nicky by Gary's brother Ian. She was 'devastated' that he could go out with someone else and that 'it was his way of trying to end us without having to face it properly'. In Heather's account to the *News of the World*, it is Nicky who leaves. Both Gary and Nicky, however, confirm that it was Heather who stormed off in floods of tears.

It was a sad scene. Gary would later describe his behaviour as his 'love-rat ways', which wasn't really the case. He might have wanted to seem like a bit of a Casanova but he has never been a love 'em and leave 'em sort of guy.

Heather set about creating a new life without him, doing normal things like going to the pub with her friends. She managed to leave Frodsham behind when she studied Fashion Knitwear Design at Nottingham Trent University. Eventually, some four years after she and Gary split up, she fell in love with someone else, a process operator in a factory; they married and had twin daughters.

Nicky, meanwhile, was filled with the excitement and enthusiasm of a teenage girl with a serious boyfriend for the first time. Within two weeks, however, she learned something that would cast a shadow over the entire four years she went out with Gary. They had been seeing each other every day of their new relationship when suddenly he turned to her and said, out of the blue, 'No matter what anyone says or no matter what happens, we must stick together.' Nicky was puzzled and her friends advised her to find out what he meant. Why was he being so mysterious?

A few days later she raised the subject again and this time he warned her that any time he had gone out with someone in the past, his mum had told him to get rid of her if she didn't like the girl. He added that if Marj didn't like somebody, she just said.

Nicky was horrified but perhaps naturally made a joke about it. She thought she was safe because she saw Gary's mother in school all the time and used to give her a Christmas card, as she did to all her favourite teachers and staff. Gary had told her that his mum had said to him that she was a lovely girl and he ought to ask her out. Surely she would have nothing to worry about.

And yet, she *was* worried, especially when he admitted he had done as his mother had asked in the past. It seemed to Nicky that Marj had exerted an influence on Gary, at least when he was younger, that nobody knew about. The whole conversation made Nicky uncomfortable, unsure how things were going to pan out with her new boyfriend. She wasn't kept in the dark for long.

Her friend explained, 'Nicky went round to his house. His mother seemed different with her than she was at school. She seemed a little bit standoffish. And it made Nicky nervous, especially after what Gary had told her. Nicky was popular, so she had never given it a thought that Gary's parents wouldn't like her. She just assumed they would be lovely to her.

'But two weeks into the relationship, he went round to her house and he was upset. Nicky's mum was at work, so it was just her there. His face looked all blotchy. He said he had had a big argument with his mum and that Nicky was "not allowed to come to the house any more". Nicky was really upset about it and burst into tears. Gary tried to comfort her and tell her that she hadn't done anything. He said his mum hadn't given him a reason but she didn't want Nicky coming round. Nicky never went back to the house again.'

Incredibly, from that day on Gary's long-term girlfriend never shared so much as a cup of tea with his mum or dad. Sadly, she didn't have the chance to get to know his dad because she never spent any time with him. In subsequent years, she would see Marj in the VIP section at Take That concerts but they would always be at opposite ends.

Gary

Marj Barlow has rarely spoken about her talented son, preferring to let his achievements speak for themselves. Other than referring to his mother as 'the boss of the house', Gary has had little to say about her either. She has been very supportive of his endeavours and is obviously proud of him. They are a close and private family. He has never mentioned her banning other girls from his house, before or after Nicky. If there were previous incidences, then it might explain why he stayed with Heather for so long.

It's not exactly clear what happened to his first serious girlfriend in this regard. They did have to see each other in secret in the latter part of their relationship but Gary has hinted that this was more to do with their respective parents falling out than anything specific regarding Heather. Nicky thought Marj didn't like Gary being with anybody who might prove a distraction. Perhaps she didn't want Gary straying from his upward career path with one of the best-looking girls in town. Marj had no cause to ban her son's girlfriend.

The picture that Nicky painted to her pals is of a son extremely embarrassed by what had happened. So much so, in fact, that she was flabbergasted when he subsequently told her he thought he must be adopted. It was completely unexpected. Her friend explains, 'Gary said to her, "Well, I don't look like my parents and I'm nothing like them. I'm not like my brother and I have this musical ability and it doesn't run anywhere in the family." Nicky told him that didn't mean anything because you can be a brilliant musician and have nobody in the family who plays an instrument. She told him talent wasn't genetic!

'Nicky found the conversation upsetting. She was only fifteen, after all. It sort of reveals how troubled Gary was about what had happened. He was embarrassed about how his mum behaved. He knows it wasn't reasonable. She thought he was ashamed.'

Fortunately the ban didn't stop Gary and Nicky's relationship from moving forward agreeably. They continued to see each other every day – he would go round to her house when she'd finished school and she would accompany him if he had a local gig. If it wasn't a school day, Gary would drive them to Delamere Forest to take his family's two golden spaniels, Pete and Olly, for a walk. They made sure they passed their favourite ice cream parlour on the way. During their time together they tried all the flavours at least once, although Gary was always partial to a traditional Cornetto. He still had the Ford Orion in which he always kept a stash of chocolate to munch on. He loved Cadbury's Dairy Milk.

Nicky was too young to drink, so they didn't go to pubs. Gary wasn't a drinker then either. He was too involved with his music to want to go out for a pint or two with his mates. Her friend observes, 'He wasn't ever a guy that you saw hanging out with other groups of guys. He tended to do a lot of stuff on his own. So when Nicky and him got together it was just the two of them really.'

His new relationship was like a breath of fresh air for Gary. They were inseparable – as he had been at first with Heather, but they had both been very young then. Nicky's mother Christine was as alarmed as Heather's parents had been about the intensity of the love affair. Her concern was heightened when Gary bought her daughter a solitaire diamond ring for Christmas the first year they were going out. They had bought it together at a little out-of-the-way jeweller's when they were driving around Cheshire one afternoon. Nicky thought it wonderfully romantic. Christine thought it looked remarkably like an engagement ring and Nicky had to reassure her it was just a ring and she and Gary were not getting married. They were still too young, although Gary often talked to Nicky about getting married and having ten children, which made her gulp.

It became a running joke between them but Nicky would grow to realize that Gary really did expect her to become a wife and mum when the time was right. He would talk a lot about his ambitions but seemed unmoved by his girlfriend's aspirations. Her mother was concerned because she knew her daughter had ambitions of her own and wanted her to fulfil her dream of becoming an actress.

Gary

Nicky had no complaints about the way Gary treated her. If he drove past a flower seller by the side of the road on his way back to Frodsham, he would invariably stop to pick up a bunch of her favourite pink freesias. She loved their honeyed scent and vibrant colour. Barely a week would go by before he would be knocking on the door of her mother's house and presenting her with a little posy or bouquet.

They never argued and she appreciated how romantic he was, especially when he announced in the car one day that he had written a song for her and put it on for her to listen to. 'Every Part Of Me' was Nicky's personal song from Gary, complete with a big key change in the middle, which he knew was something she really liked. It was a gloriously romantic ballad; it's a shame that he has never released it because it's probably one of his best songs.

Nicky also loved Gary's original version of 'Babe', which apparently was very different from the one Mark Owen later sang when Take That took the track to number one. Where Mark's was sweet and could bring a tear to the eye, Gary's original that he gave to his friends was very raw and passionate.

Nicky left Frodsham High to study for her A levels in theatre studies, English and contemporary dance at a private tutor's in Chester with the intention of going to drama school as soon as possible. It didn't change the dynamic of their relationship. She would be at every gig. When he wasn't performing, they would go to the movies or pop down to a local restaurant, the Chinese Delight, where Gary would order his favourite crispy duck and pancakes. He would munch away, telling Nicky all about the progress he was making in his quest for fame – or, more precisely, the lack of it.

He was trying hard to get a record deal. He was earning good money gigging around northern clubs but was never going to be content earning £600 a week playing Barry Manilow songs for the rest of his days. He wanted to be on *Top of the Pops*, but nobody seemed interested.

One of the stumbling blocks to Gary moving forward was that record companies couldn't see past Rick Astley when it came to young northern singers. Rick was from Newton-le-Willows in Lancashire, about twenty miles from Frodsham. He had been phenomenally successful in the late eighties, when he had been taken under the wing of the Stock, Aitken and Waterman hit factory that also launched Kylie Minogue and Jason Donovan.

Unfortunately for Gary, he was never going to sound like Rick Astley, who had a rich baritone voice and sang in a distinctive soulful manner. When the record company executives realized Gary wasn't the next Rick, they rapidly lost interest. He didn't help himself when he turned up to meetings in London wearing a conservative suit and carrying a leather briefcase full of song sheets and demo cassettes. On one now famous occasion an A & R man with Rocket Records jumped out of his seat while Gary's tape was playing, tore it out of the machine and threw it out of the window with the verdict that he would never make it in the music business. It's a great story but, at the time, it was very harsh on Gary and tested his resolve.

Not everyone was so negative. A manager called Barry Woolley was among a gang of people who saw Gary performing one night at a club in Ashton-under-Lyne on the outskirts of Manchester. Gary sang a couple of ballads and did the Michael Jackson moonwalk, which he had now perfected. Barry recalled, 'He was brilliant and brought the house down.'

Their association was the start of one of the strangest periods of Gary's musical life, when, for a short time, he became a performer called Kurtis Rush. He somewhat naively appointed Barry as his manager, with the incentive that he would have a record released within weeks. That looked like it was going to happen when he was booked into a recording studio in Nottingham to sing the vocal on 'Love Is In The Air', an old disco hit for John Paul Young that he knew well from performing it with John Tedford.

Gary

Gary was understandably excited about this turn of events, even though he had to agree to be called Kurtis Rush for the purposes of the project. It's never been properly explained who thought up this corny name. Gary Barlow may not be the most charismatic name – sounding like a cross between a professional footballer and one of the comedians he used to accompany at the Halton Legion – but it was much better than Kurtis Rush.

The newly named Kurtis was despatched to London to film a video and he excitedly set off for the day with Nicky going along to support him. The video didn't go exactly as he had expected. To begin with, he had to mime to a vocal that wasn't actually his. Goodness knows why they thought it was better than anything Gary could do. The most interesting detail about the shoot was the identity of one of the two female dancers, although more so in retrospect. Sheffield-born Dawn Andrews was the pretty pencil-slim one, wearing a black crop top and skirt, who more than ten years later would become Gary's wife.

Nicky and Gary travelled back home on the train, looking forward to watching the finished recording together. They settled down at Nicky's mother's house to enjoy the video that would turn him into a star. Only it didn't, of course . . . They both agreed it was terrible.

The video is arguably the low point of Gary's career. He looks rather demented as he tries to sing and show as many teeth as possible at the same time. The dancers don't do much but wave their arms seductively in his direction. It was very dated – even in 1989. It was probably a pitch for the Rick Astley audience but, if so, it failed miserably.

For a while Gary tried to promote himself as Kurtis Rush but that didn't really work, especially when the track, released as a 45 rpm vinyl, barely registered. Gary sent Nicky around to all the different record stores to try and make it a chart hit but that strategy failed too, and his first-ever single lapsed rapidly into obscurity.

One of the better insults an *X Factor* judge can throw at a contestant is that he or she sounds like a cruise ship entertainer. After the Kurtis Rush debacle, Gary was seriously thinking of packing in the relentless grind of working men's clubs for a season sailing around the Caribbean. He was still grafting away in Frodsham though, sending showcase packages all over the country to potential agents and managers. There had to be someone out there who would take him on. He needed something to happen.

Typically, the man who would change his life and have the greatest influence on Gary Barlow's career lived close to home – just half an hour away in Manchester.

PART TWO

The Heartbeat of Take That

6

Nice Sweet Northern Lads

Nigel Martin-Smith was an ambitious entrepreneur who ran the Boss Agency in Chapel Walks and was well known in the city's blossoming gay scene. He had established a foothold in the entertainment world in the early eighties, working as a casting agent and trying to overcome the traditional London bias in showbusiness.

Fortunately for Gary, he harboured ambitions to be a player in the music industry, as he realized there was big money to be made there. His initial venture was managing a local singer and drag queen called Damian, who had a top ten hit in 1989 with 'The Time Warp', an energetic and flamboyant cover of the song from the hit musical *The Rocky Horror Show*. It wasn't a big breakthrough but did reveal a patience and persistence that would serve Nigel's future music ventures well. 'The Time Warp' was released in 1987 and 1988 before finally reaching number seven the following August. A follow-up single, 'Wig Wam Bam', crept into the top fifty before Damian Davey slipped off the radar. Damian's most significant achievement was appearing on *Top of the Pops* – just the thing to impress aspiring young pop stars.

Nigel needed fresh inspiration. He found it when he saw the latest American teen sensations New Kids on the Block at a television studio in Manchester. He didn't really like what he saw and told pop columnist Rick Sky: 'I couldn't help but feel how obnoxious they were. They seemed to be very big-headed, strutting around the studio as if they owned it.' While he wasn't taken with the boys in person, he was shrewd enough to be very impressed with the scale of their success.

In 1990, New Kids were the biggest band in the world, scoring three top ten albums, including the number one *Step by Step*, and eight top ten singles in the UK. That year alone they grossed a reported $861 million worldwide, making them the highest-earning boy band of all time. It was a rare teenage bedroom wall that wasn't filled with posters of the band from Boston: Danny, Donnie, Joey, Jon and Jordan. No wonder Nigel left the TV studio thinking he should find some local lads who could grab some of this action – and his Manchester Kids on the Block would be a much nicer bunch. He explained, 'I was looking for five level-headed, professional, well-balanced young guys. I didn't want five obnoxious little twats. I wanted five nice sweet northern lads.'

When Nigel first met Gary, he had no clue that the young man from Frodsham was a one-man musical tour de force. He just had Gary's picture and a short CV. His strategy for putting a band together was simply based on how they would look. For his part, Gary had no idea when he presented himself at Nigel's offices that the agent had an interest in music. He thought he was going along to sign up as a film or television extra. He had always fancied himself as a bit of an actor and thought he could earn some extra money sipping a pint in the background of the Rovers Return or strolling past Barry Grant in Brookside Close.

He was more than a little surprised, therefore, when Nigel started telling him about his plans to put together a new band. Gary wanted to be a solo singer, so he wasn't especially interested. He did notice Damian's gold disc for 'The Time Warp' hanging on the wall behind Nigel, however. He recalled in *My Take* that his whole attitude changed when Nigel said the magic words, 'He was on *Top of the Pops*.'

Gary never went anywhere without a cassette of some of his songs and so was able to leave one with Nigel at the end of their meeting, not knowing if it would end up on the Manchester pavement. It contained '1 Million Love Songs Later'. Next morning he was washing the Ford Orion when Marj shouted out the window that Nigel was on the phone. He sounded a lot more enthusiastic than he had in the office the day before when he'd met Gary for the first time.

'I've listened to the tape you gave me and it's really good. Who's singing on it?'

'It's me, Nigel.'

'OK. Who wrote the songs?'

'Just me, Nigel.'

'OK, so who's playing on them?'

'It's just me, Nigel.'

'OK. What about the arrangements and everything?'

'I did it all in my bedroom, Nigel.'

'Do you want to pop back in to the office?'

It is now a famous conversation, a great place to start a history of Take That. When they met for a second time, Nigel expanded on his plans for the future. He played Gary a videotape of New Kids on the Block and told him that was the sort of sound and style he was looking for. Gary had never heard of them – or so he said. They were all over the charts, on *Top of the Pops* almost weekly and in the pop columns of the newspapers daily, so it seems highly unlikely that an ambitious teenager craving a career in music wouldn't have been aware of them.

Nigel told Gary that he wanted to form a band of five down-to-earth, good-looking lads. He wanted a modest bunch of self-improvers, maybe unemployed, who would come across as the sort of likeable guys one might meet out on the town on a Friday night. To his credit, he realized pretty much straight away that Gary was the golden ticket as far as his plans were concerned. He had been handed someone who could write the music for the new band, thereby generating a far greater income from music publishing royalties. That was where the big money was.

Gary found himself being swept along by Nigel's enthusiasm for the project. He had his heart set on becoming a star like George Michael, who had used the teen-friendly eighties duo Wham! as a stepping stone to becoming one of the biggest solo artists in the world. Perhaps, when the time was right, Gary could ditch his four Andrew Ridgeleys and follow a similarly smooth path to superstardom.

Gary apparently told Nigel that he was 'crap at dancing' and could only do a few hand gestures. He was confident in his abilities and is most unlikely to have underplayed his talents. He wasn't a supremely gifted dancer like Jason Orange but he wasn't half bad, as anyone who had seen his moonwalk would testify, and the karate he had practised as a child is based around fluid movement, grace and power. Gary acquired a born-again modesty in his later career that was not especially self-evident in the early days.

The origins of Take That have become confused and muddled over the years because the band, under Nigel's watchful eye, put out a load of old rubbish to try and cloud the fact that they were five strangers put together in their manager's office. These days there is no stigma attached to manufactured bands, as the success of Little Mix and, in particular, One Direction clearly demonstrates, but twenty-five years ago it wasn't so accepted.

The most ludicrous claim was that Gary and Mark Owen were already in a band called The Cutest Rush, presumably a less than hilarious play on Gary's former alter ego Kurtis Rush. The story of how they met was reprinted so many times it became part of their accepted history. It was Nigel's plan to make the formation of the group seem more spontaneous, as if it were a case of all friends together.

In this Disney account of the birth of Take That, Gary met Mark at Manchester's Strawberry Studios, where he had been given some studio time as part of his BBC songwriting prize and where Mark used to hang out with a friend of his sister, making tea. He and Gary, so the story went, got on well together and Mark would trail along to Gary's gigs, carrying equipment and making a brew. Eventually they formed The Cutest Rush to perform a mixture of Gary's songs and some corny standards. It all sounded so plausible, but it wasn't true.

The first time Gary set eyes on Mark was when Nigel produced his photograph at that first meeting and told him he was a model on the books of the Boss Agency. Nigel also showed Gary pictures of two other young men he wanted in the band: Howard Donald, an aspiring model and dancer, and Jason Orange, who was already established as a dancer in Manchester. They were both athletic, muscular and six-pack heaven.

Mark Owen met the criteria for the band on two counts: he was a very good-looking teenager, just turned eighteen, and he was a working-class northern lad. He was brought up in a small council house in Oldham, where his father worked as a decorator. He was quite an extrovert at his Roman Catholic school; he loved acting and was mad about football. While Gary would be composing songs in his bedroom studio and singing at the Halton Legion, Mark was an Elvis fan, even dressing up as 'The King', which must have been quite funny to witness because he is only 5ft 5in tall.

As a young teenager, Mark's big ambition was to become a professional footballer but trials with Huddersfield Town, Rochdale and even Manchester United failed to provide the career breakthrough he wanted. Then a groin injury ruined any long-term plans and he ended up working in a local boutique, Zutti of Oldham, where he was well known for being fashion conscious and spending most of his wages on clothes. One of his schoolteachers, Fred Laughton, observed, 'He was very good at soccer but he was a little bit of a poser. He used to prepare his looks and comb his hair before he went on the football pitch.' Nowadays every player has some mirror time before a game but back in the eighties David Beckham had yet to introduce Armani underpants to the world of football.

After leaving the boutique, Mark worked for a while as an electrician's mate before moving on to a job in Barclays bank. He didn't want to settle for that, though, and so signed on with Nigel. The manager recognized that Mark had a cuteness about him that would be very important in the development of any band: girls wanted to pick him up and cuddle him. Mark, to his credit, has always loathed being described as 'cute'.

Fast-forward twenty years and you would probably have caught Jason Orange and Howard Donald as part of a dance troupe like Diversity on *Britain's Got Talent*. They were two of the best dancers in Manchester, although Howard seemed more inclined towards a career as a model. He had already done some modelling when he sought representation at Boss and left Nigel a comp card.

Another strand of the Disney story of Take That was that Howard and Jason had already formed their own dance duo when they met Nigel. In career terms, Jason was well ahead, working on the popular late night Granada television show *The Hitman and Her*. The 'hitman' was the influential producer Pete Waterman, while the 'her' was TV presenter Michaela Strachan. The programme would trawl around the clubs of Manchester and surrounding towns, showing enthusiastic clubbers dancing to the latest hits, and featured games and guest stars, many of whom, like Sonia and Sinitta, were signed to Stock, Aitken and Waterman. Jason, as a regular dancer, would miraculously choose the right club to be seen in every week wearing the show uniform – red vest, cycle shorts, red socks and red trainers. It may have been fashionable at the time but in retrospect looked pretty gay.

Jason, who was very handsome, was the son of a Manchester bus driver and had five brothers, including a twin, Justin. His parents divorced when he was a boy and all six brothers stayed with their mother in Wythenshawe. He was brought up in a Mormon household in which alcohol and caffeine were banned and, perhaps as a result, had put all his energies into dancing and keeping fit as a teenager. He didn't show much enthusiasm for academic work and left his South Manchester High School with no O levels. Instead of college, he joined a Youth Training scheme as a painter-decorator and started earning pocket money busking as a dancer in the city centre.

When he came to the attention of Nigel Martin-Smith, he was living with his older brother Simon, who worked in financial services and would later look after Gary's money for a time. Jason wasn't exactly a loner but was secure in his own company. Gary would be a close second in that regard.

Howard, too, was from a large Manchester family with three brothers and a sister. He was born in the district of Droylsden and was brought up by his mother, a school secretary, and stepfather after his parents divorced and his mother remarried. He and Jason had quite similar academic backgrounds in that neither was the least bit bothered about school. Howard even bunked off for five weeks, explaining to Rick Sky, 'I only intended to have a few days off, but I kept taking another day, then another day, till the days had run into weeks.'

More often than not Howard would be skipping lessons to practise breakdancing. You could imagine him with his friends on a street corner in New York, earning dollars by showing passers-by their moves. As part of that culture, he would draw graffiti on various targets, usually buses, around Manchester. That ceased when a diligent bus driver realized that Howard and his mates were writing on seats; he stopped the bus outside a police station and locked the doors. Spending some time in a cell put paid to any future ambitions of becoming a Banksy.

Like Jason, Howard left high school with no O levels and began a YTS as a vehicle painter. He too would supplement his meagre income by dancing and could often be seen on the podium in popular local clubs like the Apollo. He also loved house music and hip-hop – tastes that would later serve him well as a solo DJ.

The band would need a fifth member if they were going to follow the blueprint of New Kids on the Block, which was lucky for Robert Peter Williams, who at the time was smoking his days away, sitting on a wall with his mates while he was supposed to be out selling double glazing in Stoke-on-Trent.

Nigel decided to advertise for possible band members. He would choose the best two or three to join the others at an audition. He was not yet 100 per cent sure that Mark was ready for the band because, although he looked the part, he had no experience of singing, dancing or performing in front of an audience. The audition would be the chance for everyone to meet and see how they gelled.

It wouldn't really be an audition for Gary, Jason or Howard, however. They were in.

Nigel didn't place the advertisement solely in the Manchester papers. Robert's mum, Jan Williams, saw the story in *The Sentinel*, the local paper in Stoke, that a Manchester-based talent agency was seeking a candidate for a new boy band: *Singers wanted. Singers and dancers wanted for a new boy band. If you have what it takes, call Nigel Martin-Smith*. It's always the mums who see these things. She pressed her son, who was more likely to be reading the back of a fag packet than a newspaper, to send in his picture and details of his stage experience in the hope of getting an audition.

Rob, as his friends all called him, was a sensitive and sociable boy whose father, the comedian Pete Conway, had left the family home when his son was three. He wanted to be accepted by the boys in his class and loved to join them playing football in the park after school. He was just sixteen and may not have had the professional background of a teenage Gary Barlow but he had appeared in leading roles at two of the biggest theatres in his home town.

When he was eleven, he had played Jeremy, one of the juvenile leads in the Stoke-on-Trent charity production of *Chitty Chitty Bang Bang*, and had sung 'Truly Scrumptious', one of the more famous numbers from the show. After the performance at the Theatre Royal, Hanley, he had been overjoyed when the Lord Mayor came back-stage and shook his hand.

His biggest success as a young performer was playing the Artful Dodger in a local theatre group's production of Lionel Bart's Tony-winning musical *Oliver!* It was a role he was born to play but it was a struggle for him. The director of *Oliver!* was a stern figure who treated his actors, both adults and children, equally harshly. Rob found it very hard being bawled out by him in front of the rest of the cast and was close to walking out several times. He reacted badly to what he perceived as unfair or bullying treatment.

Gary, by contrast, was a boy from a very stable family background who had an unswerving belief in his own abilities. He was self-sufficient, spending hours in solitary confinement writing and record-ing songs that would build the foundation of his future. Nobody ever needed to give him a dressing down.

While Gary would later claim he did suffer from nerves inside – although nobody ever witnessed them – Rob always had a touch of stage fright. His close friend Zoë Hammond, who appeared with him in all his theatre work, had to gee him up before he went on, making him recite, 'I'm going to be good.'

On the first night of *Oliver!* she realized he wasn't himself. During the interval, he started crying and told her, 'I just said my first spiel and I looked down into the pit, like, and, bugger me, but I looked up and there is my fucking old man in the front row.' Rob had put his dad on a pedestal and was surprised and upset to see him. His reac-tion is fascinating not just because he was emotional but also because he told Zoë about how he felt. Robert Williams wore his heart on his sleeve, as Gary would later discover.

Rob's mum had to take the day off from her florist shop to drive her son to Le Cage, a gay nightclub where the auditions were going to take place. Gary didn't have to do much other than introduce himself to everyone. He had met Jason at Nigel's office the previous week but went up to Rob and introduced himself: 'Hi, I'm Gary Barlow and I'm the singer.' Rob later recalled that Gary was carrying his trusty briefcase. He also noticed he wore 'uncool' trainers. More importantly, however, he remembered being 'shit-scared' of Nigel Martin-Smith.

Nigel had invited one other lad to try out for the band but, after hearing his voice, he told him to go and then there were just the five left. They all had to sing a version of Jason Donovan's 'Nothing Can Divide Us', which had been the Australian soap star's first UK hit in 1988. Jason and Kylie were very popular in gay clubs and this was perhaps an early indication of the type of music Nigel wanted his boy band to perform. Gary was note perfect; Rob, who was an old hand at auditions, was more than passable. The other three were terrible, but that didn't really matter. They had never been asked to sing before and this is a hard song to master.

When it came to dancing, Gary was self-conscious in front of the others. They all had to show some moves, which made him realize he would have to work hard not to trail behind them, Jason and Howard in particular.

Jan Williams, who ran her own business and was quite astute about money, interviewed Nigel to find out exactly what it was all about. Nigel, who was more at ease bossing around five lads, admitted, 'She fired twenty questions at me and gave me the hardest time.' Jan was reassured by his businesslike manner and the size of his £80,000 personal investment in the boys.

The audition concluded with Nigel taking everyone across the road for lunch at British Home Stores.

7

Cycle Shorts and Leather

The yet-to-be-named band were under the complete control of Nigel Martin-Smith. He didn't tell them the final line-up at the audition, preferring to wait a few days for tension to build before letting everyone know. This wasn't a passport to instant fame but Gary felt optimistic that at last someone was taking him seriously. There was never any doubt that Nigel was in charge, even though it was also clear the band was being built around Gary.

Nigel was the master of the withering put-down and the five unworldly lads were in awe of the older man. Even Gary, who had the most self-assurance of the five, was nervous around his new manager. One of the first things Nigel did was to gather the boys round and tell them he was gay; they were not so naive as to think otherwise. A confession about his sexuality was not the point of the meeting, however. Nigel wanted to share something with the group so they would feel they could reciprocate. He wanted to know if there were any skeletons that he needed to know about. He knew he could deal with anything as long as he was aware of it. In particular, he wanted details about any girlfriends. Nobody had much to confess, although Jason had apparently not paid his poll tax.

Nigel also wanted to make sure all the boys involved their parents before they signed anything with him. He didn't want any later repercussions about the contract. His share would be 25 per cent, which meant, in effect, that he would earn more than any of the others individually. He would later reduce the amount of his cut when they started to become successful. He also had strong advice about the importance of financial prudence and promised to look after their earnings with great diligence so none of them would walk away broke. He always paid the band an allowance even when they were amassing huge sums and they needed his approval before they could spend a large amount.

Under Nigel's direction, the initial incarnation of Take That presented a gay image to the outside world. His first move was to send them off to his hairdresser, Pierre Alexander, for some new trendier styles. When Gary left the salon, he was a spiky peroxide blond, looking a little like the brothers Luke and Matt Goss who, as Bros, had been very popular in the late eighties. The process was extremely painful and Gary's scalp was red and sore where the chemicals had burned his skin.

Gary laughed about it on the day, although he soon became sick of the maintenance his new hairstyle required, especially when his roots started to show through after a couple of weeks. He also finally had to bin his favourite shirt – the white one with black stars he had worn on his last night at the Halton Legion – and get used to wearing cycle shorts and leather – not the usual sort of attire for a stroll down Frodsham High Street. Next, they had pictures taken so Nigel could start trying to drum up some publicity.

Gary didn't appear to be the least bit fazed by his introduction into the gay world. He even admitted in *My Take* that he was aware that all the girls in Nigel's office thought he was gay for the first year and he went along with it.

It was exciting to feel he was getting somewhere, even if it meant rigorous physical training with an instructor at a dance studio in Manchester. This was not just the odd spinning class and a wind-down in the sauna; it was full days, from early morning to 7p.m., which included all manner of press-ups and push-ups, aerobics, gymnastics and dancing. When they had a weekend off, they were all under strict instructions from Nigel to go to the gym or play some sport.

The new band still needed a name. You would have thought it would have been the first thing on everyone's mind, but Nigel wasn't that bothered, believing that nobody would care what they were called when they were famous in two years' time. The only person's name he wasn't happy about was Robert Williams and he decided right away that the youngest member was going to be called Robbie. The man himself hated it and to this day never answers if someone calls it out in the street. If you want to get Robbie's attention, you call him Rob. Gary always called the youngest member of the band Rob and it's not true that he used to refer to him as 'son'. The new Robbie Williams also acquired an extra forename – Maximilian – another of Nigel's total inventions. Gary acquired a nickname, Gaz, which nobody had called him at school; at least he could put 'Goose' in the bin.

The name Take That was finally chosen when the five boys were in Nigel's office one afternoon. He suggested that they should be called Kick It, which nobody liked. They realized they would need to think of something quickly or end up being stuck with his idea. They were leafing through some magazines, wondering what to do, when they came across a sexy picture of Madonna that had the caption 'Take That' underneath. Mark explained, 'We thought it was snappy and had a punch. We wanted to make sure our name was original.' Mark was right that the name was original but not in a good way. Now it is one of the most famous names in music but then it came across as rather lame and half-hearted. The boys genuinely liked it though.

To start with they called themselves Take That and Party but dropped the extra two words when they heard of a minor American group called The Party. Instead, *Take That & Party* would become the title of their first album.

Amazingly, considering they were an unsigned band, Nigel managed to use his contacts to set up a string of television appearances. He despatched Gary to a studio in Cheadle Hulme on the outskirts of Manchester to produce two recordings that would be of good enough quality to use on TV. The process was similar to the recording he did of 'Let's Pray For Christmas'. He worked on two songs that had featured on the original demo he had given Nigel, 'Girl' and 'Still Waiting'. They were quite catchy but sounded as if Gary had sat in his bedroom and decided he was going to compose songs in the style of Stock, Aitken and Waterman. Neither of the songs was a knockout and, sadly, even Jason Donovan would have rejected them.

They were good enough for the appearances Nigel had lined up, however. First up, they were filmed miming 'Girl' at a dance studio in Manchester for the BBC magazine programme *North West Tonight*. Gary's camp ensemble consisted of a red neckerchief, no shirt, red satin cycling shorts and a black leather studded belt.

The next day they featured on *Cool Cube*, a short-lived music programme on the now defunct BSB channel. Nigel was friendly with the producer, Rosemary Barratt, who worked under the professional name of Ro Newton. She was a former *Smash Hits* journalist and TV researcher. He persuaded Ro to see the boys and she was impressed with their dance routines and Gary's singing. The show was filmed on the back lot of Granada Studios on Quay Street. Gary had swapped his red shorts for black ones matched with a black hoodie and no shirt.

Take That were filmed in front of an unenthusiastic crowd of about a hundred people who looked like they had come across a bunch of performers while they were strolling round a shopping mall. You couldn't fault the boys for effort though, with Howard doing a back flip while Jason and Mark executed some back spins. They began the show by singing 'Girl', which had a soppy lyric about wanting to take a girl home. Then they introduced themselves to Michaela Strachan, who was one of the show's presenters, and Gary said he was the singer and did all the writing. He said he thought it would take between six to eight months for them to become major stars; it would be nearer two years. He confided that various record companies were interested and they expected to have their first single out in the new year.

Next up, Gary and Jason, still in their cycling shorts, were on a studio couch with various youngsters asking them questions about the band. Gary told them they were going to be the next New Kids on the Block and Jason said that it was Nigel, their manager, who inspired them. They closed the show in more demure white trousers and red shirts for 'Still Waiting'.

It was all pretty innocuous but fifteen minutes was an amazing amount of airtime for a band that had recorded only two songs in a studio and admitted they were still rehearsing. Throughout the show they impressed with their enthusiasm and professionalism, which was remarkable in a band that had been in existence for less than three months. They were well received and were asked back a few times, although even Ro admitted being 'a little dubious' about some of their outfits.

They appeared for the first time on *The Hitman and Her* on Halloween night. Pete Waterman was away, so the programme was presented by the ever-present Michaela, this time joined by Damian as co-presenter – further proof of how proactive Nigel was on the Manchester entertainment scene. They went for the black cycle shorts and bare-chested look and performed the same routine to 'Girl' as on *Cool Cube*. Gary seemed to be having no trouble with the dance steps, although he was safe in the knowledge that he didn't have to do any breakdancing in the middle of the song.

Again, they were asked back from time to time and Pete Waterman recalls how pleased they were to do the show. He observed, 'They saw it as a big step forward.' Pete, who is never afraid to be outspoken, added, 'All I know is that on *The Hitman and Her* they were one of the worst groups we had on – without a doubt.'

While the band was in development, Gary continued to build his nest egg by taking as many gigs as he could. He already had £4,500 saved, whereas the other four barely had the cost of a round of drinks between them. Rob's mother Jan, for instance, subsidized her son's ambitions for two years before he was able to provide for himself. Gary kept his solo options open by having new cards made up: *Gary Barlow (formerly Kurtis Rush) is pleased to announce his new exclusive representation: Nigel Martin-Smith Personal Management.*

Sometimes Nigel would travel with him and talk about his plans for the band. On one such occasion he invited Gary to join him on a short break he was planning to Florida. Back in Frodsham, Nicky Ladanowski was looking forward to a two-week holiday in Biarritz with Gary and her mum, Christine. She was taken aback when Gary told her he would have to fly back early to go to Florida with Nigel. A friend explained, 'He told her it was work, but she was surprised when she found out none of the other boys were going.'

The holiday in the south of France was lovely. They drove their hire car along quiet French roads listening to 'their song'. Every couple has one. Gary and Nicky's was 'Me And Mrs Jones', which had been a soulful hit for Billy Paul in 1973 and had grown in stature since it was first released so that it eventually became a classic pop song.

Despite enjoying these idyllic days with his girlfriend, Gary flew back early, repacked his suitcase in Frodsham and set off to meet Nigel to fly to Orlando. Just a day later he was driving in the Florida sunshine with his manager. Absolutely nothing untoward happened between the two of them – they shared a room but had single beds – but you can imagine what the tabloid press would have made of the jaunt.

Gary was able to fulfil his childhood dream of going to Disneyland and other famous tourist destinations like SeaWorld and Epcot. When he arrived, Gary found a note from Marj in the back pocket of his jeans in which she told him how proud she was of him and that she and his dad had always wanted to take the boys to Florida but could never afford it. She was pleased he would now be able to do these things thanks to Nigel.

Marj and Colin Barlow weren't touchy-feely people but the hand-written letter was a tender gesture from a mother to her son and something to treasure. It's easy to speculate that Marj was worried about Gary's connection with an openly gay man and that she was letting him know it was OK with her if he decided to go down that route, but a more sensible interpretation is that she was simply acknowledging that her much-loved son was growing up and starting to live his life away from the shelter of home.

Gary remembered to ring and send Nicky a postcard every day. When he returned he presented her with two cuddly toys – a Mickey Mouse and a Jiminy Cricket.

Gary's trip to Florida may have contributed to the general feeling within Take That that he was Nigel's favourite but much of what is written about those early days is done with twenty–twenty hindsight. It is clear that Nigel had a huge influence on all of them but he specifically needed Gary for the venture to be a success. Gary was the beating heart of the band.

The most likely explanation of the whole Florida saga is that Nigel wanted him to be happy and in a good place because he was shrewd enough to realize that the young man needed to be at the top of his game in the coming months if Take That was going to be a success. Gary would have to work as hard as the rest of the band put together.

The priority in December 1990 was to prepare for the band's first-ever live gig at Flicks nightclub in Huddersfield. It wasn't a gay club but a suitably obscure venue for Nigel to assess how much more work they needed to do before they were ready to reach a wider audience. The short answer is: a lot.

Gary described the occasion to Rick Sky: 'There were about

twenty people in the audience and a dog. Only about ten of them were watching but to be honest I felt I was messing up a lot.' It was probably just as well that it was a small crowd, as the five were trying to work out the dance steps and the songs at the same time. They were also having to get used to their leather look, which made them all look like the biker guy in the Village People. They even performed 'Can't Stop The Music' by the famous New York group. As Gary wryly observed, 'At least we didn't do "YMCA".'

Take That underwhelmed the crowd for twenty minutes – hardly the exhilarating start they had hoped for. Undaunted, Nigel began to book them into a series of gay clubs up and down the country to try and build a groundswell of popularity. The boys, in their tight leather gear and tassels that left little to the imagination, would have to run the gauntlet of wandering hands but they took it in their stride. Howard would later recall that at most of the venues they would have their 'arses pinched or their front bits pinched'. For his part, Rob rather liked going to clubs where he wasn't going to get his head kicked in.

Nigel now set about the next stage of his plan: signing a record deal. He secured a meeting with Mike Stock, hoping that he would want to add Take That to the list of acts at Stock, Aitken and Waterman. Pete had been unimpressed by them on TV and Mike also wasn't interested. He recalled, 'We were busy with our own stable of young stars like Kylie Minogue and Jason Donovan. We felt we had enough all-boy bands with Brother Beyond, Big Fun and Dead or Alive.' It seems astonishing now to think Take That were ignored in favour of these forgotten bands.

The boys had no better luck with Simon Cowell, then an ambitious A & R man working for the BMG group. Simon would drift in and out of the Gary Barlow story over the next twenty years. His first impression was that Take That looked good but their songs weren't strong enough. During an interview with Jonathan Ross in 2012, Cowell recalled he had said, 'I'll sign them without the fat one.

But then actually I realized I'd made a mistake and I called up the manager a few months later and I said, "Do you want the deal?" and he told me where to go. So that was the end of that.'

It's a good story but none of the boys had an ounce of fat on them during these dancing days, and it was Rob not Gary who had been on the chubby side growing up. At least Simon actually saw the band. At RCA they didn't make it past reception.

The rejections had Nigel scratching his head. He decided that Gary needed to write new material. When they had the right song, he would start his own record label and release it on that. He arranged for Gary to go down to London to work with an up-and-coming producer called Ray Hedges. Gary enjoyed these trips because it meant he could indulge in his twin passions: composing and spending time with his girlfriend Nicky when she was able to join him.

Ray and Gary came up with an easy listening disco tune, 'Do What U Like', which Nigel arranged to bring out on his Dance UK label. That sounds grander than it was. Nigel's commitment to the band should not be underestimated, as he remortgaged his house to finance this venture. Gary hoped the song would be the Take That equivalent of the New Kids on the Block number one 'Hangin' Tough'. Unfortunately, it was one of those inoffensive songs that tried to be current but was almost dated by the time it was released.

The other four were still rehearsing hard to improve their singing, so while he was at Ray's studio Gary recorded both the lead vocal and all of the backing ones as well. For the first few months Gary admits that he had 'no real respect' for the others because, to his mind, they were just dancers and actors and so, musically, he had to carry them.

While the single had its limitations, the accompanying video achieved notoriety and did more to get the boys noticed. It was a camp classic and became known as the 'jelly video'. Nigel asked Rosemary Barratt if she would be interested in making the first video for his new band for the princely sum of £5,000. She brought in Angie Smith, who had worked with her on television, to direct the shoot at the imposing Vector Studios in Stockport.

Ro was impressed with the boys: 'They were so professional. They were a joy to work with. They would just do anything you wanted them to.' Take That were pros right from the start for two reasons. First, Nigel stood no nonsense and made sure they rehearsed conscientiously and worked hard. Secondly, Gary was already immensely professional. He was only twenty but had been working in the business for seven years.

The video began with some high-energy dancing, with the boys in their leather, Lycra shorts and codpieces, but degenerated somewhat when the whipped cream came out, swiftly followed by jelly, jam and custard. Angie was doing her best to interpret Gary's lyric that included lines about jam, cherry pies and recipes. Nigel wasn't especially happy and told Jason off for singing Gary's lines when they were being filmed. He had been carried away in the general excitement of making the video and looked suitably sheepish when he was told to stick to his own lines.

Nigel wanted the video to be more daring so that it might get banned and generate greater publicity. Halfway through the song the boys were all topless, writhing around in jelly and frolicking in foam. Two pretty models from Nigel's agency were there too, massaging them with squirty cream. Then someone had the bright idea that the track should end with the camera firmly focused on a band members' bare bottom surrounded by some wobbly jelly. The problem was which bum to choose. The boys, always competitive, started to argue about who had the most photogenic *derrière*. In the end Angie decided to audition each behind: 'I have never seen five people strip off so quickly in my life. Gary was the most embarrassed, while Robbie was very keen!' The choice proved difficult, so she decided that they should all lie face down on the floor, naked with just a small towel covering their modesty.

Ro, who would later make a film about shooting the video for her company Little Wonder Television, also remembered that Gary was the least enthusiastic when it was decided that the video should end with them all joyfully throwing their towels into the air. He was, after all, a serious songwriter: 'He was clinging on to his towel for dear life and looked distinctly embarrassed when his bum was mopped by one of the models.' At least nobody had to show their dangly bits.

Everyone was delighted with how it went. Afterwards Nigel treated everyone to a meal at nearby Bredbury Hall. They had a grand piano and Gary wasted no time in getting up and serenading everyone with a few Lionel Richie and Barry Manilow classics. Angie noticed that even the waiters thought he was great: 'I realized then what a talented singer and musician he was.' Rob added to the enjoyment by making everyone laugh with his impressions of Norman Wisdom and Frank Spencer.

When the final cut of the video was ready, the boys couldn't wait to show their parents. Nigel, however, insisted that each of them pay a tenner to purchase a copy. He was probably joking with them but they fell for it and all scrabbled around in their pockets to find enough money to buy their own video. No wonder Nigel and the equally canny Gary got along so well.

The video, which had an adult's and children's version, was seen for the first time on *The Hitman and Her* on 12 July 1991, just ten months after the band had been formed. Years later Rob, who had loved every minute of it, saw the whole thing in a different light when he showed his wife Ayda the film. He explained to his friend Chris Heath, 'She pointed out there was something wrong about a naked seventeen-year-old on film with his arse out, writhing naked on the floor with four other boys.'

Their image as conveyed by this video was completely homoerotic and one that the DJ and former *Pop Idol* judge Neil Fox described as 'hysterical'. The video, a collector's item, seems more like knockabout fun these days but the purpose at the time was very serious: they wanted to capture the free-spending gay market.

The first Take That single was released the next day. Gary sent Nicky off to buy the record wherever she could find it, and the rest of the band did the same with their friends and family. The boys all crowded round the radio the following Sunday to listen to the charts. Expectations were high, especially when the rundown reached the top ten and their song had yet to feature. Their excitement built as the countdown continued. Disappointingly, they hadn't heard 'Do What U Like' because it didn't factor in the charts at all. The song only managed to crawl to number eighty-two.

Despite that disappointment, it would be just two months before Nigel finally secured them a record deal.

8

Missing a Hit

Take That had a eureka moment when they appeared one evening at a club in Hull called Lexington Avenue. They had their usual bondage-lite gear in the back of the yellow van Nigel had hired to take them to gigs, but when they arrived for their six o'clock show it was clear that their full-on raunchy look wouldn't be appropriate: the place was packed with underage teenage girls.

They still had to wear Lycra shorts, as that's all they had with them, but they made sure they buttoned up their jackets. The boys were mobbed. Gary had barely started singing before the teen girls were clambering over each other to get to the stage. It was bedlam. They couldn't believe it. Nigel wasn't with them that night and Gary couldn't wait to tell him what had happened.

Nigel booked them into an under-18s club near Manchester and went along to see for himself. He was astonished and realized the boys had stumbled onto something. The leap from appealing to a gay audience to one consisting of teenage girls is not a difficult one. From that evening on, Take That had a twin approach to building their fanbase: they still played the gay clubs but now they played as many younger clubs as they could as well.

They had to make sure they didn't get muddled. They were booked onto a children's television show called *8.15 from Manchester*.

The presenter, Dianne Oxberry, recalled that they were concerned about whether Take That were going to be right for the programme after they saw the video for 'Do What U Like' but, as she observed, 'They were pros.' They sat, good as gold, on the sofa and Rob did his Michael Crawford impression and Howard demonstrated how to do the splits.

Nigel hired a full-time press officer for the band, Carolyn Norman. It was her job to broaden Take That's appeal and transform them from a northern band into a national phenomenon. She secured profiles of the band in *My Guy, Jackie* and *Just Seventeen*, while the hugely popular *Smash Hits* featured them for the first of many times.

The former editor of *heat* magazine, Mark Frith, remembers how bemused he was by the antics of the band when he worked on *Smash Hits*. They were so well trained and determined to be agreeable. He told *Gary Barlow: Real Lives*, 'Take That were desperate to be famous. They would turn up at the office with a pen and Post-it note and take people's tea order. You would have a member of the band in skimpy leather gear asking if you wanted one sugar or two. It was really weird.'

It worked. Take That were an unsigned band whose manager risked losing his house in their bid for glory. There was no *X Factor* or *Britain's Got Talent* to guarantee press coverage. They had to use their charm and their 1,000-watt smiles to win over a traditionally sceptical and battle-hardened press. Carolyn observed, 'We bullied and cajoled people to get them to see the band but once they did they were full of support.'

Carolyn's media blitz began to work. She made a conscious effort to promote the band as fan friendly. One teenage girl, who won a day out with Take That, was forbidden by her father from going when the five hunky lads turned up at her house in their rickety old yellow van. It took all Carolyn's powers of persuasion to coax him into allowing his daughter to go, saying it would be all right because they were only going to Alton Towers.

Gary had his first taste of stage success when he played the lead in his primary school production of *Joseph and the Amazing Technicolor Dreamcoat*.

The teenage Gary spent all his free time learning old songs and composing new ones in his bedroom studio at the family bungalow in Frodsham.

Greenall Whitley Weekly News
CLUB ACT of the YEAR

All that practise was worthwhile when, at sixteen, he won Club Act of the Year with drummer John Tedford at the Ball O'Ditton Royal British Legion Club, in Widnes, in 1987.

Soon after winning Club Act of the Year, Gary's composition 'Now We're Gone' won a nationwide schools music competition sponsored by EMI. The first prize was a trip to London to watch his song being recorded at the world famous Abbey Road Studios.

At the start of a thrilling day out (top). Gary couldn't resist having a go himself (middle). Gary shows off the finished record, with presenter Bill Buckley (left) and form teacher Martin Smiddy.

Gary went out for four years with local girl Nicky Ladanowski, who later went on to become an actress and a familiar face on TV. They kept their relationship secret when he started in Take That.

Gary's first image in the band involved him becoming even blonder than his girlfriend. He hated the amount of maintenance his haircut needed.

Gary spent many happy evenings at Martin Smiddy's house in Frodsham. He looks a natural holding Martin's baby son Richard.

Three years later and he was cuddling up on the same sofa with Richard and new baby Helen.

Gary made sure he kept in touch with old friends even after he had achieved success. Here he is pictured at the go-kart track in Warrington with Dave Mort, who used to drive him to concerts.

He proudly showed off his gold record for *Take That & Party* when John Tedford went for dinner at his house in Knutsford.

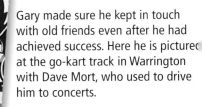

The early image of Take That in 1991 was all bare chests, leather and codpieces, aimed at attracting the important pink pound.

Gary shows his domestic side by doing some ironing. It would be another couple of years before he employed Maurice the butler.

With Take That's manager, Nigel Martin-Smith, whose vision to build a boy band around Gary set the group on the road to success.

Take That proudly give 100 per cent on tour. Gary reaches out with Robbie and Howard at the Manchester G-Mex in July 1993.

Performing at the Birmingham National Exhibition Centre the next night, he was always the star of Take That.

The five on ITV's *Gimme 5* in 1993: the leather had been replaced by teen-friendly leisurewear but they still wore the clodhopper boots that made dancing hard work.

On the *Party* tour it became a Take That tradition that the boys would wear white during their concerts.

Gary dressed as his musical hero Elton John for the show-stopping number 'Apache' during the *Party* tour in August 1993.

Elton already had a shelf full of Ivor Novello Awards, but Gary was thrilled to win his first two in May 1994.

Gary has long enjoyed an easy rapport with the Royal Family. Here he shares a joke with Princess Diana before her *Concert of Hope* at Wembley Arena in December 1994.

Gary doing his best to look hard in January 1995.

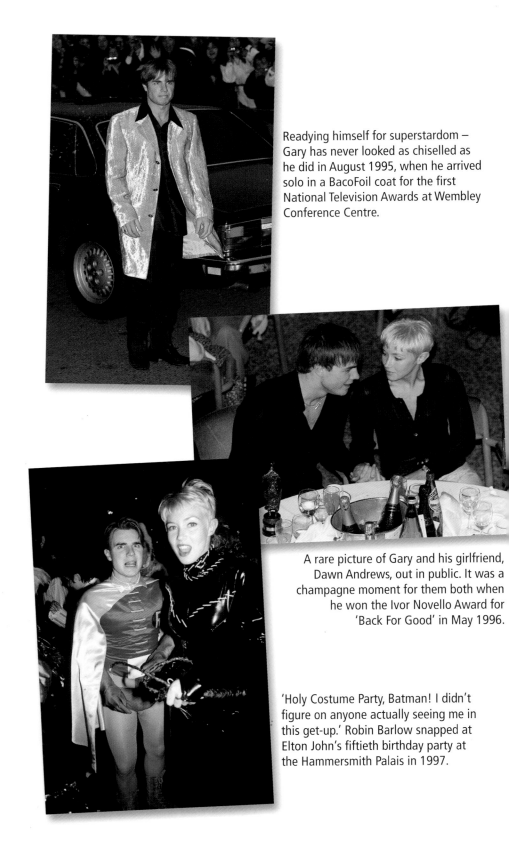

Readying himself for superstardom – Gary has never looked as chiselled as he did in August 1995, when he arrived solo in a BacoFoil coat for the first National Television Awards at Wembley Conference Centre.

A rare picture of Gary and his girlfriend, Dawn Andrews, out in public. It was a champagne moment for them both when he won the Ivor Novello Award for 'Back For Good' in May 1996.

'Holy Costume Party, Batman! I didn't figure on anyone actually seeing me in this get-up.' Robin Barlow snapped at Elton John's fiftieth birthday party at the Hammersmith Palais in 1997.

The most important thing was to keep the band's name in the columns, particularly the ones written by the tabloid newspapers, which had finally realized pop news was a way of attracting younger readers. Piers Morgan in the *Sun*, Rick Sky in the *Daily Mirror* and Linda Duff in the *Daily Star* were very important in the early days of Take That. They would lap up stories like the one in which girl fans smashed a plate-glass window at a nightclub in a bid to see their new idols. It may have been made up but it was just the sort of story that kept interest running high.

Nigel's strategy was to keep the band on their toes. They felt that at any time he could dispense with one of them with the click of his fingers. That excluded Gary and Howard, who were undoubtedly his favourites and became good buddies, spending time together on their days off.

Sometimes they would meet up in Warrington for a night out at the go-kart track. Gary would invite a group of friends over from Frodsham for a competition. Graham Hitchen would go and so would Dave Mort, who recalls, 'It was just a normal night out with the lads – nothing fancy. Gary and Howard always won. Nobody ever beat them.'

Although he was not a go-kart fan, Jason was in Gary's camp at this time, while the younger boys, Rob and Mark, stuck together. These three were the least happy when the band started up. Intriguingly, the rumours in the music world then were that Nigel fancied Jason. That may or may not be true but Nigel certainly gave him the toughest time.

On one occasion Jason was a few minutes late for his pick-up in the van – something guaranteed to frustrate Nigel, who understood the importance of punctuality. They were on their way to London for a photo shoot with *Number One* magazine. It was a big day because this was going to be the first Take That front cover. Nigel was annoyed and his bad mood festered for a while before he ordered the van to turn round when they reached the M6 and dump Jason back at his home in Wythenshawe. Jason, he announced, was out of the band, which would continue as a four-piece. The others did the shoot as planned. By the evening, Nigel's mood had brightened and he phoned Jason to tell him he was back in. The only problem was that there was no time to reshoot the photos, so a separate picture of Jason had to be dropped in for the cover. It's a completely bogus shot.

Rob had his problems as well, because he had been struggling with self-doubt. He had begun defining his Take That persona as the cheeky one but he hated being picked on either by Nigel or by the rest of the band. He saw himself as a bit of an outsider – a view not helped by niggling little things, not least by being dropped off at junction 15 on the M6 motorway whenever they were on their way back north from a personal appearance. It would drive him mad that they would never listen when he explained it was not out of their way to drive through Tunstall and continue on to Manchester.

Quite early on Rob went to see his father and told him he wanted to leave the band and take a job as a bluecoat in the holiday camp Pete Conway was working in. His dad told him he would regret it when the others were number one, which was the best advice he could have given his son. Rob stuck it out but the others, with the possible exception of Mark, never realized how sensitive he was. Gary certainly didn't, because he was so focused on his own destiny. Rob described it memorably in his book *You Know Me*: 'Gary was single-minded back then, and bloody-minded.'

Nicky Ladanowski also detected a subtle change in Gary since he had come under the influence of Nigel. She was concerned at what was happening to her boyfriend. It wasn't a huge thing at this stage but she was alarmed he seemed to be giving Rob a hard time. A pal explained, 'Nicky thought Gary was quite nasty about Robbie, who she thought was sweet. Robbie was just very young and he irritated Gary because he would never shut up. But the first time Nicky met him he was sitting in the back of the Orion and hardly said two words. She thought he was really quiet!'

On one occasion the boys stayed over at her mum's house in Frodsham. Nicky gave up her room to Rob. In the morning, when she took him in a cup of tea, he had been rummaging about in her photograph album. He had all her photographs out on the bed. He was looking through them and started pointing out to her the ones he thought were nice. She just laughed because Rob was a cheeky lad who could get away with something like that. It was the sort of behaviour that people loved him for.

Nicky liked all the boys. They were much more typical 'lads' than Gary. He was strait-laced, at least at the beginning of Take That. She and Gary usually socialized with Howard and his long-standing girl-friend Gillian, and they would all head off to the cinema to unwind. Sometimes Jason would tag along with his girlfriend, Juliet. Jason probably had the widest social circle from his days as a dancer and had lots of female friends. More often than not, however, it would be just Gillian and Howard, who, perhaps because he was older, told very funny stories and had everyone in stitches.

One of Nigel Martin-Smith's unbreakable rules as the band became more widely known was that the boys weren't allowed to have steady girlfriends. He was very serious about it. They firmly had to deny that they were with anyone when they gave interviews. He had known about Nicky from day one and he didn't like it. He was paranoid about reading something for the first time in the newspapers, so he didn't want any surprises or dark secrets.

Clearly Nigel thought that their newly discovered young girl fans would stay loyal if they believed Take That were available. The thinking behind it was that every girl could dream of being 'the one' who would steal the heart of her idol. They could all be the princess to their Prince Charming. If the boys were revealed to be in steady relationships, then the girls would quickly switch their allegiance to another act. Nowadays, a desirable partner makes the star more appealing – a stunning girlfriend like Nicky Ladanowski would have done wonders for Gary's credibility – but nobody seemed to realize it at the time. It also might be argued that a certain ambiguity about Take That's sexuality would make them more appealing to the gay market.

Nigel, it seemed, never quite got over Nicky's existence. His apprehension about girlfriends didn't stop Gary and Nicky from seeing one another. At least Nicky was an open secret because Gary had told Nigel about her. Rob, though, was striving to keep his girlfriend Rachael, back in Stoke-on-Trent, entirely hidden from him. She had still been at school when Take That were launched and was dividing her time between modelling and sixth-form college when the band began gigging up and down the country. She was always introduced as Robbie's cousin when she turned up at the small gigs around the country. Both girls were well liked by the other band members. All five of them signed a birthday card for Rachael, which she kept. Jason had written, 'When you've finished with Cousin Robbie, let me know and I will take you out.' Nigel would have had a fit.

While the boys were striving to keep some normality in their private lives, they were grafting away, playing small gigs for not much more than petrol money. Their lives were about to change, however, when a new A & R manager at RCA records, Nick Raymonde, saw a video of them on television and thought they had something. He told the author Martin Roach that he immediately saw an opportunity: 'They were sort of boy-next-door, just dead ordinary, and they gave off the vibe that they were really enjoying what they were doing.'

Back at his office in London, Nick already had an ally in his appreciation of Take That. Nicki Chapman, who would later become well known as a TV presenter and a judge on *Pop Idol*, was then part of RCA's publicity team. She had seen a picture of the band in their underpants in *Number One* magazine and had pinned it to the door of Nick's office.

Nick went to see the boys perform at a small club in Slough, where they were supporting Right Said Fred, the over-the-top duo who were in the charts with their debut hit, 'I'm Too Sexy'. He was impressed. They were only showcasing a few numbers but the reaction from the watching girls was exactly the same as it had been at Lexington Avenue in Hull: they were mobbed. The teenage fans didn't seem to care that they were wearing their bondage gear.

It was the record company's hesitation about the leather look that had originally led to RCA passing on the band. Fortunately, Nick Raymonde had not been part of the initial rejection and he took a demo of the band into a meeting with the head of A & R, Korda Marshall. The demo consisted of three tracks: 'Do What U Like', 'Take That And Party', which was new and written by Gary deliberately to promote the band's name, and 'A Million Love Songs'.

Korda loved the last of the three, the renamed '1 Million Love Songs Later'. He thought it would be a smash hit. A cliché of popular music that is entirely true is that it only takes one song. This composition, more than any other, defines Gary as a great songwriter. It has always been a song that makes the hairs on the back of your neck stand up.

G-A-Y would have been the ideal venue in which to showcase Take That but the popular West End club wasn't launched until 1993. Instead, Nick took Korda to see the band live at The Limelight, the cavernous club in Shaftesbury Avenue. They just did the three numbers, which Korda thought 'so gay it was funny'. Like his colleague, he could see that the band had something that could fill a void in the music scene – they were a pop group that could make records unashamedly for the charts.

One of the key factors that shouldn't be overlooked is that RCA liked dealing with Nigel. He was determined, had a vision for Take That and was very businesslike. Record companies despair of having to deal with a lot of egos flying around. In this case, they only had to deal with Nigel and they could trust him to deliver. Negotiations moved swiftly, with Nigel agreeing a £75,000 deal with the record company that was a fairly standard contract. After he took

25 per cent, Gary, Robbie, Mark, Jason and Howard were left to split £50,000. They each received £10,000 minus Nigel's deductions for the things he had bought for the band. It wasn't much of a return for the year of hard graft they had put in.

Gary, however, was about to move into a different league from the others. While negotiating the recording contract for the group, Nigel had also been trying to find a publishing deal for his protégé. Just four days after the RCA signing party at the Hard Rock Café on Old Park Lane, Nigel took Gary aside and told him that he had landed a £150,000 songwriting contract with Virgin Music Publishing. This was an incredible break for Gary. Already, even after deducting Nigel's cut, he would be considerably richer than all the other boys put together.

The financial arrangements behind this last deal may have sown the first seeds of discord within the band but they weren't apparent then. Instead, the other four loyally signed the Virgin contract because the company wanted them all to do so, even though it was Gary alone who received the advance because he wrote the songs. Everyone knew and accepted that. They realized that if they did well, they would all be millionaires; it was just that Gary would be a multimillionaire.

RCA didn't want to waste any time and, probably too hastily, rushed out 'Promises' as the label's first Take That song. The song was recorded and practically ready to go, so it seemed the obvious choice. Thanks to Nigel's London contacts, Gary had joined forces with a young producer called Graham Stack to come up with a catchy dance track. Graham would go on to achieve much greater recognition as the producer behind a string of *X Factor* hits, including 'Impossible', James Arthur's winning song in 2012. In retrospect it was a poor decision to go with 'Promises' but everyone was enthused by the prospect of releasing a record. They couldn't wait for Take That to be the biggest band in the country.

They threw themselves into the promotion, which included

making a video that was considerably tamer than 'Do What U Like' and nothing like as memorable. They were filmed rehearsing in a dance studio. There was no jelly or jam and just one naked bottom, as one of the band splashed out of a swimming pool wearing a G-string. Rob would later confirm that this was his backside, which came as no surprise, as he has never been embarrassed about showing the world his rear view.

Gary was still peroxide blond but at least he no longer had to wear the leather bondage costume. The overall impression was that the band had jettisoned the Village People look without being quite sure what to put in its place.

This dilemma was never better illustrated than when they appeared as the closing act of *The Disney Club*, which was a Sunday morning show on children's ITV for the under-tens. The boys all looked like they had stepped off the set of *Seven Brides for Seven Brothers* – a bunch of wholesome ranch hands. Gary sang in front of the children, while the others gamely did their usual back flips and dance moves, and the young audience wondered what was going on.

The PR machine behind Take That was working wonders. One minute they were on *The Disney Club*, the next on *Wogan*, which at its peak boasted an audience of twelve million before it was axed in 1992. Then there was *Going Live!*, *The O-Zone*, *Motormouth* and *Pebble Mill*. You could barely turn on the TV or open a magazine without Take That grinning at you. Surely 'Promises' was going to be an enormous hit?

The Sunday after its release, in November 1991, the boys all crowded into Nigel's room in the Metropole Hotel, Paddington. This time there wasn't the huge let-down of their first single. They entered the charts at a perfectly respectable number thirty-eight. Everyone was ecstatic and Nigel cracked open the champagne. Rob jumped up and down on one of the beds so enthusiastically that he broke it. Disappointingly, though, the song failed to climb any higher and disappeared from the top forty the following week.

'Promises' was a good song but it wasn't a great song. The band was a work in progress, trying to find the right song to go with the right image. Nick Raymonde had taken a big chance with Take That, so he wasn't going to give up on them after one record. This was lucky for them because things got steadily worse before they improved.

Nick's next move was to persuade Gary that he needed to write new material and he brought in a producer called Duncan Bridgeman to work with him on the next single. Duncan was a young producer who had first seen Take That on Saturday morning TV and thought they had potential: 'Something went off in my head and I thought I'd like to work with them. I got my manager to find out what label they were on and from there I met Nick Raymonde.

'To be honest, the impression I got at the time was that he was the only person taking it seriously. Boy bands hadn't really happened and I think everybody thought it was a bit of a joke. Nick took me to see them at a gig in Burnley. They were doing their usual thing of spinning on their heads with their tops off and I told Nick I would love to work with them. I was very excited about it.'

Duncan had his own studio on the Uxbridge Road in Acton, so Gary left Frodsham to spend three weeks in London with him working on songs, in particular one he had written in his bedroom called 'Once You've Tasted Love'. He stayed at the La Reserve Hotel near Stamford Bridge, the Chelsea football ground, but spent a lot more time at Moody Studios than he did lounging about in the hotel.

Duncan's first impression when working with Gary was of a man who had done his homework: 'He knew the chords; he knew how to put things together. He had a demo of the song and I started building on the programming he had already done. I remember getting a few session guys in to play some squiggly techno noises. I think I helped him, showing him how to arrange, stick extra chords and stuff in, but basically he knew what he was doing and the whole thing was built around him.'

A few days before the end of the session, the rest of the boys came down to sort out their vocals. Duncan recalls that they weren't very confident about singing in a studio but it did prove a landmark for Robbie: 'I am very proud that I gave Robbie his first vocal. He did a rap.'

It wasn't groundbreaking or particularly clever but Rob was 'chuffed' that something he had written was going to be on a record. When Nick Raymonde raised the question of Rob receiving a writing credit and royalty for his contribution, Gary told him that if he wanted that, then they would drop the rap.

Gary's apparent meanness about a relatively minor thing was nothing to do with money, although there were signs he was cautious about such matters. He had put his publishing advance into a savings account that needed a co-signature from Nigel before he could withdraw any money. The songwriting credit had more to do with achievement: Gary needed the recognition that he was the songwriter. He wanted the sleeve-notes to read 'words and music by Gary Barlow'. 'I wasn't ready to share the glory.' Rob never forgot.

After Christmas Duncan travelled up to a studio in Bury in Lancashire to work with Gary. RCA wanted to bring an album out as soon as possible to cash in on all the publicity the group was receiving. It was hard work. Duncan recalls, 'We worked really long hours, laying down the tracks, working out arrangements and rearranging choruses and stuff. I don't think Gary was much of a late-nighter. He used to take the mickey out of me quite a lot.

'But I was very impressed by his professionalism. He gets properly prepared and doesn't seem to be that nervous about it. He just comes in and it's a job and it's what he wants to do. And he just does it.'

Gary is very complimentary about Duncan in *My Take*, saying he owed him a 'huge debt of gratitude' for improving his vocal technique and getting rid of any lingering cabaret vibrato. For his part, Duncan thought Gary's vocals were 'fantastic' and he was a 'natural'.

Duncan was also very patient with the others, trying to build confidence in their singing ability. They spent about a month producing six tracks for the as-yet-untitled first album, including one called 'Satisfied' that Duncan still thinks is his personal best. The track is a very danceable piece of electropop but sounds like it's by a band that had yet to find a strong identity.

All appeared to be going well until 'Once You've Tasted Love' was released as the next single in February 1992 – and promptly flopped, reaching number forty-seven in the charts. The critics were not that impressed, with *Smash Hits* condemning it as being 'as funky as a cauliflower'.

RCA had invested more than a million pounds in the band, so this was a disaster that needed a major rethink. The first thing that happened was Duncan was sacked. He acknowledges graciously that he didn't get it right: 'I was going for a George Michael grown-up classy kind of sound, which I think was a bit of an error.'

Even Gary was feeling less sure about the future. He wryly observed, 'We're becoming the most famous group in Britain for not having a hit.'

9

Top of the Pops

Gary could go to the hole in the wall at any time and check the six-figure balance in his savings account to cheer himself up. He had just turned twenty-one and was extremely well-off for his age. He had a lovely girlfriend and masses of fans but he needed more than that: he craved recognition and acclamation as a great songwriter. He was hurt, therefore, when the record company decided to bring out a cover as their next single. It's what happens when things aren't going well.

'It Only Takes A Minute' changed everything for Take That. Now that RCA had become part of BMG, Simon Cowell came into Gary's story again when he suggested that they should work with a producer called Nigel Wright, who had achieved a good reputation working with the jazz-funk group Shakatak in the eighties. Nigel formed an enduring association with Andrew Lloyd Webber after he produced the cast recording of Gary's old favourite *Joseph and the Amazing Technicolor Dreamcoat*, which was revived in 1991 with Jason Donovan.

Gary instantly liked Nigel, a larger-than-life character. Gary's musical world is amazingly small. Nigel, for instance, enjoyed a long-standing connection with Simon that would lead to him becoming musical director of *Britain's Got Talent* and *The X Factor* and producer of many of the contestants' solo albums. His was a friendly face when Gary later joined the top-rated programme.

Their first contact came at Nigel's studios in Chertsey when he suggested recording 'It Only Takes A Minute'. The song had been a disco favourite in the seventies for Tavares and, less notably, a top ten hit for the notorious Jonathan King in 1976 under the name of One Hundred Ton and a Feather. The track was no weightier than Gary's own efforts but it did at least have the virtue of familiarity.

'It Only Takes A Minute' is one of those songs that instantly makes you want to get up and dance. Duncan Bridgeman concedes, 'The new producer got it a lot more right than I did. Suddenly they had got the sound right.'

Gary was unhappy that his songs were taking the blame for the band's lack of success: 'To me it felt like everyone had lost faith in me as a songwriter. I believed that we had at least partially got our record deal on the strength of my songs.' The only consolation was that his composition 'Satisfied' was the B-side of the 7-inch single and two others, 'I Can Make It', a lush ballad, and 'Never Want To Let You Go', featured on the CD single.

Gary didn't have time to mope around. Part of the plan to re-invigorate Take That involved them working harder than before – if that were possible. The first thing Nigel Martin-Smith did was to make sure the record company provided them with decent transport. Gary had driven literally thousands of miles ferrying the band around in their yellow transit. Occasionally they all squeezed into Nigel's Ford Escort XR3i. Now they had a Toyota Previa people carrier.

They would need it, because Nigel had the brilliant idea of joining up with the Family Planning Association. He sent the boys on the *Big Schools Tour*, preaching a safe sex message and plugging the band relentlessly with as many as four mini concerts in a day. Gary wasn't driving any less but the tour proved to be a groundbreaking success, with the band getting the message across to 50,000 youngsters before the release of their next single. It was PR gold, especially as the young fans could leave their names and addresses so a coherent fanbase could be built. It was before social networking and email made this sort of thing easy. These days pop stars will have a comparable number of followers on Twitter the very day they open an account.

They were touring light – two speakers, an amp, a tape deck and a microphone were all they needed. They would sing a few songs, give out the FPA leaflets and then chat with the schoolchildren about anything they wanted to talk about: sex, drugs or smoking. Take That were very approachable, which is one of the main reasons their fans stayed so loyal. Gary said simply, 'I felt like we were helping.'

The Family Planning Association were struck by the boys' responsible attitude to sex, which would have pleased Nigel. Fortunately, the FPA were not involved with the boys when they later bragged about their female conquests on tour.

Gary contacted Frodsham High to ask if Take That could visit but his own school turned him down. The identity of the killjoy has never been revealed; perhaps he had watched the notorious jelly video and thought the band wouldn't be suitable. Gary never returned to the school before it closed in 2009.

Take That's publicity machine continued to work tirelessly to promote the band. In May 1992 they bounced on stage at the Dominion Theatre in Tottenham Court Road to perform 'It Only Takes A Minute' at the Children's Royal Variety Performance. The timing was perfect, as the single was due out on 1 June. Any lingering gay image had completely vanished. Gary wore a horizontally striped sailor's T-shirt that would have been a good choice if he had been presenting *Blue Peter*.

The stage was filled with so many children and dancers that there was barely room for Howard to do a back flip. By coincidence, one of the dancers was Dawn Andrews, who Gary immediately recognized from the dreadful video for Kurtis Rush. Her career had moved on since those days and she was in great demand as a session dancer. She had been one of the Itsy Bitsy girls chosen by Arlene Phillips to appear as Bombalurina with Timmy Mallett in the video for his 1990 number one 'Itsy Bitsy Teeny Weeny Yellow Polka Dot Bikini'. The video, shot in a cold north London garage made to look like a beach, was so popular that Dawn had been on the front cover of *Smash Hits* before Gary had.

Gary went up to her to say hello, but Dawn was so embarrassed that she went bright red and couldn't speak. The way their paths crossed over the years was like something out of a movie. It was destiny. Another three years would pass, though, before Gary met her again.

He had a better conversation with Princess Margaret, who was guest of honour at the show. As is customary, she came backstage to meet the performers afterwards. Gary introduced her to the band and she said she had enjoyed their dance routines. The best thing about the show was the knowledge that it would be televised on the BBC, so an audience of millions would watch it.

Neither the band nor the record company was leaving anything to chance. The song *had* to be a big hit, so the boys started an exhausting round of signings and personal appearances up and down the country. Thousands of excited teenagers would turn up for an in-store signing, with the resultant hysteria and publicity being just what the band wanted. Girls who fainted were looked after by St John's Ambulance volunteers, while police smuggled Take That out the back door.

When 'It Only Takes A Minute' was released, it reached number sixteen at the end of the first week. This time a Take That single went up the charts the following week, peaking at number seven. Rob described it simply as a 'momentous day'. They celebrated at the restaurant of the La Reserve Hotel where, a sign of good things to come, a mass of girl fans gathered outside with their noses pressed up against the window, hoping to catch a glimpse of the band.

Gary's mother Marj was listening to the radio a week later when they appeared on a *Radio 1 Roadshow* live from Alton Towers. She couldn't believe the screaming she was hearing: 'I realized all that Gary had been working for had come to fruition. There were tears in my eyes.'

Even better was to come: they were booked for their first appearance on *Top of the Pops*, the fulfilment of one of Gary's principal ambitions. He sang live, which meant he had to do very little dancing, while the others hurled themselves around the set in their usual athletic fashion. Apparently, the camera crew and production staff were taking bets on whether any of them could actually sing. Gary was incensed when he heard and sang his heart out: 'It does make you want to try harder.'

He was thrilled when he discovered that Lionel Richie was in a neighbouring dressing room. Gary had been singing his songs for years but managed to restrain himself from giving a rendition of 'Hello' outside his door. He approached Lionel's manager and asked if he would sign a CD he had brought with him. Lionel came out and introduced himself. Later, as they were leaving, Lionel passed with his entourage and shouted over, 'Hey, Gary, how's it going?' The other four couldn't believe it.

Rob was astonished that nobody on the show seemed to be as excited as they were: 'Everybody else looked so bored. I couldn't understand why they weren't excited to be working on *Top of the Pops*. We were!'

Take That were a breath of fresh air for the programme, which was looking tired with so many faceless grunge and dance acts. One of the show's producers, Jeff Simpson, observed, 'They were a godsend. At last there was a buzz about music again. They regularly delivered what the show desperately needed – excitement.'

Not everyone was impressed. Simon Mayo, who presented the breakfast show on Radio 1, described 'It Only Takes A Minute' as 'crap', although he would later recognize Gary's songwriting abilities.

Smash Hits liked it enough to put Take That on the cover. They were photographed and interviewed on a day trip to the beach at Camber Sands. Gary told them, 'If we hadn't had a hit this time round, we'd have been a laughing stock. I can't tell you how happy we are.' For once in an interview, he was being entirely truthful.

The other inescapable observation was that Gary seemed to eat a lot more than the others. He was forever munching on Pringles while he chatted with whoever was next to him. The suspicion that he liked his food was enhanced when he had three extra helpings of toast with his pâté at dinner. He confided that he hated his legs and wasn't as conscientious about working out as the others. He also had the annoying habit of flicking his bandmates' ears when they were sitting next to him.

He was asked to describe himself for the magazine: 'I'm quiet, interesting and thoughtful. I enjoy eating out and going to the pictures.' Rob, taking a break from playing football with Mark, was also truthful in the interview, revealing, 'I'm not very good at taking criticism' – something he had to take plenty of and that would gradually undermine the unity of the band.

Gary loathed their next single, 'I Found Heaven'. Once again, he hadn't written it and this time he didn't even sing the lead – Robbie did. The song was written by Billy Griffin and Ian Levine. The former had replaced Smokey Robinson as lead singer of The Miracles in the early seventies. The latter was yet another producer who had been brought in to help Take That find their sound. Gary wasn't impressed with the result and never plays it on stage. 'Truly fucking awful' is his succinct opinion.

His view was vindicated to some extent when the track peaked at number fifteen, which was yet another step backwards. The plan had been to top the charts as the first album was released. That didn't work. When their debut album *Take That & Party* reached the record stores, however, it was an instant hit, reaching number five in the first week of release.

Buoyed by this initial success, the band began a nationwide tour of HMV shops. The thirst for publicity was more than satisfied early on when several thousand girl fans went on the rampage at their first couple of appearances. In Manchester, where 5,000 turned up to see their new idols, the boys donned police disguises to slip out of the shop and avoid being torn to bits. It was all good fun and their growing reputation was further enhanced when HMV cancelled the rest of the tour for safety reasons. Perfect.

Take That & Party eventually climbed to number two and stayed in the charts for seventy-three weeks – a fantastic result. Gary's lack of grace over Rob's rap was put into perspective when it turned out he wasn't going to be the sole writer on the album after all. Instead there were three tracks he did not compose: 'I Found Heaven', 'It Only Takes A Minute' and 'Could It Be Magic', the Barry Manilow standard that he had played a hundred times at his teenage solo gigs.

Ten out of thirteen songs had been written by Gary either in his bedroom in Frodsham or in hotel rooms, which was still a good percentage, but he was especially peeved that 'I Found Heaven' was the opening track. Many long-term fans of Take That cite this album as their favourite but that's probably more to do with nostalgia than merit. The album lacks a sense of cohesion although it did help that they ended up using the six tracks Duncan Bridgeman had already produced. That improved the overall sound, even if the decision not to re-record was reached mainly for financial reasons.

The relative failure of 'I Found Heaven' gave Gary more leverage when the record company wanted to rush out another single to cash in on the album's initial success. He fought for 'A Million Love Songs', which in retrospect was by far the best track on *Take That & Party*.

Even normally cynical DJs found themselves praising Take That. Simon Bates, then an influential Radio 1 presenter, observed, 'There's one reason why Take That are such a success – Gary Barlow's songwriting talent. Now he is going to take over from George Michael.'

Gary

Some critics did think that Gary was attempting to copy the feel of George Michael's first solo number one 'Careless Whisper' but that was more to do with the use of the rich saxophone than any similarity in the tunes. 'A Million Love Songs', produced by Ian Levine and Billy Griffin, was a mature song with a powerful chorus. There is nothing like a classic ballad to improve public perception. Gary acknowledged that the song changed the band's career: 'A lot of people thought it would be the kiss of death but in the end we got our way.'

'A Million Love Songs', written when Gary was fifteen and premiered at the Halton Legion, is a once-in-a-lifetime classic that transformed Take That from being just another pop group into something far more substantial and long-lasting. A million romances were sealed when it was the slow number at the end of an evening out. The brilliant 'Angels' would have a similar effect on Robbie Williams' solo career. Sadly, when Gary needed something equally memorable to ignite his own solo career, he didn't have it.

When 'A Million Love Songs' equalled the highest chart position of 'It Only Takes A Minute', Gary's decision to fight for its release was entirely vindicated. He celebrated by buying his first house, a three-bedroom bungalow in Bexton Road, Knutsford, a desirable Cheshire town eighteen miles from his childhood home. He paid £60,000 and didn't need a mortgage. The property required a lot of work but Gary was able to keep it in the family by employing his brother Ian as renovator and his father Colin to improve the look of the garden. Ian had completed a YTS scheme when he finished school and now worked as a builder.

Gary's new home was within walking distance of Knutsford's well-heeled town centre but, more importantly, it was just a few minutes from the M6, so he could be back in Frodsham in twenty minutes. Gary moved partly because Nigel convinced him it was a sound financial investment and also because he would have more space for his home studio and the important task of writing the next album. He was already under strict orders to start composing to cash in on Take That's popularity in case it didn't last.

Take That fans quickly discovered Gary's new address. They always seemed to be there when he was enjoying a romantic evening with Nicky. Having his own home made it easier for the couple to spend time together. Gary had started to cook and would light candles all over the house to make it romantic. The drawback, however, was that if he peeked round the curtains, there was always a group of girls outside. Take That fans were very good-natured and never caused any trouble or gave Nicky a tough time. Gary would go out from time to time to make sure they were OK and not catching cold. He would sign autographs and pose for pictures before telling them sternly, 'Go home now. Your parents will go mad.' One loyal fan recalled, 'He was lovely to us.'

In the morning Gary would go out to start his car and find a pile of love letters and cards underneath the windscreen wipers. That also used to happen when he and Nicky went for a meal at the Chinese Delight but the fans were always as good as gold and never disrupted his crispy duck by setting foot in the restaurant.

10

Reason to Party

When *Smash Hits* published the Take That life story over two editions in October 1992, it was Nigel's storybook version – the one that included Gary and Mark spending two years building their partnership at Strawberry Studios. Other myths were trotted out. One of them was the rules they had laid down for themselves: 'Lots of sleep, very little drink, plenty of working out and absolutely no girlfriends.'

Gary came over rather blokish when he declared, 'We have relationships whilst we're away. You know, we're young lads.' *Relationships* was rather a nice way of suggesting they had one-night stands, which wouldn't have been music to the ears of Nicky Ladanowski as she was smuggled into his hotel room during their first nationwide tour. She would only attend when Nigel was nowhere to be seen.

It was a touch of bravado from Gary, who wanted to appear less strait-laced than he actually was. He had also had his nose pierced to help conceal his natural conservatism, ironically one of the characteristics Nicky most admired about her boyfriend. When they started going out, he didn't drink, smoke or take drugs. It was on tour that he started to smoke Silk Cut and enjoy a nightcap or two. Nicky told her friend how surprised she had been when he pulled out a bottle of Jack Daniels in his hotel room: 'Nicky said it was really weird seeing him drinking because he just never had a drink. He was not like the other lads.'

Nicky had a simple system for getting to Gary's room. All the fans would be outside and she would slip into the lobby to be met by Gary's bodyguard, James, who was huge, and he would walk her to the lift. Somebody else would take her to another floor of the hotel and she would be shown to a room where she would wait. This was not Gary's room or even on his floor but a precaution so that fans couldn't follow her to the room he was in. Eventually, James would arrive to show her to the right floor and Gary would suddenly appear in the corridor, invariably laughing because he found the runaround hilarious.

They would go back to his room to order a club sandwich from room service, sometimes watch a movie or just talk through their day. By now Nicky had started at the Central School of Speech and Drama near Swiss Cottage in London. She would tell him about her acting classes and he would tell her about being a famous pop star. She particularly enjoyed it if they were staying in one of the best London hotels, like The Rembrandt in Knightsbridge or The Conrad in Chelsea Harbour.

Take That approached a concert as if it were an important football match. Nigel Martin-Smith was the manager, getting the boys in a huddle before he sent them out on the pitch. He would tell them, 'Work for each other and take no prisoners.' Their first proper concert on the *Party* tour was in front of 2,000 'shrieking girls' at Newcastle City Hall on 2 November 1992 and went so well that nobody noticed Robbie had a bad throat.

The *Daily Mirror* was impressed and said the boys 'could give Michael Jackson a run for his money when it came to dancing'. Piers Morgan in his column in the *Sun* was equally enthusiastic: 'The dance routines were slick and energetic. The singing was tight and in tune. The overall effect was polished and exciting.

'Yes, it's simple and poppy. But the stale British music scene needs a breath of fresh air like Take That.'

They played all but one of the songs from *Take That & Party*. You could have guessed the missing track was Gary's least favourite, 'I Found Heaven'. In its place a new one, 'Apache', was arguably the most exciting of the night. Mark, Howard and Jason performed a dancing tour de force, while Gary played keyboards wearing a T-shirt with 'Gaz' written on it. Rob came on with a hat that made him look like one of Ken Dodd's Diddy Men and proceeded to rap. The fans, who now called themselves Thatters, lapped it up. The boys closed the show with 'Could It Be Magic', 'It Only Takes A Minute' and, inevitably, 'Take That And Party'. It was pretty much all action from start to finish. Rob spent the entire tour hoarse and even Gary was struggling after twelve consecutive nights around the country without a break.

There's no doubt that they were more like a lusty sports team on the road in their tour bus than the 'intelligent and modest' young men that Piers Morgan first described meeting a year earlier. On one occasion, bored with the endless motorway, they decided to have a wanking competition in the back of the bus. They all enthusiastically entered into the spirit of the contest and tried hard but Rob came first.

The record company was anxious to squeeze another track from the album to coincide with the tour. 'Could It Be Magic' became the sixth single from *Take That & Party* but, despite that, was their biggest hit to date when it was released in November 1992. Once again Gary had to grit his teeth that it was a well-known Barry Manilow song and not one of his. He also had to take a back seat on vocals, with Rob singing the lead. Nor did he have much to do in the video that was set in an aircraft hangar decked out like a large American garage full of cars. He is glimpsed only a few times, as Rob is very much centre stage, with a smattering of Mark's cheeky smile and Howard's abs. It was very much the Robbie Show.

Nowadays it's commonplace to have all sorts of mixes of a song but it was quite rare in the early nineties. Ian Levine had done a disco-style mix for the vinyl but Nick Raymonde brought in the renowned Italian producers The Rapino Brothers to work on a club mix. They had earned a reputation for producing exciting mixes of dance tracks during the house music revolution of the late eighties. Originally it was going to be credited as The Rapino Brothers featuring Take That but in the end their version was launched in a CD format under the group's banner. The Radio Rapino Mix would be track twelve on the album.

It is one of the classic Take That songs and possibly best represents their music in these very early years – it had vitality, verve and *joie de vivre*. In years to come, this song would always feature whenever there was a Take That night on *The X Factor*.

Intriguingly, Ian Levine was at the *Top of the Pops* studio when Take That performed it in December. He told Martin Roach that they had changed: 'In my opinion they'd changed completely and they just weren't the same people any more. I just felt like I didn't know them; I felt a bit alienated.'

Ian's observations reflected those of others who knew the band better than he did but, for the moment, everything in Take That world was completely positive. Mark Owen said he knew the band had truly arrived when they won seven prestigious *Smash Hits* Readers Poll Awards. They might not have had the kudos of the Brit Awards but they were an excellent barometer of popularity. Mark always did best on these occasions because he would win awards like Most Fanciable Male Star and Best Haircut.

The *Smash Hits* Poll Winners Party, held that year at the Royal Albert Hall, was more than satisfying for Take That because they beat New Kids on the Block into second in the Best Band in the World category. They also received the award for Best Single from Jordan of New Kids. Gary had just performed 'A Million Love Songs' seated at a piano while the others sang the chorus sweetly – not a back flip in sight. He could obviously play, which was something the fans might not have fully realized. The renowned saxophonist Snake Davis belted out the famous signature sax melody next to them. When Jordan Knight came on, he decided to hand the award to Gary because 'you're the one who actually wrote the song, right?'

The ceremony was even more pleasing for Gary because 'A Million Love Songs' won the award for Best Single ahead of the cover versions 'I Found Heaven' and 'It Only Takes A Minute'. Gary had been under pressure to write stronger and more current lyrics, so this was a welcome vindication of a great song at last. Gary thanked everyone who voted and then said, 'A special thanks to the best manager in pop, Nigel Martin-Smith.'

1992 had been a stupendous year for Take That. It had started off unpromisingly but ended with the band arguably the biggest in the UK. Their debut album had sold more than one million copies and also been the best-selling video of the year despite being released only three weeks before Christmas.

Gary began the new year completely knackered. The tour had put an enormous strain on his voice and he was continuing to write new material in what little spare time he had. He always made sure he spent Christmas with his mum and dad, but no sooner had he wished them a 'Happy New Year!' than he was at a chateau outside Paris filming the video to 'Why Can't I Wake Up With You', the eighth single from *Take That & Party* – or, to put it another way, the first single from the yet-to-be-released second album.

The first album used Duncan Bridgeman's original production. The second would include a new version by Paul and Steve Jervier working with Jonathan Wales that resulted in a smoother, more soulful interpretation of the song. Steve had first come to Nick Raymonde's attention at RCA with a remix of Boyz II Men's 'Motownphilly'.

The video was also more relaxed – just individual shots of the boys in the chateau. Gary was seen playing the piano and looking wistful. Even though every fan had a copy of *Take That & Party*, they still went out and bought the new single, taking it to number two in the charts, just kept off the top by 2 Unlimited with the club hit 'No Limit'. The boys also won their first Brit Award for Best British Single, although for some reason they weren't booked to play during the ceremony at Alexandra Palace.

Gary had no time to rest, with plans in motion to project Take That internationally. They had travelled abroad for the first time in the summer of 1992 for some gigs in Sweden. It was the beginning of their enduring popularity throughout Europe. Another short tour of Sweden was followed by trips to Holland and Germany. Then they were quickly on a plane for their first promotional visit to the US and Canada and then on to Japan without drawing breath. They much preferred Japan to the States, where they felt their music didn't fit in. They were booked into schools as they had been in the UK but there was a world of difference between a New York inner-city high school and its provincial English equivalent. Take That weren't hard-core rappers nor were they Nirvana, the kings of grunge and the American rock gods of the time.

The usual drawbacks about being a British band trying to crack America applied: nobody had heard of them and nobody could understand them. Gary, however, was convinced they would break through in the US: 'I think it's really going to happen here. I'm so excited. I can't believe it.' Later, when he went solo, his desire to please an American audience was a crucial factor in his demise.

Gary had been to Florida with Nigel but that was a world away from their rooms on the forty-fifth floor of the Marriott Marquis Hotel in Times Square, the hub of Manhattan. They went for Chinese food, hung out at a popular garage club called Club USA and went shopping. Gary acquired a taste for shopping abroad, always looking for antiques for his bungalow back home and, later, for his far grander house. He didn't find anything on this first trip to New York and complained about the cost of everything.

The rest of the time was made up of interviews with relevant US magazines in a bid to repeat the strategy that had worked so well in the UK. The response was lukewarm by comparison. A couple of months later they were back to try again, this time with the renowned *Smash Hits* writer Alex Kadis, who was their preferred journalist during Take That's early years.

Alex had a way of making the bonkers world of pop seem almost day-to-day and normal. She had been New Kids on the Block's writer of choice and was ideal for Take That. Her rapport with the artists served her well when she moved on from journalism to become Mark Owen's manager. Later she worked at a senior level for record companies and most recently for Simon Cowell as the project manager for Susan Boyle – another indication of how the music business is an incredibly small world.

In the US, she couldn't help noticing how different it all was for Take That. They were swamped by thousands of adoring fans at airports in the UK, but when they flew in to Boston airport they were greeted by three people – two of them from *Smash Hits* and their own press officer. The boys did their best and threw themselves into a rigorous schedule of photo shoots and handshaking.

Gary was very much the leader on these short promotional tours. If Nigel wasn't with them, then he had charge of the Take That credit card, rather like a teacher having to deal with a group of impetuous students abroad. He had to be the sensible one because the others never had any inclination towards responsibility – especially Robbie. Barely a day would go by without the cry going up, 'Has anybody seen Rob?' When the boys went out to Club USA, Rob disappeared and went to the club next door. He was still a wayward teenager.

A typical New York day began in the Marriott hotel lobby at 6.30a.m., then on to *Live! with Regis and Kathie Lee* for 7.30. This was the US equivalent of one of the breakfast shows like *This Morning* with Phillip Schofield and Holly Willoughby. Rehearsals for the show began at 8a.m., then it was magazine interviews for an hour before the live show began at 10.15. The studio audience consisted of middle-aged matrons who thought Take That were from outer space.

A complete waste of time was saved by Gary striking the first familiar chords of the most famous song of the city, 'New York, New York', his final number at the Halton Legion four years before. Rob also knew the song well, having sung it often with his father around the pubs of Stoke-on-Trent. Together, they gave a rousing rendition as if they were Frank Sinatra and Dean Martin live in Las Vegas. The matrons loved it.

There was no time for an encore, however, as they had to be at RCA by 11.30 for more handshakes and some radio interviews. They were bundled into cabs for more radio interviews, then a quick lunch before an interview in Central Park with Simon Bates from Radio 1. As they were setting up, a girl walked by and said in a northern accent, 'Hello, lads, what are you doing here?', which seemed a bit surreal. At teatime there was a photo shoot until 6p.m., when it was back to the hotel for a quick shower before dinner with record company executives. Gary, in his role as the teacher, insisted they all have some singing practice in his room and, in revenge, Jason would make him try out some new dance steps. Then it was time to go to a club.

When he had time off, Gary walked the ten blocks to Macy's department store to look at the furniture. He was taking his role as homeowner very seriously. Afterwards he would go back to his hotel room, where he had his keyboard set up, and work on some songs. When he needed a break, he would leaf through one of the copies of *Homes and Gardens* that he had packed and eat one of the KitKat bars that had found its way into his suitcase. Gary was notorious for travelling light. His leisure gear usually consisted of three track-suits, so there was always room for some emergency supplies of chocolate.

After the painfully slow progress in the US, Japan was a breath of fresh air. They all loved it. Everyone was so polite and it rained every day, which reminded them all of Manchester. The young girl fans were as noisy as their British counterparts but when the boys said, 'Shush!' they all fell silent. Gigs in Japan were like no other place in the world. For fast numbers, they stood up and danced; for ballads, they sat down and listened so intently you could hear a pin drop.

Touring and being away from home for extended periods of time is not a recipe for a long and healthy relationship. Despite inevitably seeing less of him, Nicky wasn't unhappy about her relationship with Gary. It was exciting and fun watching a gig from the VIP seats or dodging the fans at the hotel afterwards. She was looking forward to starting work when she finished drama school, however, and she had the impression that her desire to have a proper career didn't register with him. She felt that her ambitions didn't really fit in with what he wanted: a loving wife at home looking after the kids – lots of them.

One episode that she found out about later was particularly revealing. Gary had heard that they were looking for a new, fresh-faced young presenter to host *Top of the Pops*. He immediately thought Nicky would be perfect but decided against telling her. She was disappointed when he finally confessed one evening at the Conrad Hotel. Nicky told her friends that she was 'really surprised' he had done that: 'He told her he felt bad about it and should have said. She didn't think it did her any harm because she wanted to be an actress but she thought it was really bad of him. She thought he probably just didn't want her going off and living a life that didn't include him.'

She also felt that he had changed a lot in a short space of time. Perhaps anyone would have with all the attention and adulation Take That were receiving. One of Nicky's friends explained, 'She thought Gary had become very dismissive towards people in his life – even his friends. He wasn't very nice about people who had been important to him. Nicky thought it was temporary and everything would go back to normal but I think their lives just became more different.'

Nicky's misgivings came to the surface unexpectedly one evening when they were on their way back to Manchester from London. She told Gary she was finding the Nigel regime increasingly difficult to deal with and she was worried about what was going to happen in the future. Her friend explained, 'They were becoming more and more famous and Nicky just wanted to let Gary know how apprehensive she was about everything. But there was nothing he could really say to reassure her.'

A couple of months later they were in the Chinese Delight for dinner when the question of their future together arose again. They went back to Nicky's mum's house for a heart-to-heart that didn't go well. Nicky would later tell her friend that it was 'horrendous': 'She said she cried and he did as well, and they had a big hug and she told him that she didn't want the relationship to end but felt that everything was changing beyond their control every day. They were very upset about it but sort of mutually decided that they couldn't go on. Nicky didn't say that she wanted to break up with him but it seemed like the only solution for them both. It just came to an end.

'I think Nicky and Gary believed they would get back together when things with Take That calmed down. They still saw each other and spoke on the phone all the time.'

The problem with that good intention was neither of them could have foreseen how much bigger Take That were going to become.

11

Everything Changes

'Pray' is a classic Gary love song, full of longing for something just out of reach. In the lyric he is praying that he will be part of his lover's life again one day. When he recorded the demo in the bungalow in Knutsford, it was a poignant ballad with a beautiful melody. By the time it reached the shelves of the record stores, it had grown into a great pop song thanks to an uplifting and invigorating tempo that had given it previously unrealized power. 'Pray' had become an anthem and, as such, would be a blueprint for many of Gary's greatest songs: you wanted to shout the chorus as loud as you could.

The final version owes much to the work of Steve Jervier, whom Nick Raymonde had brought in to work on the single. Gary was astute enough to realize it had been improved, although he was beginning to become a little fed up with his songs always being taken out of his hands. He was very proprietorial about them.

He was right to support the reworking of 'Pray'. The song went straight to number one when it was released in July 1993. These were the days when it meant something to debut at the top of the charts. The Beatles always used to do it but otherwise it was a rare achievement. Eventually the song would sell 410,000 copies, more than enough to earn them their first gold disc.

The video helped and was an indication that they had moved up a division. They were filmed in Acapulco, where they took part in a pop festival that also featured Sting and Gloria Estefan. Gary is anguished on the beach, singing to the heavens in an open black shirt and trousers. The other four showed off their dance-hardened bodies.

The female fans loved it, unable to resist their heroes as Gary sang about being so cold and all alone – which was a pity because the weather looked rather sunny in Acapulco. In between takes, Rob and Mark enjoyed playing football on the beach in their bare feet.

The song topped the charts for four weeks and was perfectly timed for their first arena tour. Any concerns that Take That might not sell out the larger venues disappeared in a matter of minutes. The first night at the G-Mex Centre in Manchester was significant for several reasons. Rob snorted his first line of cocaine before they went on stage and spent the entire performance flying. That didn't matter to the fans, who invited him to 'Point Your Erection in my Direction' or waved a giant inflated condom with the banner 'Rob – Fill this'.

Everything was getting more (hetero)sexual with Take That. Their adolescent fans had hormones flying all over the place. The boys finished their encore of 'It Only Takes A Minute' by bending over in their underpants on which the letters of Take That were spelled out. Each of them had two letters of the band's name on their pants except Gary, who was in the middle and just had a star on his.

Many of Gary's old friends from Frodsham, including Martin Smiddy and Dave Mort, made the short trip to watch him perform. Marj Barlow would always make sure that there were tickets available for the Frodsham faithful. Chris Harrison was there too, as well as Heather Woodall, whom Gary's mum had helped fix up with a backstage pass.

Heather complained to the *News of the World* that when she went to see him there, he looked straight through her: 'The man in front of me wasn't the Gary I knew any more. He was cold and distant and treated me as if I was after something when all I wanted to say was "have a good gig, I'm rooting for you". He looked straight through me as if I was just one of his groupies.'

Heather said she couldn't face going to the after-show party and she never went to see Gary again. In his defence, she could have had no conception whatsoever of the sort of life he was leading. In any case, after she told her story to the newspaper in 1996, the chances of her ever being welcome were nil.

The gigs at Wembley Arena a couple of weeks later were a turning point for Gary – he met Elton John for the first time there. As a singer-songwriter Elton had already been at the top for more than twenty years and was the benchmark for all Gary's ambitions. After the show, they were introduced backstage by Paula Yates, who was married to Bob Geldof. At the time, the late television presenter was the band's most famous fan. She seemed to have a particular fascination with Jason Orange after she interviewed the boys on her bed – a regular gimmicky feature on Channel 4's *The Big Breakfast*. She described him as Take That's answer to Gandhi because of his fascination with healthy living. Rumour has it that Jason's devoted mother, Jenny, warned the presenter, then thirty-four, to back off.

Elton was a hero to Gary, who admitted to being tongue-tied in the great man's presence. He may have been a little embarrassed by the ensemble he wore for the dance number 'Apache', which was unashamedly a pastiche of one of Elton's famous stage costumes, complete with a long purple military-style coat and a large pair of sparkly red specs.

After a friendly chat, Elton invited all the boys for dinner at his grand estate, Woodside, near Windsor. They took their tour bus down the M4 and were greeted at the front door by two butlers in full livery. It made the bungalow in Knutsford seem a little dowdy. Gary was going to be a millionaire by the end of the year but this was a rock star experience that he could never have imagined. He realized he had a long way to go when he studied Elton's array of gold and platinum discs on the wall.

Elton showed Gary some of his multimillion-pound collection of great art, including works by Picasso, Bacon and Magritte. Gary's big ambition at the time was to buy a new bed from the Harvey Nichols store in London but that changed after he saw the grand furnishings at Woodside. He lapped it up, especially when Elton praised his talent and said specifically that he could make a career for life out of songwriting. He observed, 'From that day on my life changed.'

Nigel Martin-Smith was there as well. Usually he was reluctant to let the band mix with other celebrities in case it diminished their focus but even he could not resist this invitation. Perhaps he was worried that Elton's long-standing manager, John Reid, was going to try and steal the band away and wanted to keep an eye on proceedings.

The evening was a brilliant success. After dinner Gary sat at Elton's white grand piano and played a song, as he had done many times when they were staying in hotels. This time he chose 'The Party Is Over', a ballad that has never been released. Elton, who doesn't like to be upstaged on these occasions, promptly ushered Gary away so he could play 'Your Song' for the millionth time.

Before the evening closed, Elton gave the boys a stern lecture about the perils of taking drugs. 'Stay away from fucking cocaine,' he said, apparently looking hard at Rob the whole time.

Gary has only once ever admitted to becoming involved in drugs. He told the *Sun* in an interview three years after Take That had split that he had taken cocaine and tried ecstasy, and that a drugs binge had made him ill for a week so he had knocked drug-taking on the head. It may or may not have been true. Gary was undoubtedly trying to make himself appear more interesting and rock 'n' roll than he was. His friends didn't believe it. One observed, 'It was a stupid interview.' In his autobiography, Gary, perhaps more accurately, admits to trying the odd substance but says that he and drugs are a bit of a non-story.

Gary had already fulfilled so many of his ambitions, from being on *Top of the Pops* to having a number one hit record. He left Woodside with a new aim: to be the next Elton John. He didn't just want to have a long career and write lots of hits; he wanted the life – the houses, the paintings, the sculptures and the antiques. He wanted the luxury and the opulence. At the moment all he had space for was a grandfather clock. He had to move.

The best time to find a house in keeping with his new status would be when the royalties came in at the end of the year. Take That were due a month off at Christmas, so he would be able to search properly then. He didn't want to leave his home patch, even though he loved visiting Woodside. He was always welcome there from that first dinner onwards. The two songwriters would walk out to Elton's Rolls-Royce parked in the driveway and sit in the back, where they would listen to each other's new songs on the brilliant sound system.

The next Take That single was the group's last nod to the camp world of their origins two years before. 'Relight My Fire' was a gay club classic. Nigel Martin-Smith loved the Dan Hartman song, which had been a number one dance hit in the US in 1979. He thought it would be perfect for the boys, even though Gary took some convincing, especially as it would be the only cover on the album and would again spoil his ambition to have 'words and music by Gary Barlow' on the sleeve.

Originally the idea was that the track would be Rob's big number on the new album but he couldn't master it. He spent two nights trying to get it right. On the third, Gary went into the studio to record a guide vocal for Rob to copy. It quickly became apparent that it should have been Gary's song all along, so his version was used on the record. Looking back, he believes this was a key moment in Rob's growing disillusionment with his role in Take That.

They needed a female vocalist to feature in the middle of the song. Nick Raymonde was in favour of a big-voiced black singer like Kym Mazelle but Nigel, who proved to be the driving force behind this song, suggested Lulu, one of the great female vocalists of the sixties. She had won the Eurovision Song Contest as far back as 1969 with 'Boom Bang-A-Bang'. She was enjoying a revival in 1993 with a couple of minor hits but, more importantly, she was one of the great belters in pop. When Lulu sang a song, it stayed sung.

She proved to be an inspired choice. When she came on after two minutes, 'Relight My Fire' suddenly became ten times more exciting. The video was shot in the Ministry of Sound nightclub in Elephant and Castle and used real clubbers mingling with the boys. Lulu showed Gary how to warm up his voice properly and advised him to drink water with ginger and lemon to keep the vocal cords happy.

The song repeated the success of 'Pray' by going straight to number one in October 1993 – the perfect advertisement for the new album, which was due out a couple of weeks later. In a sad postscript, Dan Hartman died of an Aids-related brain tumour a few months after-wards at the age of forty-three.

There was a last-minute panic with the album when everyone realized that Rob no longer sang a lead vocal. Gary needed to write something for him quickly and immediately thought of a talented Sheffield-based producer and songwriter called Eliot Kennedy whose company he had enjoyed when they had worked together on another track for the album called 'Wasting My Time'. Earlier in the year Eliot had produced Lulu's comeback single 'Independence', a track she had recorded a few months before 'Relight My Fire'. Gary usually worked alone but this was an emergency. Eliot had a phone call from his publisher asking if he wanted to do it and jumped at the chance.

The very next day Gary drove over to his house. Eliot recalled, 'Twenty minutes later, in the kitchen, we wrote "Everything Changes". Gary came along with the title, we sat down and I put "but you" in brackets. After a couple of hours, we had the whole structure and song – so it was a very quick process.'

Now all they had to do was coax a star vocal out of Rob. The result was so good, with Rob developing his mid-Atlantic sound, that the album ended up being named *Everything Changes* as well and the hastily put together title song became the first track. It gave the whole record a sense of direction – smoother and more mature than *Take That & Party*.

The fans loved the new album, buying 300,000 copies in the first week and sending it straight to number one. Eventually it would sell more than 1.3 million copies in the UK alone and was the third biggest-selling album of 1993. The reviews were more than positive. *Smash Hits* enjoyed the mixture of 'disco swingers and moody atmospheric love songs'. The magazine gushed, '*Everything Changes* is a masterpiece of pop and the must-have album of the year.' It doesn't get much better than that.

Gary, who featured alone on the cover of the magazine, was chuffed to read that 'Wasting My Time' was singled out as the 'absolute' highlight. In all, he wrote eleven of the thirteen tracks on the album. For the first time another member of Take That had a songwriting credit but it wasn't Rob. The funky 'If This Is Love' was co-written by Howard with producer Dave James.

Gary may have been reluctant to share songwriting credits but he didn't mind about the vocals. Howard, naturally, handled the vocal on his own song and revealed a pleasingly mellow tone. Mark Owen sang lead for the first time on Gary's teenage classic 'Babe' and everyone loved his interpretation. He could barely sing a note when the band had begun but since then he had developed a unique style that was half spoken, half sung. You could never mistake a Mark Owen vocal.

On the *Everything Changes* tour in the autumn of 1993, 'Babe' was the favorite of many of the girl fans, who were all in love with Mark. Gary had developed an endearing, self-deprecating way of dealing with his lack of popularity – he and Jason competed for last place in terms of fan mail. He would stand alone among the throng of fans trying to kiss Mark, Rob or Howard and exclaim loudly, 'Gerrof me!

Go and bother the others.' It always got a laugh. On tour he would often slip out for a quiet meal by himself and look out the window and see the number of girl fans building. Eventually he would get up, go to the door and tell them, 'Sorry, girls, it's just me tonight. The others aren't coming.' And they would go home disappointed.

The 21-date UK leg of the tour began, for some reason, with three nights at the Bournemouth International Centre at the beginning of November 1993. The last night was at the Whitley Bay Ice Rink. The set included a rock 'n' roll medley that involved Gary doing his impersonation of Jerry Lee Lewis performing 'Great Balls Of Fire'.

'Babe' was another highlight and was a good choice for their bid to have the Christmas number one. Howard commented, 'I think Gary knew straight away when he wrote this he wanted Mark to sing it.' That would have been psychic, as the two hadn't met when Gary wrote it in Frodsham and gave it to friends to listen to.

'Babe' made the top of the charts but missed out on the Christmas number one to Mr Blobby, which said everything you needed to know about seasonal hits. There was some consolation: Take That won eight awards in the *Smash Hits* Readers Poll, beating the previous year's record. Gary placed fourth as Most Fanciable Male Star but, as usual, he was beaten by Mark, Rob and Howard. He did finish above the last named in the Best Haircut category.

Gary could take a month off at Christmas safe in the knowledge that the band was comfortably the biggest in the country. Before tucking into the Christmas pudding, however, he had a house to find. He didn't have far to look. He paid more than £300,000 for Moorside, a four-bedroom detached house in the village of Plumley, four miles away from Knutsford on the other side of the M6. Today it would cost more than a million pounds. The railway station was a couple of hundred yards away and trains ran every hour into Manchester Piccadilly or Chester. The location was perfect for someone who travelled around the country a lot.

His new home may not have been on such a grand scale as

Elton's, but it was a start. As well as the bedrooms, there were four bathrooms and five reception rooms, so Gary had plenty of space for his home studio and the lavish furnishings he intended to buy. His father Colin couldn't wait to get his hands on an impressive garden at last. He retired, aged fifty-five, from his job at the fertilizer company to join his son's staff full time.

Gary could also keep the fans at arm's length behind some impressive iron gates and a private driveway. They soon found out the address, however, and on any given day there might be a hundred girls who had made the pilgrimage over from Europe to camp out in the driveway. Italian girls, in particular, liked to travel over and tour round the Take That homes. They treated it like a day at a pop festival without the music.

Unfortunately, it wasn't just the young girl fans who would loiter outside. When the local TV news revealed his new address, he phoned them up to complain. 'Thanks very much,' he said. 'What you don't realize is there's girls under fourteen years old who'll stand here until one in the morning and I have to clear paedophiles off the car park outside my house on a regular basis. Wherever our fans go, you get this little network of perverts as well. So I've got this sleaze and smut round my house where I live thanks to you.'

Gary set about turning his home into a mini Woodside – at least in his own mind. Elton was on hand to lend advice to the younger man. On one afternoon during tea at Woodside, he told Gary he should get a butler. He convinced him that there was nothing better than hot buttered toast with your morning cuppa in bed, having your bath prepared with soothingly scented bubbles and putting on a freshly ironed shirt.

Gary couldn't wait to find his personal Jeeves, a gentleman's gentleman. He placed an advertisement and interviewed a selection of candidates at Moorside before settling on Maurice, who could live at the house in Knutsford ten minutes away. It was a perfect arrangement.

The band, unsurprisingly, found his new grandeur hilarious. His mum and dad never let on what they really thought of the lad from Ashton Drive living in his own scaled down version of Downton Abbey and Gary never asked. Perhaps Marj was grateful she didn't have a pile of ironing to deal with whenever she came to visit. Instead, they would often arrive with friends from Frodsham to be greeted formally by Maurice, who was a bit theatrical with a distinctly military bearing. He would then disappear into the kitchen to prepare an impressive dinner party for any number of guests. There was nothing shepherd's pie about Maurice.

12

The Two Garys

Nigel Martin-Smith was the first person to point out that there were two Garys. He told *Smash Hits* that the first Gaz was a 'sensible, mature husbandly-type man who's very into his business and his money'. The second was a 'giddy, excited little boy' who would scream and jump up and down when he topped the charts.

The mature Gary was the one who had spent his teenage years working among adults and achieving success in a grown-up world. The little boy Gary was the kid in a sweet shop who had come out of his shell since Take That had become a phenomenon and was determined to have a slice of sex, drugs and rock 'n' roll while he could. He may not have been up for quite as much mischief as Rob but he had more than his fair share, particularly on tour.

Gary was still great friends with Nicky Ladanowski, although they were no longer an item. She had a new boyfriend but remained very much part of Gary's entourage, speaking to him all the time on the phone and going to his concerts and after-show parties. He would proudly tell her of some of his escapades, particularly with girl fans – like the one he picked up in Japan who would let him drive her father's Ferrari. Then there were the girls in Italy and Germany when they toured Europe. Nicky listened encouragingly but, privately, she didn't recognize the person Gary had become.

The Two Garys

His new dedication to imitating the lifestyle of Elton John meant that he would have to dip into his wallet – a lot. Elton had always been cavalier with his vast wealth but Gary had a reputation for extreme caution in all financial matters. The image of Mister Mean is far from accurate, even if he has played up to it a little over the years. Gary is generous to his family and friends and always treated his girlfriends to the very best, but he is a northern man who knows the value of a penny and of a pound.

Growing up, he watched his mum and dad make the most of their money, ensuring their children could have a nice telly and holidays abroad. It's a generational thing, like the grandparent who will scour the supermarkets for the cheapest sliced loaf but will stump up the cash for a new school uniform without a moment's thought. Gary was exactly like that, caring more about the money he had in his pocket than the sums in his bank account.

Gary's reputation for being tight first came about when it was revealed that in the early days he used to charge his bandmates £1 upfront to use his mobile phone to call their mums. He was the only member of the band who could afford one. These were the days when mobiles were bricks and you could use them in smash and grab raids. This was the same Gary who charged his schoolmates 50p to buy one of his cassettes with 'Let's Pray For Christmas' on it. Notching things up a degree, he charged Take That £1,000 a week for the use of his keyboards on tour, claiming they would have to pay more if they hired them elsewhere.

It didn't help when Gary became instantly wealthy following his publishing deal. With a six-figure sum in his NatWest savings account, he decided to treat Nigel and the boys to a slap-up Chinese meal. That was generous but he spoiled the effect by declaring that everyone could have either a starter and main course or a main and a sweet; they couldn't order all three.

Much of Gary's reputation for thrift was perpetuated by Rob's stories about the man he dubbed 'Ebenezer Barlow'. They are legendary. A favourite was that Gary liked to save on the central heating, so he would perch at his piano in a thick duffel coat. He would apparently keep some expensive Arabica coffee beans at home for his personal use, while visitors were treated to an instant from an industrial-sized tub of Nescafé. One of Rob's best stories was that Gary had put a more exclusive Mercedes 500 badge on his new Mercedes 350, which he had bought to replace the trusty Ford Orion. All good fun but it helped Rob to chip away at Gary's credibility.

A very different Gary would be on a mission to spend whenever they went on a promotional trip, particularly to Europe, where he would think nothing of splashing out £75,000 on some paintings for the lounge. His general rule of thumb was that the sky was the limit if it was an investment that would grow in value. His new house would do that, as would the art and antiques.

Gary liked to relax in two ways on tour: he would find the hotel piano and play some songs or he would go on a shopping spree to improve Moorside. His only condition about purchases was that he liked to haggle. Alex Kadis amusingly described him as 'Bargain Barlow, expert shopper and renowned bargain hunter'. She witnessed him in action, in his uncool anorak, buying an antique silver cigarette box at a shop in Copenhagen and delivering his killer opening line: 'Ooh, that's far too dear.' The days when Gary disliked smoking and the smell of cigarettes were long gone. In Take That world, where everybody smoked, he had become a chain smoker, which didn't do wonders for his voice.

By the end of 1993 none of the boys had the same girlfriend they'd had when they joined the band. Gary did see a girl in Frodsham for a while but she went off to university and he didn't much care for being sneaked into her room. No men were allowed in the women's halls of residence, even if they were in Take That. The girl, called Rachel, was someone to hang out with on the relatively rare occasions he had time for a drink in the pub, but it was nothing serious. Gary was too busy enjoying the attentions of the female fans on tour to fall in love. This was the golden age of Take That. Their performance at the 1994 Brit Awards is arguably their most famous live show from this period of their careers. They performed a Beatles tribute, which was a daring move for a boy band, because the Liverpool legends were quite simply the biggest-ever pop group. They wore Beatles-style suits in bright blue with black collars, white shirts and black ties. All the dancers looked as if they had stepped off the set of *Ready Steady Go!* circa 1964.

Gary was no stranger to medleys of this sort and smoothly began 'I Want To Hold Your Hand' before Robbie took over for 'A Hard Day's Night', although Gary sang the tricky, higher-pitched middle eight. They finished with Howard and Gary singing 'She Loves You' and left the stage at Alexandra Palace to deafening applause. It was inspired. Their two awards for Best British Single and Best British Video for 'Pray' seemed almost incidental after their performance. Not winning Best British Group was disappointing, although for a boy band to be nominated in this category was an achievement in the early nineties. They were beaten by the hip-hop group Stereo MCs.

From Gary's point of view, a Brit Award for 'Pray' was vindication of his songwriting ability. Even better was the news that he was going to receive an Ivor Novello Award for the song. The Ivors were introduced in 1955 in honour of the Cardiff-born entertainer, one of the most popular musical stars between the two world wars. He wrote many standards that were sung around the pub piano, like 'Keep The Home Fires Burning' and 'We'll Gather Lilacs'.

Over the years the Ivors have come to represent the pinnacle of a songwriter's achievement, although Gary hadn't fully appreciated that when he took his mum along to the awards ceremony at the Savoy Hotel in May 1994. He wore a Versace suit that some commentators said resembled the notorious Liz Hurley safety-pin dress that she showcased the same month. He won Songwriter of the Year, and picked up a second award for Best Contemporary Song for 'Pray'. Rick

Sky remembers his face was a picture of joy when he received the main award from Elton John. Gary said simply, 'I was made up.'

A month earlier the track 'Everything Changes' had become their fourth consecutive number one, a feat that hadn't been achieved since The Beatles. The classy ballad 'Love Ain't Here Anymore', another Steve Jervier production, was a song the critics liked but, disappointingly, failed to make it five in a row at the beginning of July. The main reason for the track reaching only number three was that the album had been in the charts for nine months and it was probably one single too many – the fans already knew all the words. It also didn't help that 'Love Is All Around' by Wet Wet Wet topped the charts for a record fifteen weeks throughout the summer. Some consolation for Gary was that Elton John said 'Love Ain't Here Anymore' was his favourite Take That song, perhaps because it most resembled one of his compositions.

Gary should have paid more attention to Rob. If he had, he might have realized that the younger man was not only very sensitive but also talented in a way that he wasn't encouraged to show during his time in Take That. Rob's mother Jan perceptively observed that her son had missed out on his teenage years by joining Take That.

In Gary's defence, he wasn't Rob's dad nor his big brother and there was no obvious indication that the two didn't get on. Rob had always been the joker in the group, the lad who would shock but would do it with a grin that would endear him to the world. Rick Sky recalls that on the many occasions he interviewed the band Rob was by far the most charismatic. He didn't follow Nigel's careful code of behaviour. The others stuck closely to a dull script that didn't reflect their true personalities. Gary can be very funny but kept his dry sense of humour hidden.

Any thoughts of leaving Take That were probably more in Gary's mind than Rob's: 'It really depresses me when I think of all this coming to an end.' Keen-eyed observers noticed Gary was looking a little fitter and more chiselled, as if he were thinking ahead to when he would be centre stage and the eyes of the audience wouldn't automatically be drawn to Mark's smile or Howard's body.

For the most part Rob was concealing his problems from the world – it was the Take That way. He was left in no doubt that under no circumstances should he go to the annual Glastonbury Festival in June 1994. The premier summer event for Rob's generation was a three-day extravaganza of drinking, drug-taking, fabulous music, police arrests and mud. It represented the antithesis of everything Take That stood for. To be seen at Glastonbury would be the ulti-mate transgression for a member of the band – Rob went anyway. He wasn't yet brave enough to flaunt the rules completely, so he spent the duration of the event hiding in a tent getting drunk with the Irish singer Feargal Sharkey.

Gary, meanwhile, was at Moorside, taking his new dog, a rescue Alsatian called Jess, for walks and being looked after by Maurice. The butler would frequently have to take care of Rob as well after one of his drunken weekends in Dublin, which were becoming more fre-quent. Sometimes, when Rob was in good form, he would bring his new girlfriend, the *London's Burning* actress Samantha Beckinsale, over for a dinner prepared by Maurice. Gary was completely unaware that there was any resentment eating away at Rob beneath the surface.

The two men were being equally decadent in different ways: Rob existed on a diet of drink, drugs and sexual excess; Gary had been seduced by the trimmings of wealth, the fine wines and fine art that he splashed out on with carefree abandon. Unless he was on tour, Gary wasn't bothered about the rock 'n' roll lifestyle. He preferred to invite Mark, Howard and Jason over and the four of them would head off to the cinema. Rob was usually too busy.

On one occasion Gary was keen to see the new Quentin Tarantino film *Pulp Fiction* and asked his old mate Chris Harrison if he would like to join them at the cinema in Bury. Nobody liked sitting next to Gary because he would buy the biggest tub of popcorn and sit there munching it throughout the entire film. They settled down to watch the adverts and the trailers and were in high spirits, when all the lights went off and the projector stopped. There had been a power cut and everyone had to troop off home. The rest of the audience were surprised to see Take That stumbling out into the street.

It would have been a welcome break for Gary, who was working furiously on the new album, while Rob contributed precious little to the record. Rob did get together with Mark to write a rap for the middle of the single 'Sure', which went to number one in October 1994. It was the first occasion when other members of the group received a joint songwriting credit with Gary – perhaps he agreed because there were two of them this time.

The song was by no means the most successful from the band but at least Gary was trying something different – a more relaxed, American-friendly sound, known at the time as 'New Jack Swing'. The new style suggested that at last this was the big push for US success, which had so far proved elusive. The song could have been performed by one of those smooth soul outfits like Earth, Wind & Fire or the R & B singer R. Kelly.

The seven-minute video was completely weird, with the boys looking after a little ginger-haired girl for about three minutes while Gary pretended to finish composing the song on the piano. Rob and Mark were quite natural but Gary needed some acting lessons. Then, for no apparent reason, they change into fishnet see-through vests that harked back to the old days – you can take the boys out of the gay clubs but you can't take the gay clubs out of the boys! Howard summed the video up succinctly: 'It was absolute shite, to be honest.'

Although it made number one, 'Sure' was probably a touch bland and too much of a departure from the uplifting choruses of 'Pray' and 'Relight My Fire'. It achieved only silver disc status, with just under 250,000 copies sold.

The following month there was some consolation for this minor disappointment when they were asked to perform at Princess Diana's *Concert of Hope* at Wembley Arena for World Aids Day. They were invited round for drinks at Kensington Palace the day before. It would be the first of many informal royal meetings for Gary over the years but, sadly, the only time he would spend time with Diana, who died in 1997. He recalled, 'She was fantastic.' Afterwards, it was reported that Mark had asked the Princess out, which made sure they gathered lots of useful headlines from their visit.

Gary worked with Elton John for the first time when he sang on the soundtrack of *The Lion King*. Elton had composed the music for the Disney film and invited his friend and fellow composer to sing backing vocals on the stand-out track, 'Can You Feel The Love Tonight'.

Listening to the song, you could almost have imagined Gary writing it, although his lyric would have been more anguished than Tim Rice's at this stage of his career: 'Why Can't I Feel The Love Tonight'. He was thrilled to take part, however, especially when Elton later presented him with a gold disc for sales of more than 500,000 in the US.

American success had come easily to Elton John and Gary was determined to follow suit. The attempts to break Take That in the US had been directionless and lacking intensity. The band had been spread too thinly around the world and that half-hearted approach would never work across the Atlantic.

Gary was more optimistic about the next song, which he had written in a hotel room when they were on tour in Europe. 'Back For Good' was number one in thirty-one countries and was by far the biggest-selling single for Take That first time around, shifting more than a million copies. Gary told everyone he had written it in fifteen minutes – and that included the coffee break. He was immensely proud of the track, composed around just four chords. He played it to Nick Raymonde, who had joined them on tour.

Nick loved it, telling Martin Roach, 'I couldn't believe what I was hearing.'

Gary originally thought it would make a great new song for Mark after his success with 'Babe' and invited him over to Moorside to make a demo. Mark didn't get on with the song, so Gary decided to record it himself. He also shared the producing duties for the first time with Chris Porter, who had engineered many of George Michael's songs, including 'Wake Me Up Before You Go-Go' and 'Wham Rap! (Enjoy What You Do)'.

The result was a pop classic: dreamy, contemplative and very singable. The intro alone is unmistakably Barlow, with a lightly strummed guitar leading to some lush strings before Gary's voice floats in. Again, the lyric is one of anguished love – 'the twist of separation' – that so appealed to the hearts of Take That fans.

They wanted to perform the song at the Brits in February 1995 but the organizers wanted acts to perform either a duet or a song they had been nominated for. That was no good for Take That, who wanted to showcase their next single. Nigel Martin-Smith had the chance to show his strength as a manager. He gave the producers the single and suggested they listen to it because it would be the one the boys would be singing if they were required on the night. Needless to say, the producers were on the phone the next day pleading with Take That to perform 'Back For Good' – the song had that effect on people.

Take That were the stars of the night and there were no back flips on view. The five of them sat on stools in front of a stringed orchestra of young women in gold dresses. Gary was looking leaner than he had ever done before. He also had a better haircut and a sharply cut suit that gave a hint of how he would grow into a new image as an older man. There were no frills – it was a beautiful song simply sung. The next day, radio stations were falling over themselves to play the song, even though it wouldn't be released for another month. Gary's night was made even better by watching Elton John receive the premier award for Outstanding Contribution to Music.

After the lacklustre video for 'Sure', it was important that the one for 'Back For Good' was memorable for the right reasons. Once again, keeping it understated worked well. Shot in black and white, the boys just danced and splashed around – a variation on the old 'Singin' In The Rain' number. For once Gary looked like the coolest guy in the band. He sang poignantly, as if he were about to burst into tears. It worked. As well as helping to propel the song to the top of the charts, the video has been watched nearly six million times on YouTube.

Gary believes 'Back For Good' represents the pinnacle of Take That's early years. It is the only Take That song that he included on *Milestones: The Songs That Inspired Gary Barlow* for his MITS Award in November 2012. His faith in 'Back For Good' would be further justified when it won two Ivor Novello Awards in 1996. How different his career might have been if this classic had been his first solo single – and it wasn't even the last great song he wrote for Take That during those early years.

13

That Was Take That

From a personal point of view, life could scarcely have been better for Gary. He was no longer seeing Rachel, so a new girlfriend was on his wish list, but as a songwriter he couldn't have been happier that he was receiving so much acclaim. The money, too, continued to pour in and his first million had multiplied many times, so he was already thinking he should move to a bigger house. By the time the other four had made their first million, Gary had made seven.

He was aware that the Rob situation within Take That was getting worse but it wasn't particularly on his radar. He was enjoying the release of the band's third album, *Nobody Else*, in May 1995. For the first time he was listed as co-producer on eight out of the eleven tracks. He worked mainly with the ultra-fashionable producers Steve Anderson and Dave Seaman, who were known as Brothers in Rhythm. The previous year they had been responsible for 'Confide In Me' and 'Dangerous Game', which had given Kylie Minogue a richer and more mature sound. They helped do the same for Take That's third album.

It was nearly 'words and music by Gary Barlow'. He shared the credit on 'Sure' with Mark and Robbie and on 'Sunday to Saturday' with Mark and Howard. The only non-Take That writer was David Morales, the house music DJ and producer. He co-wrote with Gary

'Hanging Onto Your Love'. All three tracks were smooth pieces of eighties-style soul funk. Gary was pictured alone on the opening page of the jacket sleeve, while the other four shared a later page. You might be forgiven for thinking this album was by Gary Barlow featuring Take That.

His pride did take an amusing fall, however, when he went into a Chester store to check out the new Take That dolls that featured on the front jacket. By common consent these were awful and didn't remotely look like any of the band. Gary could only find the other four on display, so he asked an assistant if they had a Gary Barlow doll. 'Oh yes, sir,' said the attendant, reaching below the counter to produce the Gary doll. 'You buy the other four and you get this one for free.' Gary loves telling this as part of his self-deprecating image.

He could afford to laugh at himself when the album went straight to number one, selling more than 160,000 copies in the first week. He had dedicated the title track to his mum and dad – a touching tribute to their enduring love for each other and their sons.

For the first time Rob didn't sing a lead vocal on the album. According to Gary, he had been given twelve songs to see which suited him but didn't learn any of them. The official version was that he had been concentrating more on the writing side of things, but the reality was that Rob's voice had cracked up under a barrage of late nights, boozing and cigarettes. He would later admit, 'I abused my voice and I paid the price.'

Gary first realized the extent of Rob's unhappiness when they started rehearsals for the *Nobody Else* tour, which was due to begin in the summer. Rob confided in Gary that he was thinking of leaving the band. Gary was genuinely shocked Rob would want to give up something that had been such an astonishing success.

Rob was at Glastonbury again in June 1995. This year he appeared to be past caring what the world thought of a member of Take That turning up with a case of champagne hoping to be admitted to the inner sanctum of rock. When he arrived, he walked into the bar where Oasis were having a drink. Liam Gallagher took one look at him and memorably announced, 'Take fucking what?' You could imagine Nigel Martin-Smith choking on his cornflakes at the sight of Robbie Williams in sublime drunkenness, with newly peroxide blond hair and a front tooth blackened out with marker pen, jumping on to the stage where Oasis were performing.

The band held a meeting at Moorside to discuss the year ahead and Rob was more specific about his plans, saying he would probably leave after the tour but he would make sure he fulfilled those commitments. Each of the other four tried to get through to Rob as he sat on a swing in the back garden. It was clear that they weren't having any success when they asked him if he had anything to say and he went, 'Wheeeeee.'

Soon afterwards, Rob was no longer a member of Take That. The Cheshire Territorial Army barracks in Stockport in mid-July was the unlikely setting for his last day. He had slipped out of dance practice for a McDonald's. On his return he was told the others wanted a word with him. It was a court martial. They were clearly unhappy with him dictating at what point he would leave the band. Jason told him, 'If you are going, go now so we can get on with it.'

Rob, concealing that he was upset, swaggered over to the fruit bowl, grabbed a melon from the pile and asked, 'Is it OK to take this with me?' With a spring in his step and a smile on his face, he left. He didn't burst into tears until he was safely inside his mother's house in Newcastle-under-Lyme. He was still clutching the melon – a fruit he didn't even like.

Was he pushed or did he fall? Jason Orange said in 2010 that it was half and half. He told the ITV documentary *Look Back, Don't Stare*, 'Half because he wanted to go and needed to go and fulfil his destiny and half because people got annoyed with him and encouraged him to go and effectively threw him out.' That is probably a fair appraisal.

Nigel Martin-Smith, who would carry most of the blame in Rob's eyes, had said with uncanny accuracy two years earlier that they would have problems with Rob when he could no longer get through to him: 'He'll just fly off and we won't be able to catch him.' The legal fallout, particularly that involving Nigel and Rob, would go on for years and end up in the High Court.

Secretly Gary and the other three were relieved that Rob had gone because it had got to the point where he was 'doing our heads in'. Howard and Mark were a good deal more upset about it than the other two and the former revealed in *Take That/Take One* that he had cried when it sunk in that the youngest member of the band had left for good and wasn't coming back.

The official line from Gary was distinctly formal and unemotional: 'The four of us are 100 per cent committed to this band and are looking forward to a long future together. We feel we owe it to the fans as they want us here.' In the end the 'long future' would last a little over six months.

'Never Forget', one of the best-loved Take That songs, was released exactly seven days after the official announcement of Rob's departure. Howard sang the lead vocal for a change and the opening of the song suited his soft style. The lyrics were taken by devoted fans as marking the end of an era, focusing on how far the band had come and indicating that in the future the journey would be someone else's dream. The words certainly seemed poignant after the trauma of the past weeks. It was as if Gary was trying to let the fans know that they were only human.

Brothers in Rhythm and David James had done the original production for the track but Nick Raymonde decided to bring in one of the best-known American producers, Jim Steinman, to rework it. He had been responsible for Bonnie Tyler's 'Total Eclipse Of The Heart' and the Meat Loaf classic 'I'd Do Anything For Love (But I Won't Do That)'. He had a considerable reputation in the US as a Grammy Award-winner. His involvement in Take That and the six-figure sum it cost was further evidence that Gary was being perceived as a serious talent across the Atlantic.

Gary

The timing of the release almost guaranteed a number one, especially as it was the last single to feature Robbie Williams. 'Never Forget' sold close to 500,000 copies but, more importantly, it became one of the focal points of a Take That concert.

The remaining four had the *Nobody Else* tour to prepare for, hastily reworking the show to expunge all traces of Rob before the first night. That wasn't going to be easy because he had already been rehearsing to sing the vocal to two unusual tracks for Take That: 'Smells Like Teen Spirit' by Nirvana and Pink Floyd's 'Another Brick In The Wall'. Gary, professional as ever, decided he would take the first one on. Jason, who wasn't that keen on singing solo, stepped up for the second. They didn't have much time to learn the new routines because they were opening at the Manchester NYNEX Arena on Saturday, 5 August, just two weeks away.

The tour would be easier than previous ones, as it was only taking in two venues in the UK – ten nights in Manchester followed by ten more at Earl's Court in London. All the concerts had sold out when Rob was still in the band so there was the added pressure of not knowing how fans would react to them performing without him. They need not have worried.

From the moment Jason, dressed in skintight crimson PVC shorts, began proceedings by descending on a wire onto the stage, this was a £2 million show that combined the pyrotechnics of a rock tour with the slick showmanship of Vegas. The *Manchester Evening News* described the first night as one in which 'Take That come of age as pop's consummate showmen'. The paper's reviewer won't want to remember his comment that Robbie Williams may yet go down as the Pete Best of Take That – a reference to the forgotten man of The Beatles.

The rock purists were no doubt horrified when Gary, a boy band singer, ripped off his shirt and launched into the Nirvana grunge anthem but the fans, who had paid good money to see their heroes, loved it. Howard, also shirtless, played drums, Mark was on bass, while Jason banged out the chords on guitar. Gary, in black PVC trousers, charged around the stage in demented rock 'n' roll fashion. *Smash Hits* noted that the crowd went 'mental' and called it 'utterly fantastic', although the magazine was almost a Take That fanzine by then.

Gary put a shirt back on to accompany Mark on piano while he sang the last track from the album, the heartfelt ballad 'The Day After Tomorrow', complete with a sixty-member choir. Mark's vocal abilities were improving all the time but the song also revealed how Gary's songwriting was maturing. The choir stayed on stage for the last two numbers: 'Pray' was even more of an anthem live than it had been on record, with the audience clapping enthusiastically, arms reaching to the sky; 'Never Forget' was the perfect song to bring the evening to an end. Rob's solo towards the end of the song was sung by all four.

The benefit of playing so many nights in Manchester was that after the concerts the boys could go home. There was no late-night partying with girls queuing around the block in the hope that tonight might be their night. The band had moved on from those days. Mark was missing his mate Rob's involvement but he had become absorbed in Buddhism and was more interested in regular meditation before a gig than a kickabout. Jason, too, had grown more introspective and would join Mark to meditate so they were mentally refreshed for each concert. At home Mark was reading the *Tibetan Book of the Dead*, Buddhism's guide to the afterlife.

Gary went home to Moorside to unwind by playing the piano. He wouldn't be doing that for much longer because he had bought a magnificent £1 million mansion called Delamere Manor on the outskirts of the village of Cuddington. He would move only about ten miles but would be that much closer to Frodsham. He wouldn't have to worry about visiting his family, though, because he bought the lodge for his mum and dad, as well as the house next door for his brother and his wife. Delamere would be the Barlow family enclave.

Ian set about organizing the extensive refurbishment that needed to be carried out before Gary could move in.

The main house had six bedrooms and five bathrooms and was set in 117 acres of parkland and woodland. From his bedroom window Gary looked out over a seven-acre lake. Staff quarters above the garage would be ideal for Maurice. The manor may not have been on a par with Downton Abbey but Gary now felt he was on a level with the bigger superstars. He had some way to go to match the opulence of Elton John's mansion but set about spending £1 million on antique furnishings and art. He vowed to make it a northern Woodside: 'It's my very own copy of Elton's house.'

Gary had little time to make plans for his new house before he had to fly out with Mark, Howard and Jason to promote Take That in the US. At least this time they had a single to promote that was a hit. Arista, which was under the umbrella of BMG just as RCA was in the UK, also released an album *Nobody Else* that had a different songlist from the one that had reached the top of the British charts. The American version was more like a greatest hits collection, including old favourites like 'Babe', 'Pray' and 'Love Ain't Here Anymore' as well as 'Back For Good' and 'Never Forget'. It was a strategy record companies often try when launching an established band stateside but it seldom works, as the result feels like a jumble of styles and doesn't account for how artists have evolved.

Annoyingly for Take That, there had been such a tepid effort to introduce them to the US in the preceding couple of years that when there had been a real gap in the market earlier in the year someone else, Backstreet Boys, had filled it. Groups like 'N Sync and Hanson were about to crowd the marketplace with music that was far more formulaic than Gary's. The American audience, it seemed, like their boy bands bland. They also liked them to be boys not men, and Howard and Jason were big strapping men, not pretty blond teenagers from Disney.

Gary gamely said he was determined not to compromise their

sound: 'Many groups feel the need to remix their music to make it sound more American. Why? We wanted to break America sounding British.' That sounded good in theory but the album didn't follow 'Back For Good' into the charts. The only consolation for Gary was that Arista had an option to sign him if he decided that Take That was no longer working and turned solo. The boys' commitment couldn't be faulted; criss-crossing America for personal appearances and interviews was exhausting and demoralizing. It was one thing doing that when you were still starting out but it was quite another battle when you were the biggest band in the UK.

Gary's mood wasn't improved when they toured their show in the Far East and Australia, where they played to practically empty venues. He complained that for the first time being in Take That felt like a job. They went on stage in Adelaide and played the whole show, complete with all the pyrotechnics and paraphernalia, for two hundred people – about the same number who would be trying to get a drink at the bar in Earl's Court. Gary observed, 'It was not good for morale.'

They were out of the country for three months but at least on their return they had the boost of winning their now usual eight awards at the *Smash Hits* Poll Winners Party at the London Arena. Gary sang 'Back For Good', which won Single of the Year, perched at a piano, half turned to the audience in an Elton John-type pose. His hair had been restyled with a fringe sweeping across his eyes. He gave the impression of caring more about his appearance, another sign perhaps that he was preparing to be the sole focus of attention.

Despite all the spirited words when Rob left, Gary had realized by Christmas that it was time to move on. His ambition wasn't the only factor. Nigel was reportedly unhappy at the financial involvement that Jason's brother Simon had in the band. He had been making investments for Gary, as well as advising Jason, and Nigel wasn't happy about it. As a result, Nigel told Gary that he needed to go solo right away, as he felt he could no longer manage the band.

Matters weren't helped by the complicated financial situation involving Rob. Nobody was keen to carry on paying him when he was no longer a member of Take That. Robbie, in effect, would continue to be a shareholder in the band until it ceased to exist.

The original plan was to make an announcement that they were splitting up at the Brit Awards in February, when they were due to perform their new single, a cover of the Bee Gees' 'How Deep Is Your Love', a song that Gary had performed on his last night at the Halton Legion when he was still dreaming of fame. He clearly didn't want to waste one of his original compositions on a group that wouldn't be around for much longer; he was now writing for himself.

Take That's last video was filmed at a quarry in Wiltshire and featured all four roped to chairs while singing to a demented-looking Paula Hamilton. She may have represented a crazed fan getting revenge for the band splitting up. Gary sang the song nicely enough but it was a pale imitation of the great Bee Gees' interpretation from *Saturday Night Fever*. He hated everything about the video. It was freezing cold for the two days and he didn't enjoy being stabbed in the neck with a fork by mad Paula. At the end she tips his chair off the edge of the cliff and into the lake, which was a symbolic end to proceedings. The video failed to develop a storyline, although that wouldn't bother distraught fans three days after they finished shooting.

News that they were splitting up found its way into the *Sun* on 12 February. The RCA press officer Kristina Kyriacou said, 'At the moment there's no truth that Take That have split.' She had chosen her words carefully because technically it was true. The newspaper's scoop forced the announcement the following day at a hastily arranged press conference at the Manchester Airport Hilton. Mark did most of the talking because Gary didn't want to take the weight of the fans' disappointment on his shoulders alone even though, in effect, he had the final word. He said, 'You've been absolutely fantastic but unfortunately the rumours are true.'

By coincidence the day was Rob's twenty-second birthday. Gary was asked, 'Have you got a birthday message for Rob? It's his birth-day today.' Gary responded, 'Is it? Oh.' The exchange sounds worse than it was because Gary was being humorous in his deadpan way and he got a huge laugh from the crowded room.

He was probably peeved that on the band's big day they were talk-ing about Robbie Williams, but it was something he would have to get used to. He would much rather have talked about his solo plans. He said he hoped to have a single ready by the summer, followed closely by an album and a tour.

Howard revealed a sensitive side to his nature that he kept hidden from the public: 'I am sure we are all a little bit upset, especially me. I'm very emotional at the moment but I know that it's the best time now to finish at the top.'

And that was that. The Samaritans immediately set up a phone line to offer counselling to the thousands of distressed girl fans. The pop magazines, as well as the record company RCA, offered similar services and many took advantage of them. One fan explained to the *Sun* the effect the news had on her. It is a fascinating insight into how the band's devoted followers were affected by the news: 'I cried into my Take That duvet for hours. The headmaster of my primary school had to organize a special assembly to tell the others to be nice to me. I never took my posters of them down and when I went to university they came with me.'

Not everyone took it so seriously. An Italian magazine mistakenly printed the number of a photocopier repairman in Northampton, claiming it was Gary's. When the fans rang it, Steve Hayne would sing them 'Old Macdonald had a farm, E-I-E-I-O', pretending it would be the band's last single. 'They thought it was wonderful and said I should release it straight away.'

Gary, meanwhile, slipped into his new black Mercedes with tinted windows and drove home. He didn't have time to be sad. There was too much to do and, in any case, his secret girlfriend was waiting for him and he was very much in love.

PART THREE

The Virtue of Patience

14

The One

Gary's love affair with Dawn Andrews was a story in the best traditions of *When Harry Met Sally*. It was definitely fate. The Hollywood script would show them *nearly* enjoying romance from year to year – but not quite. Despite her experience in the showbusiness world, Dawn was shy around Gary. If they hadn't been drawn to one another on the *Nobody Else* tour, then the film would have lasted no more than ten minutes before the lights went up and everyone went home.

Gary hadn't pursued her but once again they were thrown together by accident. Jason was responsible for finding dancers for what would be Take That's final tour and he auditioned and chose Dawn as one of the squad without realizing that she and Gary knew each other, if only fleetingly.

Dancers and stars regularly get together on tour. Usually, it's female headliners who form relationships. Britney Spears and Kevin Federline, Jennifer Lopez and Cris Judd are famous former examples, while Cheryl Cole and her backing dancer Tre Holloway is a more recent one. They don't often last.

Gary's former girlfriend Nicky Ladanowski, who knew him better than most people, realized something was up when he invited her and some friends along to a Pushca party – a themed night organized by the celebrated hostess Madame Pushca – after one of the Earl's

Court gigs. The theme for this particular event was 'White Trash' and everyone had to wear white.

When Nicky's group arrived, one of the first people they saw was Dawn dancing around. Whenever Gary was dancing, Dawn would float over and give him a bottle of water. Nicky thought she recognized her but wasn't sure, as she looked so different with a short blonde bob. She asked Gary if it was the girl from the Kurtis Rush video and he said it was. One of her friends observed, 'We could all see that she really liked him. They were obviously "friends".'

The romance didn't gather pace until Take That left for the European leg of their tour. While everyone assumed that Gary was looking fit and more rugged in preparation for a solo career, he was also trying his best to impress the willowy dancer. Even Howard, who was renowned for having the best body in Take That, thought Gary was in great shape soon after he met Dawn.

Starting a relationship abroad meant that it was much easier to keep it a secret and see how things developed. The years of being under Nigel's watchful eye meant that Gary automatically shied away from letting the world know he was romantically involved. They took their time getting to know each other and, to begin with, Gary wasn't sure that Dawn fancied him, even though she would always sit beside him when everyone on the tour had dinner together before a gig.

Dawn wasn't sure herself. She told *OK!* magazine, 'He grew on me. We ate our dinner together each night and became friends first.' She realized that the private Gary, not the image-conscious star, was a very funny man, adept at one-liners that would have her in fits of giggles. He almost blew it, though, when he bought her sushi, insisting that she would love it. She didn't, and ended up spitting the raw fish into the nearest bin.

After a couple of weeks, which is a lifetime on tour, Gary was beginning to think it was never going to happen. One night, after a show, everybody went out to a club. The boys knew he fancied Dawn by then, but he told Mark that if he didn't get a sign that evening he was going to 'leave it'. Perhaps Dawn had some female intuition or some inside information, because she danced close to Gary all night.

Even more promisingly, on the way home they were sandwiched together in the back of a small van. It was hardly rock star luxury. Gary recalled, 'Dawn ended up on my knee. This is good, I thought. When we were on our way, she turned round, looked at me and we had our first kiss.'

It was a long first kiss. They knew the moment was right and spent the rest of the ten-minute journey locked together. This was completely different from the sort of joyless encounter he had experienced as one of the lads on previous tours. From the very beginning he realized he was in love. 'I was completely besotted straight away,' he admitted.

Dawn came into Gary's life again at exactly the right time. The Take That era was coming to an end and he wanted something more. They spent every minute of the rest of the tour together and Gary was dismayed when he couldn't persuade her to follow him on the Far East and Australia legs, not to mention the American commitments he had to fulfil immediately afterwards.

Dawn was being more sensible than he was at this early stage of their relationship. She had her own career to think about and had already signed up as a backing dancer for Cher's performance of 'Walking In Memphis' on *Top of the Pops*. She did agree to join him for five days in Singapore when the band had a break before moving on to Bangkok. Gary took her visit so seriously that he insisted Mark take him out shopping for some new clothes. He wanted to look his best.

There was no Facebook in 1995. Gary didn't email Dawn or text her like a lovesick teenager. Instead, when she wasn't with him, he would sit down at the desk in his hotel suite and hand-write a love letter. He made sure he did that every day because his feelings were so intense: 'I really missed her and I didn't want to lose her. It turned me a bit crazy.' This was the romantic Gary that usually came out only when he was composing a song.

Gary knew Dawn was 'the one'. He wanted someone to give him a cuddle when he went home and Maurice didn't fit the bill. As soon as he returned from America, he asked her to move in. He had started renting a luxury flat overlooking the river in Chelsea, so they could both continue their busy lives and she wouldn't be isolated for weeks on end in the house in Cheshire. One of the first things she did was inform her new boyfriend that Maurice had to go. She said, 'I'm not having him mincing around the place.'

His mother and father took an instant shine to Dawn when they met her. She wasn't at all interested in being a celebrity. She had been brought up quietly in a village near Worcester but had always wanted to be a dancer. At fifteen she had enrolled in a dance school and had consistently found work as a dancer and part-time model. She wasn't a party girl or someone who sought fame by proxy. She knew what went on in the pop world and wasn't the least concerned by any of Gary's past dalliances just so long as there was nothing like that in the future.

She didn't mind going to the Brits with Gary in February 1996 because nobody in the media knew who she was or that they were living together. Her attitude changed when the press found out about them. They were 'spotted' by a photographer at the end of March, casually strolling hand in hand down the King's Road, wearing sunglasses and matching Adidas trainers. It was the first time Gary had ever been photographed with a girlfriend. A convenient shopper observed, 'They looked truly in love.' Dawn died with embarrassment when she was described in the newspapers as being a 'raunchy' dancer and decided from that moment she would stay very much in the background.

Gary didn't deny Dawn's existence when he was inevitably asked about her in subsequent interviews but he said he would prefer it if they didn't mention his girlfriend by name because 'it just creates problems for her'. He was quoted in several places as saying, 'I don't think I ever communicated with any of my girlfriends before Dawn,' which may have been truthful but wasn't especially kind to Nicky, who was still in contact with him.

Nicky realized it wasn't appropriate for her to stay in close touch with Gary after he became so serious about Dawn. She was also with somebody else and decided it was time to call a halt to the friendship, despite her strong feelings for Gary. They didn't speak again but he followed her career with keen interest. He particularly enjoyed it when she was a regular in *Coronation Street*, playing a character called Merle Jackson who dated Jason Grimshaw's father, Tony. She would often pop up unexpectedly when Gary was watching TV, in *The Bill* or, memorably, as Les Dennis's girlfriend in a very funny episode of *Extras*.

Gary liked the evenings with Dawn when they could curl up together on the sofa, with Jess the Alsatian on the rug, and watch television like a normal couple. At least he didn't have to spend every waking moment composing at the piano. He had already written the new album and just had to finish the recording.

Take That needed to honour some final commitments before performing for the last time on a television show in Amsterdam on 3 April 1996. The whole experience was a grind. They were all so bored during the rehearsal that they dropped their trousers and finished the song in their Y-fronts. The last promotional tour of Europe was worth it from a financial point of view – the *Greatest Hits* album topped the charts in seven countries.

As the sole songwriter of most of the hits, Gary cleaned up yet again. His fortune from Take That was estimated at the time as £7 million, although more recently it was reported to be double that. He admitted, 'I've got more money than I will ever need in my life.'

Besides Dawn, Gary had much on his mind. He was under pressure the moment it was all over for the group. Nobody expected much of Robbie or the others but Gary was, by common consent, a superstar about to happen. He was favourite to have the Christmas number one before he had even released a record. Jason's father, Tony Orange, observed, 'When I first heard Take That's demo tape I told everyone that Gary was going to be an absolute megastar. He is going to be the McCartney of the nineties.'

Everyone in the music business seemed positive Gary would be the next big thing. Tilly Rutherford, then general manager of PWL, Pete Waterman's label, commented about Take That, 'Gary has got so much talent and he's the only one who can sing.' Sir Tim Rice, one of the most respected figures in British music, observed, 'Many of Gary Barlow's songs are the equivalent of George Michael's at the same stage of his career.'

The future looked promising enough when he persuaded Dawn to accompany him and his parents to the Ivor Novello Awards at London's Grosvenor House Hotel in May. He picked up two awards when 'Back For Good' was named the Best Selling Song as well as the PRS for Music Most Performed Work. He joked to the audience that it was the 'best fifteen minutes' work I have ever done'.

Gary could only hope that his first solo single, a ballad called 'Forever Love', would do half as well. The HMV chain confidently predicted it was going to be 'massive'. The song was ready to go, but the day after the Ivors Gary had to fly over to Los Angeles and impress Arista record bosses and, in particular, Clive Davis with the new album, *Open Road*. He would be performing at a private gig just for them.

Dawn went along to support him. They almost didn't make it when their plane had to make an emergency landing on a small runway in Baffin Bay, Canada, 1,000 miles north of Montreal, after a passenger had suffered a mid-air heart attack. As it landed, the plane clipped a petrol pump containing highly inflammable aviation fuel, which put it out of action. All the passengers, including Prince Michael of Kent, had to brave the arctic conditions for fifteen hours until a replacement jet could be found.

Gary was probably glad of the delay because, behind the scenes, he was becoming riddled with self-doubt for the first time since he had begun his career, aged thirteen, at Connah's Quay Labour Club. It wasn't Rob who was getting under his skin. He wasn't at all worried about Robbie Williams. Why should he be? The youngest member of Take That had been indulging in a lost year after leaving the band. He was only now emerging into the light with rumours that he would soon be signing a deal with a new record company. From time to time Rob would indulge in some sniping at his former colleagues, which prompted Gary to respond that he needed to get it together and make a 'fucking record'. Gary didn't have time to be really annoyed about him at this point.

His real nemesis as a solo performer wasn't Robbie Williams at all but the boss of Arista, Clive Davis, a man who would be collecting his bus pass if he lived in the UK but was a hugely respected figure in the US music business. He had founded Arista in 1975 after serving six years as president of Columbia Records, where he had signed Aerosmith. When he was deciding what the future would bring for Gary Barlow, he could boast of guiding the recording careers of many hugely successful artists, including Whitney Houston and Toni Braxton. Gary was a huge admirer of both singers and named Toni's 'Un-break My Heart' as his favourite record of the year. The soaring ballad had been written by the renowned Diane Warren and produced by David Foster. Gary dreamed of working with both of these Grammy winners.

That felt a world away when he took the microphone at the tiny Galaxy Theater on an industrial estate in Santa Ana, south of Los Angeles. He had a ten-song set to go through, consisting of his own songs and one favourite cover, 'Cuddly Toy', a big UK hit for Roachford in 1989. Gary, it seems, had to audition like any other wannabe and not an award-winning, multimillionaire songwriter whose records had sold millions of copies.

Despite his misgivings, he put on a show. The audience were in a good mood after the announcement that it was saxophonist Kenny G's fortieth birthday. Gary tried a touch of Halton Legion humour to keep things moving: 'Well, I've had some requests, but I'm still going to do another song.' After he closed his set with 'Forever Love', Clive, who was then sixty-four, stood up to applaud, which was a relief as it was the signal for everyone to follow suit. Ostensibly it all went well and Gary was very upbeat about things. Privately, however, he was anything but happy.

Clive Davis, he realized, was not as enthusiastic about his material as he had at first seemed. The problem is that America is considered the holy grail in British music and Gary's UK label BMG were willing to bend over backwards to make sure Clive was happy and on board. The delay would turn out to be disastrous for Gary.

The reality of his position emerged when he was summoned to Clive Davis's bungalow at the Beverly Hills Hotel. It was a comedy meeting almost as memorable as the debacle at Rocket Records before he was signed. Things got off to a bad start when Gary unwittingly ate Clive's breakfast while the record mogul took a phone call in the next room. He wanted to play Clive a cassette of his new songs but never had the chance because his host produced two tracks that he wanted Gary to record. They were country and western songs 'So Help Me Girl' and 'I Fall So Deep', both of which ended up on his debut album when it was eventually released. Gary observed rather bitterly in *My Take*, 'There I was thinking I was the star when all along it was Clive.'

At the end of the meeting Gary slunk back to the UK, having promised to record those songs as well as re-record most of the album to make it sound friendlier to an American market. Gary's problem with sounding too British for the US is exactly the same one Robbie Williams would face; being the biggest star in the UK counted for nothing. Gary would later identify working with Clive as the moment when he lost confidence in his solo career. He told *Esquire* magazine, 'Every piece of music I wrote after that was shit.'

158

Gary's UK fans were oblivious to this drama behind the scenes when his debut solo single 'Forever Love' was released in July 1996. The track was one of his heartfelt, anguished ballads with a classic Gary tuneful intro and simple but elegiac piano melody. It possessed all the ingredients of a great song but perhaps lacked the soaring quality of 'Back For Good' or 'A Million Love Songs'. You didn't want to sing 'Forever Love' in the shower; instead it was a song to enjoy with cocoa – safe rather than spectacular, although the sales were more than respectable.

Understandably, Gary was nervous about the outcome. He would be unable to share any potential disappointment with four other band members. Instead, he did an interview with *Smash Hits* and hoped for the best. He must have been feeling a little desperate because he broke his Take That rule and spoke at length about his relationship with Dawn. He was disarmingly frank, revealing they were living together but he didn't want to have children until they were married.

He explained, 'At the moment I can't give anybody the time they need for marriage. Neither can Dawn, so marriage is not spoken of yet. It won't happen because of commitments to my career, but I'm really sure now that I want to be a dad.' That didn't sound very romantic but Gary redeemed himself when he confided, 'I just fell in love with her, with her personality and her shyness and her beauty. She has helped me a lot during the past few difficult months and that's made me fall in love with her even more.'

The couple finally moved into Delamere Manor during the summer of 1996. It was a welcome distraction from biting his nails over his debut record. Gary was very proud of his house and lost no time inviting his old friends from Frodsham to come and visit. Some things didn't change from the old days because visitors still always came to the back door. Martin Smiddy remembers it well, 'We rolled up at the electronic gates and pressed the button to let him know who it was. Then you would drive up the path – I remember he had put all these statues every ten yards or so. You would park in the courtyard and knock on the back door. There was a sort of kitchen and dining area where he would entertain. It was very homely.

'From time to time he would jump up and say, "Come and look at this" and he would take you through to see one of the gold discs he had. He had *The Lion King* one there. He had a recording studio custom-built in the house and I remember he had a full-sized Storm Trooper costume from *Star Wars* standing next to the piano.'

His father Colin was responsible for looking after the grounds, keeping the lawns sweeping down to the lake in immaculate condition and making sure there were no weeds springing up on the tennis court. He had done a superb job by the time Gary and Dawn unpacked the silver. They liked nothing better than to stroll around the grounds after breakfast. This would be a wonderful home in which to start a family.

Many observers wanted Gary to reveal that 'Forever Love' was written about Dawn. He has never confirmed that, so the chances are that it was nothing more than a finely crafted pop song. The video was shot in black and white and had the feel of a French movie or perhaps one of Woody Allen's New York sagas. Gary did his tortured soul impression as he sat in a café and watched the couples, young and old, showing different ways of expressing love.

The single entered the charts at number one, so all was well. Eventually it would sell more than 500,000 copies – not far off the sales of 'Never Forget' – but, funnily enough, it did almost exactly half as well as 'Back For Good'. That summer the song was also on the soundtrack to *The Leading Man*, a romantic comedy starring Jon Bon Jovi that failed to rattle box office tills. 'Forever Love' would have been the perfect lead single for an album released in time for Christmas. Instead, his fans would have to wait until his American masters were happy.

The critics weren't enthusiastic. The *Independent* scoffed, 'Forensic musicologists have been working round the clock ever since to discern a melody in the Ivor Novello Award-winner's latest composition.'

Disappointingly, 'Forever Love' lasted only a week at the top and was swept away by 'Wannabe', the debut single from the Spice Girls. The media always wants something fresh and new to write about and the five feisty girls provided it. The whole pop world was swamped by all things spice. Nowadays, 'Girl Power' seems good fun but very dated – much more so than 'Forever Love', which has a timeless quality.

The only consolation for Gary was that 'Wannabe' prevented Rob's first single, a version of George Michael's 'Freedom', from reaching the top. Irritatingly, just before the release of 'Forever Love', Rob had called a press conference to announce his new three-album record deal with EMI/Chrysalis worth a reputed £1 million. He had spent a fortune on lawyers' fees freeing himself from his BMG contract. One of the conditions was that he could not release a single before Gary did. That didn't stop him or his canny management from using the oxygen of Gary's publicity to promote the solo career of Robbie Williams.

Rob was celebrating so many areas of freedom with the track: freedom from Take That; freedom from his contract with BMG; freedom from the dispiriting rules of Nigel Martin-Smith; freedom to party; freedom, in effect, to do whatever he wanted. The song was a statement, if a rather unsubtle one.

He took the opportunity to talk about Nigel at a press conference: 'I'd like to meet up with the manager in a fork-lift truck, souped up to 150 miles an hour with no brakes.' It was an example of the sort of funny and outrageous comment Rob would make for years to come when continuing his feud with all things Take That.

Nigel was again in his sights when Rob gave his most notorious interview for *Attitude*'s August 1996 edition. Copies of the gay magazine hit the street when 'Forever Love' was high in the charts. There was no love whatsoever in the piece. Instead, Rob started with

Nigel, 'I don't even have words for that c**t', which wasn't strictly true as he has never been short of words about his former manager. Then he laid into Jason when he was asked how many of Take That would succeed: 'It just depends what they succeed in. Jason's going to make a brilliant painter and decorator.'

Gary couldn't believe what Rob said about Take That and about him in particular. He called the band 'selfish, stupid and greedy' and referred to Gary as a 'clueless wanker'. The hostility was breathtaking but somehow, because it was Rob and he was being open and honest about his feelings, he was instantly forgiven for his outrageousness. This would only encourage him until routinely slagging off Gary became part of his 'shtick'. The media sensed a story that could run and run. In effect they joined forces with Rob to bait Gary.

A friend of both men explained why the pair were viewed so differently by the public: 'Rob is lovable because he tells the truth. They have different philosophies. Gary's thing was to make himself whiter than white. He thought people would love him if he looked squeaky clean and lovely. But Rob was like "I'm struggling. I'm on drugs. I'm drinking too much. I'm overweight. Nigel has done this to me." He just told the truth and people appreciated that life is not a bowl of cherries.'

In the eyes of the world, the whole saga of Rob and Gary unfolded like a modern version of the tortoise and hare fable: Gary was the hare, the corporate darling of his record company, about to zoom over the horizon with million-selling number ones; Rob, the drugged-up tortoise, was going round and round in small circles. Gary's coronation had the air of smug inevitability that didn't appeal to the great British public, who traditionally like an underdog. Imagine how different things might have been if Gary had said sorry to Rob for the way he had been treated, acknowledged that they had both been young and offered to give him his support in the future.

Gary's popular appeal at this time would have increased vastly if anyone had realized he, too, was struggling with insecurity and a crisis in confidence. There was no sense of smug inevitability as he tried to finish an album that would please his American masters. Unlike Rob, he was feeling far from free. Instead he was becoming more shackled by his record company and feeling powerless to do anything about it. The newspapers carried stories that his next single would be 'Open Road' and would be released on 14 October with the album, aimed at the Christmas market, following two weeks later. That would have been perfect but it never happened.

Few, if any, solo careers can have been so comprehensively botched as Gary Barlow's.

15

Unravelling

Gary fired Nigel in November 1996. The manager had been his rock and mentor from the start of Take That, so this development was surprising and dramatic. Perhaps Nigel was preoccupied with the legal action he had begun, claiming unpaid fees from Rob, but it was still unexpected and the clearest evidence yet that Gary's usually sure touch had deserted him. After all they had been through together, the abrupt end came by fax from Gary's lawyers to Nigel's office; there wasn't even a phone call.

Gary didn't criticize his ex-manager publicly, even if in private he was disappointed that Nigel wasn't protecting him from being steamrollered by Arista. He merely said that he had to move on because it wasn't right any more, although he did concede that he might have broken Nigel's heart with his decision.

Nigel was gracious about the split, emphasizing that they had enjoyed 'six great years together'. He added, 'I created Take That around Gary and I have been heavily involved with his solo album. But he wants to spend more time in America and I don't like it there. I'm more interested in discovering new acts than dealing with the problems of Gary Barlow.' The last observation was perhaps a subtle acknowledgement that Gary did have problems.

In retrospect, Gary made a big mistake ditching Nigel at this stage of his career but it looked like a forward-thinking move when he hired Simon Fuller, the manager of the moment, to take his place. Simon was guiding the career of the Spice Girls and they were the hottest property in music in the mid-nineties.

The whole world knows the name Simon Cowell. He is in the papers in his media-appointed role as the most influential person in music, but it is the other Simon who is considerably richer. The Fuller fortune is estimated at £375 million, whereas the deviser of *The X Factor* has to scrape by on £250 million. The men behind the scenes are invariably much wealthier than the performers in front of a microphone or camera.

When Simon Fuller took on Gary, he was in his mid-thirties and had been a millionaire for more than ten years. A dapper, perma-tanned figure with shiny black hair, he was the son of a primary school headmaster and was brought up in a middle-class household in Hastings. Like Nigel, he had a quietly imposing manner but he was no Svengali. He didn't create the Spice Girls nor would he have moulded five northern lads into Take That. He made his name as the manager of a musician called Paul Hardcastle, whose anti-Vietnam War song '19' sold four million copies. Subsequently, all Fuller's companies have had the prefix 19, as in the 19 Entertainment Group.

When he met the Spice Girls, Fuller was best known as the manager of Annie Lennox and Cathy Dennis. His biggest skill was in building a brand behind the scenes. He would later turn the Beckhams into global superstars but in the mid-nineties he was maximizing the impact of the Spice Girls and their 'Girl Power' slogan. When he first met Victoria Adams, as she then was, she told him, 'We want to be bigger than Persil washing powder.' He set about achieving that ambition for her.

Gary felt he needed someone who recognized the importance of the US and could fulfil his American dream. His alliance with Simon Fuller should have given him the edge he needed but, for some reason, they never gelled. Perhaps Gary at this stage of his career needed more individual attention than his new manager was able to give him. He was happy to go along with what Simon wanted, however, and so ended up attending the Brits at Earl's Court, where he watched the Spice Girls hog the limelight, winning the Best British Single and Best British Video awards. It was the evening when Geri Halliwell wore her famous Union Jack mini-dress.

Gary had to make do with presenting an award for Best International Newcomer, which was hardly the premier spot. He even had to share presenting duties with Louise from Eternal, who was wearing a revealing white nightdress, so no one was looking at Gary anyway. All he got to say was: 'Doesn't Louise look gorgeous?' She announced the winner, a DJ called Robert Miles, who was an Italian. Gary smiled gamely and nobody would have guessed that he hated the whole experience.

The papers ignored him except to note that he was spotted holding hands with a mystery 'ravishing' brunette who was definitely not Dawn at an after-show party at the Hard Rock Café. Apparently she was an old friend and there was nothing to it.

Gary was saying in interviews that one of the reasons Take That ended was because he wanted to take risks again and firing Nigel was certainly that. He wasn't taking risks, however, when he played the corporate game at the Brits nor with his debut album, which was turning into a work of complete safeness.

He first recorded *Open Road* using all his own material. He had seventeen songs written and ready before Take That's swansong in Amsterdam and had recorded them all with Chris Porter, the producer on 'Back For Good'. This time Chris stayed at Delamere Manor for a month and they worked in Gary's state-of-the-art studio. He recalled, 'It was brilliant. I learned so much from him.' Barlow/Porter seemed a sensible match.

Clive Davis and Arista had other ideas. Gary was summoned to the US to record with renowned producers David Foster and

Walter Afanasieff. They were two greats of American music and Gary was looking forward to working with them on his songs. By 2013 Foster had won sixteen Grammys and been nominated forty-seven times. In 1996, when he worked with Gary, he was best known as the producer of 'I Will Always Love You' for Whitney Houston and Celine Dion's 'Because You Loved Me'. He was the master arranger of the big ballad.

Walter Afanasieff had a similar pedigree, working closely with Mariah Carey and producing many of her best-known hits, including 'Without You' and 'All I Want For Christmas Is You'. Throw Diane Warren into the mix and it becomes clear that Gary was being treated seriously by Arista. Very few artists could boast that they worked with these three big-hitters on what was, in American terms, a debut album. Gary found it difficult working with such powerful personalities, though.

He tells a wonderful story about having lunch with Diane Warren at a restaurant near her studio on Sunset Boulevard when the multi-millionaire songwriter produced a parrot from her pocket and put it on the table. Gary must have been one of the few people in LA who didn't know Diane went everywhere with her pet bird, called Buttwings. It wasn't the sort of thing you did at the Chinese Delight in Frodsham.

Gary in the US didn't really work. He lacked the smoothness of Elton John and George Michael among premier British singer-songwriters. Trying to graft Americanization onto his Britishness resulted in a sound of quite stupefying blandness. He listened back to his day's recording with these great producers and must have wondered who he was listening to. It certainly sounded nothing like Take That – more like a collection of schmoozy ballads that Backstreet Boys might have put on the B-side.

In the end David Foster produced the two songs that Gary didn't care for – 'So Help Me Girl' and 'I Fall So Deep'. There was worse to come when Clive Davis wanted him to record a specially written

Madonna song called 'Love Won't Wait'. Successful artists like her don't hand over their best songs. The track, it turned out, was a formerly unreleased demo that didn't make it onto an album Madonna was recording in 1994.

By the time *Open Road* was finally ready to go, the original production team of Gary and Chris Porter were responsible for only three tracks out of twelve – numbers nine, eleven and twelve. Six other producers and ten songwriters were involved in the 'solo' venture.

Gary's American dream went from bad to worse when Clive drafted him in at the eleventh hour to perform at his renowned pre-Grammys party in New York. Gary's performance of 'Love Won't Wait' was probably the worst he ever gave and was met with stony silence by an audience that included George Michael and the great Aretha Franklin. It was a tumbleweed moment.

Not everything in the US was completely negative. The influential *Billboard* magazine called Gary a 'class act' and observed, 'Those who doubt his ability to become as big an international star as George Michael are likely to end up eating their words.' The magazine also pointed out that there had been 'hiccups' in the recording of his debut album, which had been due for release months ago. 'Hiccups' was a chronic understatement.

While Gary was struggling and Rob was still pulling himself together, Mark Owen beat both to the record stores when his debut solo album, *Green Man*, was released just before Christmas. His first single, 'Child', had reached the top three in November 1996 but that was the best position he ever achieved as a solo performer. *Green Man* flopped, reaching a lowly thirty-three, which didn't fill anyone with much optimism about the careers of ex-members of Take That. A year later, Mark was dropped by BMG.

Eventually, ten months after 'Forever Love', Gary brought out his second single. The powers that be had chosen 'Love Won't Wait' ahead of one of his own songs – a reminder of those early disappointments with the Take That covers. This time the producer was Steve Lipson, who had built a strong reputation in the eighties working with Frankie Goes To Hollywood and Grace Jones. Simon Fuller knew him through his earlier work with Annie Lennox. The song barely sounded like Gary.

He explained to the *Daily Record*, 'It took me a while to get my interpretation right because Madonna had written from a female point of view. It's not the kind of song I normally would write myself. But as soon as I heard it, I thought, "This is a hit."' The *Daily Mirror* said, 'It feels like a classic track you've known all your life.' The *Sunday Mirror* gave it seven out of ten: 'Take That fans will lap up another smooth one from Gary but I can't help thinking he's trying to turn into Elton John far too soon. Gary, you're a funky young man so show a bit more oomph . . .' Other reviewers found it catchy but bland, although Madonna apparently liked it.

Take That fans also approved and, despite any private misgivings, the song went straight to number one when it was released at the end of April 1997. While it wouldn't be as successful as 'Forever Love', the single sold more than 200,000 copies in the UK, again a perfectly respectable figure. When Gary toured as a headline solo act in late 2012 and early 2013 he performed all his greatest hits; he did not include 'Love Won't Wait'.

There's no doubt that Gary's solo career had lost momentum. His progress was no longer the hottest topic in the music business. When he appeared at a Prince's Trust concert in Manchester he wasn't top of the bill, even though he was the current number one. The Spice Girls, giving their first live performance in the UK, once again grabbed the limelight.

Momentum is everything in pop music and Gary no longer had it. *Open Road* was finally released at the end of May but wasn't hailed as worth the wait. Adrian Thrills in the *Daily Mail* observed, 'The music is airbrushed to perfection, but there is something missing from its soft musical hues. It often lacks musical bite, a cutting lyrical edge and is frustratingly inconclusive.' At least the serious newspapers were acknowledging Gary now. The *Independent* called it 'polished' and 'efficient' and designed for the anaemic American market.

Gary was only twenty-six but this was an album from a much older artist. Nobody seemed to say it was a bad album – it clearly wasn't – but the critical response was disappointing because more had been expected from such a talented songwriter. It was an album parked in the middle of the road. That didn't stop it going straight to number one and selling more than two million copies worldwide.

At this point Gary parted company with Simon Fuller. They had lasted less than six months together. Officially Simon was too busy with the Spice Girls, which may have had some truth to it, but Gary was unhappy at being left to sink or swim in the US while trying to promote his music. He explained, 'Wrong move hiring Fuller. My phone call was always just one of a string of more important calls.'

He decided to hire Kristina Kyriacou, someone he already knew well from RCA who had travelled with Take That on many occasions. Gary liked and trusted her. She was thoughtful and enthusiastic, although her expertise was in marketing and communications. Together they set up Gary's first production company, Globe Artists, and moved into a suite of offices near his Battersea home. Specially commissioned photographs of Gary, shot in Arles, hung at intervals up the stairs like the posters you pass on a Tube escalator.

Gary observed, 'The thing I liked about Kristina was that she was terrified about coming to work for me. She never thought she'd be able to do it. I'd far prefer to have someone who's going to concentrate on me and me alone than someone like Simon who didn't seem to care at all.'

Gary's opinion of Simon wasn't improved when he discovered he was mentioned in the Spice Girls' movie, *Spice World*. It was the funniest line in a lacklustre film. As a punishment for their big gig at the Albert Hall being a failure, the judge, played by Stephen Fry, sentences the girls to a run of pop chart failure and falling popularity. He then bashes down his gavel and announces, 'Call Gary Barlow.' This gentle piss-take was also an early indication that it was now OK to diss him. The idea that Gary's career was on the skids was a very difficult one to shift once it had taken root.

He was still focusing on the US when perhaps he should have been paying more attention to what was happening at home. After all the effort he had made, would the 'anaemic American market' actually like his album? The song 'So Help Me Girl', which had just missed the top ten as the third release in the UK, was finally selected as his debut single in the US.

Billboard magazine loved it: 'An out of the box smash that will whet many an appetite for the star-bound artist's sterling full length debut *Open Road* due to hit stores in late December.' Gary spent weeks criss-crossing the States trying to obtain airtime for his record. Despite the patronage of Clive Davis and the presence of David Foster and co, the single peaked at a dismal forty-four on the *Billboard* Hot 100. The album did even worse.

The *San Diego Vista* thought the title track 'Open Road' was the best, showcasing Gary's 'brilliant songwriting' abilities. This was the song he had written as a teenager in his bedroom in Frodsham and handed round on cassettes to his friends while he was still at school. All that input from experts and the purest and oldest Gary Barlow song was the best received. He also liked it the most.

By the time it was released in the UK at the end of October 1997, the track no longer seemed fresh enough and limped to number seven in the charts. Much worse for Gary was turning on the radio the following month and hearing Rob's life-changing single 'Angels' for the first time. He knew instantly it was a great song. The melancholic piano chords could have been Gary at his very best. 'Angels' is unusual for such an introspective ballad in that it is unashamedly uplifting and, crucially, can mean something different for everyone. It is a song about guardian spirits and rescue and, as such, rather aptly rescued Rob's career.

As Gary's career began to sink, Rob's soared. 'Angels' would become one of the best-loved pop songs of all time. *Life Thru A Lens*, the album on which it featured, eventually sold more than two million copies and became the first of four by Robbie Williams in the top 100 best-selling albums of all time in the UK. Within a year he would be the biggest-selling British artist.

Gary didn't have an 'Angels' tucked away in the back pocket. The game-changing songs he had written in the past – 'Back For Good', 'A Million Love Songs' and 'Pray' – had transformed the fortunes of Take That. Now, when he needed one for himself, all that was on the table was the cover of an old American country and western song and a dreadful version of a seventies disco hit called 'Hang On In There Baby'.

Gary saw Rob again at the *Concert of Hope* in memory of Princess Diana at the Battersea Power Station in December 1997. Originally there had been speculation that Take That would reunite, but in the end it was just the two of them performing independently. The event was slightly surreal. Rob came on and did a punk version of 'Back For Good' straight out of the Sid Vicious songbook. He sang mainly out of tune, mutilated the song and generated huge excitement. It was fantastic.

Gary, dressed in black polo-neck jumper and burgundy cords, performed two duets. First, he invited on stage a little-known American singer called Rosie Gaines and they sang 'Hang On In There Baby'. It didn't sound any better live than it did on *Open Road*. He then joined Ronan Keating for a version of 'Harvest For The World', a disco hit for The Isley Brothers in 1976. He so obviously should have sung 'Back For Good' himself instead of these uninspiring cover versions. As usual he was note perfect but that counted for nothing.

The only time Gary sounded like the performer his fans loved was in the encore when all the performers gathered on stage to sing 'Let It Be'. Gary sat at the piano and sang the first verse and it was perfect. For the second verse, Peter Andre took over. Rob gave Gary a hug and a 'well done' and that was the last time they spoke to each other for nearly eight and a half years.

16

Defeated

Somehow Barlow Bashing became a national sport. It wasn't just Rob, although he was the captain of the England team. Everyone seemed to be aiming at an easy target and there was nobody in the media prepared to stick up for Gary. He had made some wretched decisions during the year and produced an album that probably had only two tracks worthy of him – 'Forever Love' and 'Open Road'. Even someone as accomplished as Kristina Kyriacou seemed powerless to stem the tide. He complained to *heat* magazine, 'Is that the new trend, just fucking slagging me off?' It was.

Nothing encapsulated the nation's treatment of him better than the George Michael saga. Gary had made no secret of his ambition to follow the former star of Wham! to worldwide success as a solo artist. He had even featured in the *Daily Express* in an article entitled 'Why I Love George Michael'. He recalled that he was tongue-tied the first time he met his hero at an MTV Awards show in Berlin. He finally managed to chat to him in a recording studio when he was making 'Back For Good' and George showed up unexpectedly to see Chris Porter.

When Gary walked in, George was sitting on a sofa eating an apple and the two chatted pleasantly for fifteen minutes before Gary had to get back to work. He observed, 'I know they say you shouldn't meet your idols but I wasn't disappointed in any way.' That certainly wasn't the case when he met George again in November 1998 at a lunch given by Elton John at The Ivy restaurant in London to celebrate the birthday of his partner, David Furnish. They sat at the same table but George blanked him for the entire meal.

He understood why the following day when he was shown an article in *Q* magazine in which George said, 'Gary Barlow doesn't have any talent. I listened to that shit about him, someone discovered in a northern working men's club, being the new George Michael. Just because he was fat and we both have inflatable cheeks does not mean we are working in the same area. I resent it when people make out my contribution to the early eighties was influencing future boy bands.'

Gary couldn't believe how bitchy the comment was and was bitterly upset about it, particularly as it came from a hero. It was yet another knock to his dwindling confidence. In George's defence, nobody quite realized that he was struggling with his own demons. Earlier in the year he had been arrested in a public toilet engaging in a sexual act with another man and had been forced to deal with all the publicity surrounding that. The Gary comment was little more than a hurtful throwaway in a long article of navel-gazing.

To his credit, Elton was mortified when he found out and did his best to rally round his friend. There had been a great deal of publicity about how he helped Rob during his darkest drug days but he was also a support to Gary when he needed him. During his concert at the Manchester MEN Arena in November 1998, he introduced Gary on stage and the two of them sang a touching and melodic version of 'Sacrifice', Elton's only solo number one in the UK.

If only their version of 'Sacrifice' had been released, it might have changed the public perception of Gary at a time when he really needed it. Their voices were a perfect match in much the same way as George Michael's 1991 duet with Elton on 'Don't Let The Sun Go Down On Me' had been. Some years later Elton and George would start a feud over the latter's cannabis use that was almost as intense as Gary and Rob's and lasted nearly as long.

Gary had spent most of the year either touring or trying to write his next album at Delamere Manor, where he had upset the locals by banning them from fishing on his lake. He did so out of a desire for security and privacy. Gary didn't want to be spied on, especially by photographers disguised as anglers. Who could blame him?

The media's interest in Gary seemed relentlessly negative. It was a bandwagon they all jumped on eagerly. The *Sunday Mirror*, for instance, sneeringly described him as 'Mr Cheesy' when previewing his *Open Road* tour.

This unwanted reputation in the press was enhanced by his decision to light three candles on stage during his shows – the first was for Princess Diana, the second for the murdered Gianni Versace and the third for his beloved grandmother Nan Bo, who had also recently died. He then sang 'Forever Love'. The fans remained loyal and loved his shows and, as in the old days of Take That, would go to every gig in the hope of chatting to him.

If Gary had gone back to being the old Gary Barlow at this difficult time, he might have turned things around. Instead, he became a sort of poor man's Robbie Williams as he attracted the type of headlines usually associated with his now far more famous ex-bandmate. He gave the ill-judged interview to Dominic Mohan of the *Sun* that boasted of 'blowing the lid off Gary's squeaky clean image'.

The article revealed Gary's 'wild' side, although it didn't sound like him: 'The problem was, if I took E, I'd feel like shit for a week and just couldn't work . . . I've done drugs but I've never had a problem.' Gary attempted to reinforce the perception that he was a super stud during his time in Take That: 'I slept with hundreds of girl fans all over the world. But I've got all that out of my system now.'

It was as if someone had told Gary that he couldn't just talk about the music. He had to seem interesting, so he talked about drugs and sex and Robbie Williams. 'He seems to like doing things that destroy him. On our last tour, at rehearsals, he couldn't function. He was doing so many drugs and was in a right old state, like a time bomb.'

Then Gary made his debut in the *News of the World* in a kiss-and-tell story. This was nothing like the plaintive story of his first girlfriend, Heather Woodall. Instead, Youlanda Link, a sixteen-year-old schoolgirl, or a 'coleen from Bangor' as the newspaper described her, told how Gary had given her some grey woolly socks because her feet were cold and they had enjoyed a 'smouldering' kiss.

The headline that Gary had taken a 'stunning sixteen-year-old to his hotel room' while on tour in Belfast was entirely misleading because the story revealed that nothing went on – or came off – and there seemed to be no night of passion at all. The whole thing was put in perspective the following week when Rob took centre stage for another kiss and tell. This was much more like it: 'Rocker beds lap dancer Sandy'. According to the breathless pole expert, Rob had nibbled her ear, they had torn their clothes off and she lost count of the number of times they made love. It was all good knockabout fun that merely made Gary's alleged sexploits seem dull in comparison.

Even though clearly nothing had happened, the media decided that it led to a bust-up between Gary and Dawn in which she packed her bags and moved back to London. Gary has always been completely unequivocal that he has never been unfaithful to Dawn. The strength of their relationship, whatever the media tried to insinuate, kept him going through this difficult year.

The old cliché is sex, drugs and rock 'n' roll. Gary was resolutely un-rock 'n' roll. He was beginning to say in interviews that he wanted to write songs for other people as well as confirming his ambition to have a family. His statement that 'I'd love lots of children and I think I'd be a good dad' sounded like a man trying to reclaim the innocence and simpler times of Frodsham. He knew he had lost the war of words with Rob, as well as the race to see who would be the more successful solo performer. He told the *Birmingham Post* sadly, 'All his comments were very hurtful for me personally because it had nothing to do with music. It was all just bitching about me, which I took badly.'

On tour he could often be found enjoying a drink or two in the hotel bar. When Take That began, Gary locked himself away in his room, composing new songs. Now his muse seemed to have deserted him.

Gary is a great believer in confidence-building momentum. As his self-belief ebbed away, so did his creativity. He needed someone to help him write great songs again. His problem had always been lyrics. In the early days of Take That he was criticized for writing songs that weren't tough enough. He would find a word in the dictionary or the newspaper and write a song based around it. The boast that he had written 'Back For Good' in fifteen minutes was a faded memory, as he would repeatedly rub out the words to a new song because they didn't work.

Elton John never bothered with lyrics himself, and for years worked with Bernie Taupin, who wrote the words to the immortal 'Your Song'. Rob, on the other hand, was proving to be an inventive lyricist, which made one wish he had written some songs with Gary during the Take That days. Instead, he had joined up with musician Guy Chambers to compose his best-known songs.

Clive Davis hadn't entirely given up on Gary and started putting him with other songwriters to try to kickstart his new album. When that failed to work, Gary retreated to Delamere Manor to start again. The process was painful and the album that was supposed to be ready in the autumn of 1998 was put back. Things picked up only when a new producer, Jon Douglas, joined the project. Like Chris Porter, he was also best known for his work with George Michael. Gary called him Jonny D and they became good friends.

Gary's record company were getting very concerned at the length of time the new album was taking, especially when it went over budget by a reported £800,000. Simon Cowell was again a presence in Gary's life when he became the A & R man at BMG responsible for liaising between artist and label.

It's never been confirmed if he had a hand in the infamous memo that appeared in the satirical magazine *Private Eye* saying that Gary needed to be rebranded as a more exciting and dangerous character – perhaps promoting his love of Grand Prix motor racing. Gary did his bit for this new image by revealing on a Manchester radio show that he had once driven a Porsche down the motorway at 170 mph. Once again, Gary came over as more cringe than cool.

His prospects were further diminished by continued postponement of concert dates, which was blamed on a number of factors, including a problem with tickets, recording commitments involving his next album and even a reported rift with his record company. The actual problem was that Gary didn't have any new songs ready to include in the show.

The November 1998 concerts were postponed to April 1999 and then again to the following November when he finally had the album to promote. Sceptics noted that he cancelled the 10,000-seater SECC in Glasgow and replaced it with the adjoining 3,000-capacity Clyde Auditorium.

Not everything was looking bleak. He was with Dawn at their London flat one evening waiting for a Chinese takeaway to be delivered when he suddenly blurted out, 'Let's get married.' He didn't get down on one knee, recite a specially prepared poem or have a song ready. The moment was natural and spontaneous and Dawn said yes. They had been together for four years.

The newly engaged couple went to New York with his mum and dad and popped into the famous Tiffany store on Fifth Avenue and came out with a diamond engagement ring worth about £10,000. The plan was to get married at Delamere with only one proviso: they wouldn't be selling the wedding to a glossy magazine. He asked Howard to be best man.

Finally a new single was ready. Gary gave interviews confirming that he had taken a year off to write his new album but that wasn't strictly true – it was nearer two years. The track was called 'Stronger', which clearly made everyone think it was a reaction to Rob's last single, which had been called 'Strong'. The coincidence was very heavy-handed.

Gary had written the song with Graham Gouldman, one of the greats of British songwriting, responsible for some of the biggest hits of the sixties for The Hollies and Herman's Hermits. As a member of 10cc he had co-written 'I'm Not In Love', one of the most admired pop songs. They should have made a perfect songwriting match but 'Stronger' curiously didn't sound like the work of either man. It was strangely lacklustre – pleasant enough but more of a filler track on an album than a blockbuster single. A song with that title was crying out for a chorus to shout from the rooftops but it didn't have one. The video didn't help, featuring a bizarrely down-beat story of Gary pushing his car through the rain in Vancouver and causing traffic gridlock.

The online review at UKMix.org was blunt: 'Oh dear, I think Gary's feeling down about Robbie's success. And with poor releases like this one, he's going to have to carry on feeling down. The song is utterly forgettable and increasingly Gary is coming across as being some sort of twisted self-caricature.' The *Sunday Mirror* called it a 'woeful dance mix'.

The public didn't buy it and, despite Gary putting in the hours on the publicity treadmill, it reached a dismal number sixteen on the charts. He memorably described the feeling in *My Take*: 'It redefined disappointment.'

Another single was rushed out at the beginning of October in the hope that it could trigger interest in the album when it was released at the end of that month. The credentials of 'For All That You Want' were impeccable. Gary's co-writers were the Swedish pop maestros Max Martin and Kristian Lundin. Together they had written some of the best-known songs of Backstreet Boys and 'N Sync, while the previous year Max had been responsible for '. . . Baby One More Time', which launched the career of Britney Spears and is one of the best-known and best-selling pop songs of all time. They were as hot as Gary was cold.

The song was catchier than 'Stronger', with a strong jangly guitar intro, but Gary sounded suspiciously like a one-man boy band. Backstreet Boys could have recorded this song. *AllMusic* online called it 'joyless'. Further investigation revealed that Gary had already released the song two years earlier under the title 'Superhero' as his second attempt to crack the US market after 'So Help Me Girl'. It failed to chart.

It didn't do any better in the UK, peaking in the charts at number twenty-four, the worst performance of a Gary Barlow song since 'Once You've Tasted Love'. It stayed in the top fifty for only two weeks. Incredibly, that was one week longer than the album *Twelve Months, Eleven Days*, which reached number thirty-five and promptly disappeared. It had been a labour of love that was far too long in the labour. Gary came up with the title after he added up exactly how much time he had spent in the studio working on it.

The album may have been called *Twelve Months, Eleven Days* but it was actually twenty-eight months and sixteen days since *Open Road*. So where had everybody gone? Even his fans, it seemed, had forgotten to go out and buy the record. Only 28,000 copies were sold.

The critics were uncomplimentary. The *Birmingham Post* called it frustratingly bland and ultimately soporific – 'a lame collection of mid-tempo seventies soul pastiches and George Michael-style ballads'. Adrian Thrills in the *Daily Mail* observed, 'the finished product is so polished any interesting rough edges have been completely obliterated . . . background tunes that simply rush over the listener.'

Rob was very funny about it. He said that he had bought Gary's new album but had taken it back to the record store the next day and demanded his money back because it was 'crap'.

With the benefit of hindsight, *Twelve Months, Eleven Days* is nothing like as bad as the poor sales might indicate. The UK music scene of the time was in thrall to Britpop, a fascination that the public would grow tired of in a year or two. Rob embraced the trend and appeared current while Gary's music seemed old-fashioned by comparison. It was a mistake to try and change that perception by bringing out songs that didn't really sound like him and didn't please his fans. Tracks like 'Don't Need A Reason' and 'Lie To Me' are much more recognizable as Gary songs than the two that were released as singles and would probably have been much more successful.

BMG felt the need to issue a statement: 'Gary is a very important artist on the BMG roster and we look forward to a long and fruitful association with him.' That sounded suspiciously like the vote of confidence given to a football manager just before he is sacked. Disappointingly, 'Lie To Me', which Gary considered by far the best song on the album, was all set to be the third single from the album when BMG cancelled. The move looked like the record company had decided to cut its losses.

Gary still had a tour to do, honouring all the postponed dates. He had quietly given to charity all the interest that had accrued from tickets purchased more than a year ago. He called it the *For the Fans Tour*. He began at the Newcastle City Hall, as Take That had seven years before, and played nine dates before ending at the Cardiff International Arena just before Christmas.

In a thoughtful piece, John Williamson of the *Glasgow Herald* noted that Gary seemed less contrived than Robbie Williams but that the atmosphere was missing. He was technically perfect but lacked character: 'While he comes across as endearingly sincere, it still smacks of a man who is old beyond his years, struggling to come to terms with his past.'

The set consisted of half new material and half Take That pleasers like 'Pray' and 'Back For Good' and there were no prizes for guessing which the crowd preferred. The *Birmingham Evening Mail* noticed how much the temperature at the NEC rose when the fans, who were 98 per cent women, recognized one of their favourites.

Gary was unusually expansive in the sleeve credits. On *Open Road* he named nobody and wrote a tepid five-line thank you to everyone who had helped. Perhaps there were too many people he *didn't* want to thank. For the new album there were no gushing thank yous to anyone in the US or any BMG boss. If this was to be his last solo album, then at least he had thanked all the people who truly mattered to him. He thanked Jonny D and Kristina for 'keeping me safe from all the negative elements'. He paid tribute to his mum and dad and particularly noted that Marj could 'sure hear a hit!' He thanked the fans and wondered if he still sang as they remembered. And he ended: 'Dawn, I love you.'

In the interviews Gary gave to promote the album and the tour, he talked glowingly about Dawn and his admiration for her – not least her ability to eat twelve roast potatoes with her Sunday lunch and not put on an ounce. She had given up dancing professionally but was still doing promotional work for companies like Adidas and Wella. He told the *Mail on Sunday*, 'Dawn is my ideal woman.' He added that they needed to get into gear where children were concerned because time was ticking on and he wanted a string quartet of children – 'two violins, a viola and a cello'.

Dawn told him she was pregnant just before he began his final solo tour and he would become a father for the first time in the summer of 2000. They still wanted to be married before starting a family, although that doesn't matter these days, even in Frodsham. The original plan for a lavish ceremony at Delamere Manor had been scrapped when they realized it would be an organizational nightmare. The security alone would have been worthy of the Olympic Games.

They had already booked a family holiday in the Caribbean for the new year, so that seemed like a good alternative. Gary told *OK!* 'We thought, let's just run away and do it. Let's take our mums and dads and brother and do it low key and make it our day and nobody else's.' Gary's brother Ian had married his wife Lisa there and that had been a happy event.

Gary and Dawn married on 12 January 2000 on the island of Nevis. Gary wore a cream Savile Row suit while Dawn wore a white summer dress designed by her brother Stephen. They were going to marry on the beach but were worried about unwanted photographers, so in the end opted for a ceremony in a private room at their hotel. Dawn, who carried a posy of pink bougainvillea, recalled, 'It was simple and perfect. And to finish the day off we all went on a sunset cruise.'

It had been top secret, as was the party Gary had organized for Dawn on their return. Their friends were hiding in the house when he brought his new wife back to Delamere Manor. Surprise parties after a long flight home are not usually top of anyone's agenda but Dawn seemed to enjoy it.

Gary's first job when he returned was to film an episode of *Heartbeat*. The producers must have found out he had always been keen to try some acting, although he wasn't sure he would be any good at it. He joked, 'Acting has never been where my talents lie. When I was in the nativity play at school, the teacher cast me as a sheep. What finally tempted me was that I could sing on it.'

He had always had a soft spot for the nostalgic police series set in Yorkshire from the days when he used to pop round Nan Bo's house on a Sunday evening. She would always watch it, although she used to call it *Heartbreak*.

Gary's appearance as a guest star was to boost interest in the show's 150th episode. He was cast as a hitchhiker called Micky Shannon who is picked up by the series' star, Greengrass, played by Bill Maynard. Gary enjoyed Bill's company because he was the sort of northern comedian Gary had met every week at the Halton

Legion. He observed, 'He's my favourite character in the show and he's got me in stitches the whole time.' Bill decided they were going to form a new group called Take This.

His character ended up being arrested and sent down for two years for being a conman and a thief. Gary really enjoyed the change – not least his new hairstyle, a classic slicked-back early sixties mop. He also revelled in the camaraderie on set – something he hadn't had since the early days of touring with Take That. He said, 'They kept playing practical jokes on me like filling a bag I had to sling over my shoulder with rocks. When I had to be handcuffed they pretended they'd lost the key, so I was there for an hour and a half in handcuffs.'

He sang 'All That I've Given Away' in the Aidensfield Arms while the barmaid Gina Ward looked on adoringly. Gary had mixed a new version to make the song seem to fit the early sixties period and it sounded better than it did on *Twelve Months, Eleven Days*. The majority of Gary's songs would sound better if he was just singing and playing the piano. Overall, he wasn't the worst actor ever seen on television but his friends thought he was playing himself.

The day after filming, Gary was in London for a meeting with his record company when Kristina called him as he was driving down the Edgware Road. BMG had dropped him. From hero to zero had taken four years. Gary turned his car round and drove straight home to Cheshire to disappear into a black hole of depression.

17

Returning to the Light

Gary didn't leave the house for four months. He didn't shave for days on end, slobbed around in a tracksuit watching *Star Trek* movies and smoked fifteen spliffs a day to soften the reality of his profound disappointment. At the end of a long day doing nothing, he would smoke half his final spliff so that, in the morning, he could smoke the other half before he got out of bed. He lived on a diet of takeaways and Rioja, ordering McDonald's to be delivered because he didn't want to be seen queuing for his Big Mac and fries. He would order pizza, curries and his favourite Chinese by the bucketload and then become upset when he gave his name and would hear laughter on the other end of the phone.

His weight was getting out of hand as his comfort eating worsened. Eventually he touched the scales close to seventeen stone. He is only 5ft 8in – nearer in stature to Mark Owen than the strapping six-footers Rob, Howard and Jason. He told the *Daily Express*, 'It would take me three rolls to get off the bed and I was reduced to wearing XXL tracksuits.' He hated looking at himself in the mirror.

It was a classic depression, one that had been building for three years until the loss of his recording contract pushed him over the edge. Gary didn't realize he was depressed – you rarely do. He would spend hours studying his old songs to try to unlock the secret of the art he had, in his mind, completely lost. One of his old Frodsham friends observes, 'He hit a terrible depression and I felt really sad for him. I remember thinking, he is so talented, why has this happened?

'I thought, Robbie is doing really well because he is honest, because he tells the truth and he tells it like it is. Gary, on the other hand, had tried to put on this front that Nigel had kind of convinced him was the way to go. He had put on this superslick front of being something he wasn't. People aren't stupid and they didn't buy into it. He needed to show some vulnerability.'

Gary was definitely vulnerable at this time in his life even if his fans didn't know it. Dawn did her best to support her husband but she had the worry of impending motherhood. She would never have to fret about money but she was concerned about Gary's unhealthy lifestyle and the effect piling on the pounds would have on his long-term health. She wanted a fit and healthy father for her baby.

Nobody escaped Take That undamaged. The whole world knew about Rob's problems. The media loved them. They revelled in the highs and incredible lows of the most charismatic pop star in the country as he battled drink, drugs and demons. The *NME* described him as a 'bovine sex god, rehab fuck-up, cabaret clown and UNICEF ambassador'.

None of the papers obsessed by his feud with Gary took any notice of what had happened to Howard, a gentle and funny man who was so affected by the band's split that he contemplated suicide. Howard didn't tell anyone how he felt until 2005 in the television documentary called *Take That: For the Record*: 'I just wasn't ready for it finishing. Out of everybody I wasn't ready for it and I didn't want it to finish. I was really disappointed. I must have been emotional and tired about what was happening. I already knew that the group was gonna finish and, um, I decided to walk out the hotel and go to the Thames. The state of my mind at that time, I've never told anybody this, I was seriously thinking of jumping in the Thames, thinking I wanted to kill myself, but I'm just too much of a shitbag to do it.' He admits it took him a year to start functioning properly again.

Like Rob, Howard was an undiscovered talent in the band, dismissed as a dancer with dreadlocks. He too had ambitions for a solo career under the guidance of Nigel Martin-Smith, who remained his manager after the break-up. He had written only one song for Take That, 'If This Is Love' on the *Everything Changes* album, but he had set up a studio at his home in Manchester and had begun writing material. His first success was with a song called 'Crazy Chance' for Kavana, a teenage singer whom Nigel managed. It sneaked into the top twenty in 1997. Kavana turned up again on *The Voice* in 2013 but failed to persuade any of the judges to turn round.

Howard had his own songs, too. A single called 'Speak Without Words' was ready and even had a video, but before it was released he split from BMG after he sued them for unpaid royalties. Instead he took up golf and travelled with Gary on tour, sometimes joining him on stage to sing 'Never Forget'. He performed six of his songs at a showcase organized by Nigel in Manchester and two of them at the city's Albert Square during a ceremony for the Commonwealth Games. He also wrote the theme tune for a television show called *Planet Pop*. Gary and Howard remained close friends and even wrote a song together, aptly called 'Insecurity', which has yet to be released.

It seemed only a matter of time before Howard's debut album surfaced but he couldn't get a new deal. His official fan club closed in February 1999 and his ambitions for a solo career were thwarted. Instead, he wrote 'Good Times', the title track of the debut album by *Coronation Street* actor Adam Rickitt, another of Nigel's clients.

After Gary lost his record deal at the beginning of 2000, only Rob of the original Take That had one in place. Mark had been dropped by BMG in 1997 at a time when his drinking had spiralled out of control. He had retreated from public view to live in the Lake District and work on new material and, so everyone thought, embrace a tranquil Buddhist lifestyle. In reality, he was downing bottle after bottle of white wine every night. Some years later he would follow Rob's example by checking into rehab to come to terms with his drink problem. He also admitted having at least ten affairs, including one that lasted five years while he was with the mother of his children.

While Gary, Howard and Mark were getting used to solo careers going nowhere, Jason hadn't even tried. His biggest insecurity was always doubt about the importance of his contribution to the band, as well as guilt that he had been the spokesperson when they ousted Rob. It kept him awake at night and he would complain of not sleeping properly. He tried a little acting, appearing in the Lynda La Plante drama *Killer Net* on Channel 4 and having a two-night run in London in a fringe comedy called *Gob* in which he played a drug-crazed poet. He auditioned for a part in *Coronation Street* but, despite his celebrity, wasn't chosen. He decided acting wasn't for him.

Jason is probably the most private member of Take That, a thoughtful man who quietly enrolled on a course in psychology and A-level English instead of seeking further fame. He seemed to lack ambition, whereas the others had too much. While Gary moped around the house, Jason spent most of his time backpacking like a millionaire student. He told *Q* magazine that the only time he regretted opting out was on a beach in Thailand when everyone crowded round to watch the video for Rob's song 'Millennium' in which he played a spoof James Bond.

Jason explained, 'It was one passing moment – there's a whole world going on that I'm not aware of and he's the king of it, that little lad I used to think was a bit of a dickhead.' The rest of the time Jason would put his acting skills to good use by pretending to be someone else if he was ever recognized as one of the blokes out of Take That.

Howard was the first member of the band to become a father when his girlfriend Victoria gave birth to a daughter, Grace, in

March 1999. The following year it was Gary's turn and the birth of his son, Daniel, in August 2000, was hugely influential in dragging him out of his unhappy lethargy.

When he emerged nervously into the light again, Gary had given up being a performer. Instead, encouraged by friends like Howard, he started to think he could have a career as a songwriter. Those at the top of the tree, like Diane Warren and Cathy Dennis, earned millions.

The problem was that Gary Barlow's name was toxic. It was like the bad old days when he would hawk his demo tapes around record companies and get nowhere. Despite being a four-time Ivor Novello Award winner, he was having songs he thought were good rejected by faceless record company people. He still had a publishing deal – with Sony – so he did have the enticement to write songs.

His son kept him going and finally enabled him to realize that there was more to life than acclamation and applause: 'You start to think, "Well, I've tried today, and I've had three songs refused, but let's make you some egg and soldiers". And that saved me. It really did.'

He had started tentatively writing a song or two for the lightweight pop act Steps. One of the group, H, stayed at the house while Gary worked on some music for them, so it was disappointing when none of his songs ended up on their album. Even a group as low down the food chain as Steps didn't want to be linked with Gary. Then there was Victoria Beckham, who was embarking on her own derided solo career and apparently didn't want anyone to know she was working with him. She too had been a guest at his house, and after a day's work in the studio would wait to be collected by her husband David when he finished training at Manchester United.

Madame Tussaud's melted down Gary's waxwork and the annual publication *People of Today* decided he was no longer worthy of inclusion. His fan club closing down seemed like the final straw. The new executive responsible for his material at Sony Publishing,

Celia McCamley, tried sending out his songs uncredited in the hope they would be picked up. Finally she gave him the only bit of advice she thought might help and told him to leave the country for a while.

So, at the beginning of 2001, Gary and Dawn decided to close up Delamere Manor and take baby Daniel with them to Los Angeles. Making the decision to go seemed to improve things. Eliot Kennedy, one of the few in the recording industry who had kept in touch with Gary, phoned and asked him if he would like to work on some material for a new boy band called Blue.

Eliot, 6ft 6in and larger than life, had been brought up in Australia but had stayed in Sheffield all his working life and Gary enjoyed his straight-talking northern company. He and Gary were similar in that they had both been accomplished musicians as boys, although Eliot had never wanted to be a performer. His reputation had been enhanced since the days of 'Everything Changes' by his connection with the Spice Girls, for whom he co-wrote 'Say You'll Be There', their second number one. He worked well with Gary because they both crafted the whole song and not just the odd melody line here or a few words of the chorus there.

Eliot drove over to Delamere Manor with a young writer he was developing called Tim Woodcock, with whom Gary forged an instant creative rapport. They would write a number of successful songs together in the coming years. Their first was a ballad called 'Girl I'll Never Understand'. It found its way onto Blue's debut album *All Rise*, which sold more than a million copies in the UK alone.

At last, Gary could see a future in music. As a performer, he had become a liability to his now ex-record company, but as a songwriter he was still a huge asset and Celia must take some credit for recognizing that this was not the time to give up. In some ways, Gary was a poacher turned gamekeeper. He resented, while in Take That, attempts to bring in other songwriters and producers. Now he was one of those people being paid to enhance the careers of others.

He left for LA with his mood greatly improved. It became even better when the family settled into a lovely ocean-fronted apartment in Santa Monica that he had decided to rent for three months. In the end they liked California so much they stayed for nine. One of the first people to get in touch was Elton John, who was in town recording his critically acclaimed album *Songs From The West Coast*. Elton hadn't written an album this good for years and Gary went over to the studio, which was only a mile away, to spend the day with his friend. Elton suggested he should sing some backing vocals. At first Gary wasn't keen because he truly had given up singing but, in the end, he was persuaded by the quality of the material. He went back to the studio the following week and sang on 'This Train Don't Stop There Anymore', one of the finest of all Elton's songs.

Gary thrived in Los Angeles. From being a virtual prisoner in his own home, he was able to go to the supermarket or to restaurants without people nudging each other because they recognized him. His failure to make it in the US had one advantage after all. Nobody knew who the scruffy overweight figure walking along the beach with his elegant blonde wife and young son was. He told the *Daily Mail*, 'I could take my shirt off and let my belly hang out without seeing a photo of it in *heat* magazine.'

Eliot came out to visit and immediately invigorated Gary with his positive approach. They went to a writing camp together in Bearsville, a small village in upstate New York next to Woodstock, where the most famous of all pop festivals had been held. They met David Massey, the son of Lulu's manager Marion Massey and the head of A & R for Sony in the US. He promised to put work their way. With his blessing, they set up a writer-producer company called True North Music.

It was an encouraging development for Gary. He had enjoyed his American break but was keen to return to Delamere Manor and get the new arrangement up and running. Eliot suggested his long-standing manager, Martin Barter, could represent them in their new venture. Gary had parted company with Kristina simply because there wasn't enough of a career for her to manage, although her organizational skills would continue to be a great help to him in the future.

The new company's first job was a commission from Sony to fly to Barcelona and produce a track called 'Chicas Malas' for Mónica Naranjo, a hugely popular Spanish singer they were trying to launch worldwide. It was quite challenging making a record in a language he didn't speak or understand. It was made even more memorable when they turned on the TV at the end of the day to see what was happening in the world. It was 9/11.

Gary returned to Cheshire from LA in much better shape mentally. The same could not be said for his physical condition. An increasingly worried Dawn, fed up with his wheezing up and down the stairs, packed him off to the doctor, who put him on the scales and promptly informed him that he was clinically obese. Something had to be done. Gary didn't immediately go out and buy a series of diet books or celebrity keep-fit videos. With Dawn's encouragement, he was able to turn a corner by reducing his portion size.

Gary put it simply, 'Dawn knows how weight has always been my enemy, how with every mouthful of food I have always felt guilty. I realized that once I started to eat I couldn't stop.' It was a gradual process, losing the pounds not through starvation but small steps like not finishing his curry by munching on a chocolate bar. He felt better about his songwriting again and this allowed him to feel better about himself. His motivation was also improved when Dawn told him she was expecting their second child.

As part of his new regime, he started playing badminton again with Martin Smiddy and Graham Hitchen. Martin recalls, 'Neither of us were as good as Gary. I was pretty fit and Graham used to run for the county but Gary was quicker round the court than either of us despite being a stone or two heavier than he should have been. He was still good with a racket.'

Irritatingly, Gary was already exercising and eating more healthily when the *Sunday Mirror* published an unflattering picture of him leaving the Forest View pub close to his home. 'Gary Barlow is truly . . . fat for good,' it said. He would have found it funny had it been about someone else.

His partnership with Eliot, meanwhile, was going from strength to strength. The whole of Blue came up to Delamere Manor to work on material for their second album and left with the song 'Supersexual'. For their follow-up, just Duncan James was there. Tim Woodcock came in with a chorus and within half an hour the three of them had written 'Guilty', one of the boy band's biggest hits when it reached number two. The album of the same name was their third chart-topper in November 2003. For a couple of years Blue were almost as successful as Take That.

Gary wasn't exactly writing songs for Coldplay or the Manic Street Preachers. This was the world of chart-driven pop and he and Eliot were very skilful at it. The musical direction of the entire decade was set in 2001 when *Popstars*, the first of the talent shows that spawned *The X Factor* and *The Voice*, was won by Hear'Say. Gary and Eliot wrote and produced a ballad called 'Everyday' for them.

They produced a record for Donny Osmond entitled *Somewhere In Time*. Gary thought the original teen heart-throb was a complete professional and this collection of classic love songs 'a dream album'. Donny was one of a parade of famous faces who would find their way to the middle of the Cheshire countryside to enjoy Gary's hospitality. He said, 'It was almost as if we had been mates for years.'

Delta Goodrem was just sixteen and being hailed as the next big thing when she arrived at Delamere Manor from Australia in early 2003 to start work on her debut album. True North co-wrote and produced six tracks on *Innocent Eyes*, which would end up selling more than four million copies worldwide and would become the biggest Australian album of the decade. The single they wrote with her, called 'Not Me, Not I', was number one in her home country.

Returning to the Light

By the time Gary's daughter Emily was born on the last day of May 2002, Gary had re-established himself as a songwriter and producer who could be relied upon to do a good job with whichever artist came through the gates of Delamere Manor. True North wrote some of their best songs for Atomic Kitten, a collaboration that Gary had been dreading but which worked really well. He loved having the three lively Liverpool girls around because they brightened up his enormous house.

One of them, Natasha Hamilton, had been a big fan of Take That – as had her mum: 'When we were driving up to his house, I just couldn't believe it. This man was in this band I idolized and I was suddenly outside his house waiting to go to work with him. I just had a mad fit of giggles.'

Gary discovered that his absence made the media heart grow fonder. The *Daily Mail* described him as a heavyweight and for once a newspaper was not referring to his waistline. The *Liverpool Echo* called him a legend, reinforcing the thought that the tide was turning.

He probably could have continued in his new career as a man behind the scenes if it weren't for a series of external events completely out of his control that changed the future for Take That. To begin with, Mark Owen entered the *Celebrity Big Brother* house in November 2002. The first series had been a ratings success the year before when comedian Jack Dee won. The second outing, which was also for charity, featured another collection of celebrities who had seen better days, including Les Dennis, Anne Diamond and Melinda Messenger. Mark completely walked it. He had longer hair but the cheeky grin was still there. He looked like a superstar as he sat on the sofa, strummed his guitar and sang 'Street Spirit (Fade Out)', one of the most famous songs by Radiohead.

In the final against Les he secured an astonishing 77 per cent of the vote. The millions who watched were reminded over the ten-day run what a nice man Mark was. He was very humble and grateful – the same qualities that would serve Take That well when the prospect of a reunion became a reality.

195

Mark broke down in tears when Les was evicted and he was left alone in the house, waiting for the host Davina McCall to come and get him. Les commented, 'He's got a fantastic aura, a really brilliant aura – look at him.' No tool is more powerful than television to remind the nation what a star you are. Mark seemed to be genuinely astonished at the level of public support. He came out to be greeted by a screaming crowd holding banners proclaiming 'Mark: We Never Forgot'.

The second unexpected event came a year later when Take That won a *Smash Hits* poll to discover the best boy band of all time. They beat Westlife, Boyzone and Blue and all the other pale imitations that had sprung up since they had split seven years before. For the first time there was talk of a Take That reunion, and Gary joined Mark, Jason and Howard for a meeting at Nigel's Manchester house. It was too soon for Gary, who told the others in no uncertain terms that he didn't want to be a performer again.

One of the things that helped to change his mind was being in closer touch with the boys. He regularly saw Howard, who had reinvented himself as DJ HD and was much in demand in clubs in Germany and Ibiza. Howard's daughter Grace would come over to play with Gary's children at Delamere, which was something of a child's paradise, although they were under strict orders not to damage any of the priceless antiques. Gary loved having the children around.

He also got to know Mark much better when he came to Delamere Manor to work on his new album. Mark had already written a song with Eliot called 'Four Minute Warning' a couple of years before, but now specifically asked Gary to remix it. The result reached number four in the charts but the subsequent album, which Gary also worked on, didn't make the top fifty. Mark was again dropped by his record company, which was a huge disappointment to a man with genuine musical ambitions.

Gary had had little contact with Jason since the band split up. He had stopped using Jason's brother Simon for financial advice and that had led to some bad feeling. They unexpectedly caught up again when Gary was in London moving into a new flat he had bought in Kensington and discovered that his former bandmate was living nearby. They had lunch and to Gary's surprise Jason had to get something off his chest. He told him bluntly that it had been a nightmare working for him and Nigel.

Gary knew that it had been difficult for Jason as far as Nigel was concerned but was astonished to realize the depth of Jason's feelings against him. The idea that Jason thought he had been working for Gary, even if he didn't quite mean it like that, was shocking. His outburst did clear the air though, and was one of the reasons Gary mentioned the possibility of a reunion when he attended a party at the Royal Albert Hall thrown by Simon Fuller in April 2004.

The main reason he was talking about a reunion was a phone call he had received from Nigel telling him that BMG might be interested in a new greatest hits package. They had noticed a revival in interest in Take That and thought they could sell towards 100,000 copies – not a huge amount but a start. There was also the possibility of a documentary that would be gold dust in drumming up publicity. Nothing happened immediately but they thought about recording a new song so it wouldn't be exactly the same as the 1996 collection. They chose 'Today I've Lost You', a track that Gary had written ten years previously as the follow-up to 'Back For Good' before 'How Deep Is Your Love' was chosen as the final single.

The day Gary was nearly lost to the world was 7 July 2005, forever known in the minds of the British people as 7/7. He was on a crowded train on the Circle Line between High Street Kensington and Euston Square. It was a journey he took regularly so he could catch a connection home to Cheshire from the mainline station. As they neared Edgware Road, there was an almighty bang and the screaming sound of the engine's brakes as it shuddered to a halt. The carriages filled with smoke as people cried out panic-stricken in the darkness. It was a bomb, not on their train but on one that had been running alongside in the opposite direction.

When the emergency lights came on and the smoke cleared, Gary could see the other train had been ripped apart and was on its side next to them. Through smashed windows he could make out a woman lying stricken on the floor. Three-quarters of an hour would pass before emergency services opened the doors and led everyone to the front of the train and into the station. Gary counted seven bodies covered with white blankets. Other injured passengers were wandering around shocked and dazed.

Gary's face was black but he wasn't hurt and immediately realized how lucky he had been. For once this was a near-death experience for a celebrity that was real and not exaggerated by the media. Afterwards he was quoted on contactmusic.com, 'I made it home on adrenaline, I guess, and for the next three hours I was glued to the news. I don't know why there or why then, but I began to cry in the shower. Thank God I'm still here. I can't stop kissing my children. I have never been so happy to be alive.'

18

What a Beautiful World

Much to everyone's surprise, Mark persuaded Rob to take part in *Take That: For The Record*. The documentary, produced by one of Simon Cowell's companies, began filming in October 2005. *Never Forget: The Ultimate Collection* was released on 14 November, three days before the documentary was due to be aired. It proved to be perfect timing. The album of old hits sold 90,000 copies in the first week, already meeting the record company's prediction. The scale of the success was completely unexpected. The album just missed out on number one but spent three years and ten months in the charts – 199 weeks – and would go on to sell 2.2 million copies in the UK alone, easily more than Rob's album *Intensive Care*, which came out at the same time. It was an amazing result for a band that had split a decade earlier.

Each of them – and Nigel – was interviewed individually, musing about the story of Take That and where it went wrong. Gary was filmed at the piano at Delamere Manor. He invited the crew to look around his 'crib', which was stuffed full of antiques and ornaments. Nothing was out of place and he could have charged members of the public for a guided tour.

He showed off the living room, which he confessed was nothing of the kind because he had sat in it only once. The overall impression was of a slightly soulless house that would have been suitable for an older member of the Royal Family. Dawn was shown with Emily happily chatting in the enormous kitchen, and their presence helped to reduce the feeling of stuffiness.

Gary was modest and reflective and sported a goatee beard that made him seem older and wiser. He said he regretted not playing the keyboards properly for the eight years when he wasn't performing. 'I suck now when I play them,' he said. He recalled that when the band started he didn't smoke or drink and was really boring. He left the band a chain-smoker and used to get really drunk. More interestingly, he was self-aware about his state of mind when the band split: 'It was the worst part of my personality. Coming out of the band was the biggest my ego had ever been.'

Howard's revelation that he had thought about suicide gathered most headlines but Jason was charming and came across well. He was still very handsome, if a little thin. He revealed that he had been in 'awe of Gaz' from the first time he met him: 'He was a bit strange but I looked up to him and he sang beautifully. He was obviously the centrepiece, the nucleus of the band.' Jason believed that Gary was a casualty of Rob's success when the group's youngest member turned out to be the next big thing: 'The press battered him because that's what they do.'

Nigel Martin-Smith wondered who was actually the happiest – Robbie or Gary. On the one hand, Rob had a cabinet full of Brit Awards and an £80 million recording contract. On the other, Gary was pictured happily at home with his lovely wife and very cute children. Rob finished his interview, sadly, with the confession, 'I would swap everything I have for that.'

The documentary came to a climax with the boys waiting in a drawing room at Cliveden, the famous Buckinghamshire stately home, to see if Rob would turn up. Howard thought he wouldn't. Jason thought he would. Howard was right. They watched Rob apologize to them on a TV link and admit that Gary was an amazing songwriter.

The programme changed everything for Gary, Howard, Jason and Mark. They weren't boisterous boys any more; they were men with feelings everyone could relate to. When Howard declared, 'I love being a daddy', it was joyous not cheesy. Mark admitted how much he missed Rob. Gary was gracious about 'Angels'. Jason was coy when asked if he had slept with Lulu. You could imagine enjoying a quiet pint with any of them.

They were immensely likeable and it seemed churlish that Rob left them sitting around like lemons waiting to see if he would arrive. It made for great television. Commentators reflected afterwards that this was the point at which the media changed their allegiance. Rob would in the future have to suffer the press ridicule, while Take That were again the most loved. Every underdog has its day.

The four minus Rob went nervously to the documentary's premiere or, more precisely, its special screening at the Coronet Cinema in Notting Hill. They were all worried that they would again look like a bunch of losers, especially as the initial reaction to the venue was that they couldn't even find a suitable place to hold it in the West End. The audience reaction, a mixture of laughter and sentimental surprise, reassured them that it had been the right decision to resurface. Gary was unequivocal, 'It was bloody brilliant.'

Gary did have a great life. He had even more money than when Take That split – estimates put his fortune in excess of £25 million. He had bought a house near Nice in the south of France and the family would decamp there for holidays. Sometimes he would go by himself if he needed some peace. He could move around now in relative anonymity – nobody bothered him when he popped over to Dublin for the wedding of Boyzone's Mikey Graham to Dawn's best friend, dancer Karen Corradi. Gary and Dawn would often stay the weekend with them, safe in the knowledge that they wouldn't be photographed.

Gary still felt he had something more to give though. He was only thirty-five and realized that he was too young to live in the mausoleum that Delamere Manor had become. So the mansion that had represented his accession to superstar status, but had more recently become a symbol of his failure to achieve it, was put on the market and he bought a house in West London. It was time for a fresh start.

As if to emphasize that this chapter of his life was now closed, he put the garden ornaments up for auction, including water fountains, two obelisks and an antique sundial. He wasn't going to have a large enough garden in London for the statues that lined the driveway. Dawn also had a big sort-out of all the clutter in the house she had inherited. Some of the ornate furnishings went under the hammer as well, including Gary's Versace embroidered bedspread that Dawn had never liked. It went for £350, while a green Ikea sofa made £35 and a telescope £130. In all, sixty-five items from Gary's home were sold for £11,439.

It would be a wrench leaving Cheshire and a lifetime of memories. The sale of the Barlow family compound, however, would give him a huge return for his initial £1 million investment though: the main house was on the market for £6.5 million, the cottage in the grounds for £1.2 million and the lodge for £800,000. There was no rush for Gary to sell – the success of *Never Forget* was pouring money into his already bulging bank account.

Marj and Colin would have to find somewhere new to spend their retirement and look after their chickens. Marj used to sell eggs from outside the front of her house at Delamere – one of those old-fashioned honour arrangements where you left the money in a box. They decided they would stay and look after the big house until it was sold and then find a farm close to Frodsham. Gary's brother Ian would need to move too. He had established his building firm in premises next to the house and would keep those but would settle his family back in Frodsham.

Gary's new semi-detached house, costing a little over £4 million, in an exclusive area of Holland Park, was an urban world away from the fresh air and wide-open spaces of Cheshire. He sold his Mercedes and decided that he would travel as much as possible on the Tube and train like everyone else. He liked being able to squash into a taxi and take his kids to see *Chitty Chitty Bang Bang* at the London Palladium.

One of his first tasks after they moved was to look for a place where he could set up his studio, and he found a suitable building within walking distance on a fine day. For the first time he had decided to keep his work entirely separate from his family life. He was enthusiastic about the interest in Take That and wanted to produce new material but he didn't ignore his writing career, especially when it was going so well. He had added Russell Watson and Charlotte Church to the roster of artists he and Eliot worked with.

Nearly seven million viewers had watched the documentary on a boy band that hadn't worked together for nearly ten years. The question was what to do next. The first thing that needed to be done was to fire Nigel – again. Mark's manager, Jonathan Wild, had been formally approached by a promoter called Simon Moran, asking if they might consider a short reunion tour. He had been at the Coronet and had instantly recognized the potential from the fifty or so fans milling around outside on a chilly autumnal evening.

The stumbling block to performing together again was the uneasy relationship between Jason and Nigel, who had acted as executive producer for the documentary. He had positioned himself in the driving seat for Take That's comeback despite both Mark and Gary having good managers. The simmering problem between the two men came to breaking point when Jason, who couldn't even look at Nigel at the premiere, issued a 'him or me' ultimatum. It was a key moment in the history of Take That because it was clear that Jason wouldn't tour if Nigel was involved. The others chose to back him and their original mentor was out.

Nigel had been hugely significant in their careers. Many

thousands of words have been written about him over the years and he has taken the blame publicly for everything that went wrong with the band and the boys in it – particularly with Rob, who once called him the spawn of Satan – but Gary had a genuine regard for his manager and put it rather more respectfully in his memoir than Rob did in his. He credited him with doing lots of good things as well as bad. He also acknowledged how hard Nigel had fought for the band and how he had given them his 'undying attention and love'.

Nigel was understandably upset that the band had slipped through his fingers again but he was a very rich man thanks to his involvement with them and remains a major figure in Manchester, where his fashion and talent agency flourishes and he still owns two gay clubs, Queer and Boyz. He is also the manager of boy band The Mend.

The boys were now all in their mid-thirties and had simply outgrown a manager who had been able to exert control over their lives when they were teenagers. Nigel had managed to keep their egos in check long enough for them to become stars and earn – and keep – enough money never to have to work again. He had also successfully sued Rob for unpaid commission and been in a legal tangle with Gary after he was sacked in 1997. In the back of everyone's mind was the prospect that Rob would never have anything to do with the band while Nigel was running things.

In the short term, Take That were managerless while they sorted out their tour with Simon Moran. It soon became apparent, however, that Jonathan Wild was the right man for the job and he has guided them collectively and individually ever since. He is from Oldham like Mark and had been one of the few members of the audience at the band's very first gig at Flicks in Huddersfield. The band knew and liked him as a quiet and reserved friend of Mark's and he became a regular fixture at their early shows. He subsequently had been to law school and they always respected his advice.

The dilemma was simple: would this be a chicken in the basket nostalgia tour or something much more significant? The four feared the worst and hoped for the best. They held a press conference at the Berkeley Hotel in Knightsbridge at which Gary cheekily evoked the memories of their split when he declared, 'Thank you for giving us the last ten years off but, unfortunately, the rumours are true – Take That are going back on tour.'

Simon Moran was full of enthusiasm, arranging dates at Wembley Arena and the biggest venues around the country. Initially there were eleven dates, beginning with the Glasgow SECC at the end of April. Tickets went on sale at 9a.m. on 2 December 2005 and sold out within half an hour. They added more dates, including at the Cardiff Millennium Stadium and the newly built Wembley Stadium. More than 275,000 tickets for *Take That – The Ultimate Tour* sold out in three and a half hours. It proved to be the second fastest-selling tour of all time – beaten, typically, by Rob's next set of concerts. Reports said the boys had been offered £1.5 million each to do it but the scale of the demand would ensure they earned considerably more.

The euphoria in response to the sales quickly gave way to the reality that they would have to get into shape and rehearse if they were going to give the fans what they expected from a Take That show. Howard complained that his knees had gone, while Gary said he needed to lose a stone, which was considerably better than the five stone of a few years before. Jason unhelpfully observed that 'it might be a pile of crap'.

Gary had enjoyed the run-up to Christmas. There were champagne parties to celebrate Take That's reunion. Then Elton John and David Furnish held their hen party at Too2Much club in Soho and both Gary and Dawn went. At David's request, Gary sang 'Relight My Fire' with Lulu, who was also there. Finally he took the family off to Disneyland in Florida for a fabulous Christmas. In the new year, Gary was feeling more than a little jaded as he set off for the first rehearsals at a gym in Chiswick. It was hard work. Dawn, a mother of two, was by far the fitter of the couple and was hired again as one of the dancers. They were both in better shape than Jason, who sprained his ankle before the opening show.

This would be a tour of happy families. Howard now had another daughter, Lola, from a new relationship. Mark had become engaged to actress Emma Ferguson and they celebrated the birth of their son Elwood in August 2006. Jason was unmarried but his personal life appeared more positive. He had finally made it up with his father, with whom he had been distant during the first coming of Take That.

They managed to fit in a trip to the US with their acclaimed creative director, Kim Gavin, who had worked with them on the first Take That tours. They visited Las Vegas and found inspiration in the lavish stage shows there. Gary handled the itinerary with military precision, although he refused to confirm that he had fallen asleep watching Celine Dion. He was fascinated by the breathtaking performance of Cirque du Soleil.

Before the tour began, it was announced that the four-piece Take That had signed a recording deal with Polydor. Gary had been to see David Joseph, the label's managing director. The two men knew each other well from the early days of Take That, when David had been in publicity at BMG, and he had attended their farewell press conference in 1996. Record companies had realized that the Take That comeback was well on its way to becoming spectacular and were falling over themselves to secure their signature on a new contract.

The boys were concerned about their ability to produce new material. One thing that was etched in stone, however, was that Gary wouldn't shoulder all the responsibility. He had discovered that he now preferred working with others – there was less pressure. He would still be the main vocalist, because that is what the fans expected, but the other three had so much more to offer now. They had signed their new contract under the condition that they would share songwriting duties, credits and royalties. They could have resumed their relationship with Sony/BMG but Gary was impressed by David's enthusiasm. They decided to make a fresh start – a sign that they were going to be a different band in phase two. The record deal alone was worth a reported £3.5 million but additional publishing and merchandising contracts were rumoured to bump that figure up to £10 million.

Gary had also signed a deal with *Harry Potter* publisher Bloomsbury for his autobiography to come out a couple of weeks before the tour began. He was reported to have received a £1 million advance but this was pure media speculation. The actual figure was nearer £600,000, which was still a considerable sum for a book, especially when it was too early to say how successful the comeback would be. When the memoir came out, much of the interest centred on Gary's brush with death on 7/7 but his whole story was very readable and he was disarmingly honest about his previous shortcomings, referring to himself unflatteringly as 'pig-ignorant'.

More than 9,000 fans crammed into the Metro Radio Arena in Newcastle on 23 April 2006 to watch the band bounce on stage in velvet suits and launch into 'Once You've Tasted Love', perhaps a surprising choice to start a greatest hits show as it was one of their least successful songs. The *Daily Mirror* noted, however, 'They were greeted with screams the likes of which Westlife would die for.' They included a reprise of their famous Beatles' medley from the Brit Awards of 1994. All the favourites were there. They even had a plan to include Rob, which he agreed to after a visit from Mark. For 'Could It Be Magic', Rob made a sort of guest appearance – as a ten-foot hologram that sauntered to the front of the stage to sing the first verse solo. And, of course, 'Never Forget' closed the show.

Even the *Guardian* newspaper had realized this was a concert worthy of attention. Their critic, Alexis Petridis, thought Take That were the exception to the rule that few artists in pop depreciate faster than boy bands: 'Everyone of a certain age has Take That's "Pray", "Babe", "Back For Good", "It Only Takes A Minute" and "Everything Changes" burned into their brain . . . It was hard not to be impressed.'

In the *Daily Mail*, Jane Fryer was unnecessarily rude about Gary, harking back to the bad days with the comment, 'Gary's just too fat and looks more like someone's drunk dad at a wedding disco than a pop star.'

BBC Online was much kinder: 'Gary Barlow has one of the finest voices in pop; there were soaring moments of long-held notes segueing into key changes that got the goosebumps out in force.' Gary probably did more singing and less dancing than the others, but it was always like that.

The funniest review was by Tim De Lisle in the *Mail on Sunday* after the concert at the Birmingham NEC: 'This is what a hen night must be like – if the bride has 12,000 friends . . . It's like sitting on a raft in a torrent of oestrogen.' Tim rashly speculated that Take That probably weren't back for good.

The tour couldn't have gone any better. The absence of Rob turned out to be a benefit because his participation at this point would have overshadowed, or even overpowered, the other four before they had the chance to re-establish themselves. They stayed at the Conrad Hotel in Chelsea Harbour for the three dates at Wembley Arena, just across the road from the block where Rob had a luxury flat overlooking the Thames. When they arrived, they found he had sent over a bunch of flowers to wish them luck. Gary stood on his balcony and gazed across the road but couldn't see him. Apparently Rob did the same.

On the night of the concert he waited in the hotel bar for them to return so they could chat. This wasn't like in a film where everyone slaps each other on the back and acts like they have never been away. Gary and Rob were understandably awkward around one another. There was much to say and much to leave unsaid before the two could rekindle any kind of friendship. Gary's blood was still on the carpet. It was a start, however, and Rob was there again to welcome them back the next night.

Nobody had time to rest. Rob was about to embark on a punishing world tour, while the reinvigorated Take That were due in the studio to record their first album of new material in eleven years. Most of the demos had been done. To begin with, even before they had signed to Polydor, they had met in a studio to see if they could collaborate and everyone was pleasantly surprised to discover Gary enjoyed the shared responsibility.

They all contributed and it's impossible to know who thought up which lyric or which melody, but it was obvious most songs had the stamp of Gary Barlow – the quiet melodious introductions and soaring choruses.

They had a little over three weeks between the last Wembley Arena date on 26 May and the first stadium date. That was just enough time to write one of the greatest of all Take That songs. 'Patience' meant that the reunion tour was not a one-off and Take That would again become the biggest band in the UK.

Gary had wanted to write a song with that name ever since George Michael had used it as the title of his 2004 comeback album, his first to contain original material since 1996. It's fascinating how both Elton John and George Michael weave in and out of Gary's musical story.

Gary, flushed with confidence again, knew the song was a blockbuster right from the start and lobbied for it to be their comeback single. He had decided from the outset that he didn't want to be solely responsible for the album and asked Polydor to find the right man. They came up with John Shanks. After the parade of producers who had worked with Take That in the past, it was a relief to find someone who completely understood the sound they wanted to achieve.

None of the group had met John before but there was instant

rapport when they went to his studio in Los Angeles. His involvement was a statement of intent from Polydor because he had won the Grammy for Producer of the Year in 2005 and could not have been a hotter property. Besides his notable production skills, he was an accomplished songwriter and guitarist and, in recording terms, became the fifth member of Take That.

He had originally been a guitarist in smoky-voiced rock singer Melissa Etheridge's band before striking out on his own in the early nineties and working with Alanis Morissette, Bonnie Raitt, The Corrs and Joe Cocker. He was much better known in the US than the UK, working in particular with female singers like Kelly Clarkson, Ashlee Simpson and Hilary Duff.

Gary trusted John's ability. He was happy to leave everything to him. This was a completely different man from the teenage boy who had visited Abbey Road Studios all those years ago, wanting to be in control and have his hands on everything. On the new album, *Beautiful World*, he shared songwriting and vocals and played the piano – and that was it.

The much anticipated 'Patience' was released on 13 November 2006, two weeks before the album. It didn't debut at number one, reaching only number four, but that was only a minor blip because it did top the charts the following week. Fraser McAlpine in his BBC Online blog described it as a 'great big power ballad . . . with some modern indie touches'. The clever thing about 'Patience' was that while it clearly showcased Gary's anguished falsetto, it wasn't just some rehash of 'Back For Good'. It was fresh and new and made you want to listen to more, which was exactly the intention.

Gary wanted to go to Iceland to make the video because he had never been there. They were filmed, for no apparent reason, looking moody in a bleak volcanic landscape outside Reykjavik. At least it gave the track atmosphere.

'Patience' stayed at number one for four weeks. When the album came out, it went straight to number one, giving Take That a rare double. *Beautiful World* was much more than a Gary Barlow album and was better for it. It also helped that there were no covers. Jason sang solo for the first time on the folksy ballad 'Wooden Boat', which BBC reviewer Julie Broadfoot thought was a stand-out track. Howard took over on 'Mancunian Way' and the uplifting title track. Best of all, Mark had clearly matured in the intervening years into a singer of substance. He has one of the most recognizable voices in pop music and excelled on 'Shine' and 'Hold On'. 'Shine', in particular, was the track in which Mark emerged from under Gary's shadow.

Gary's vocals seemed to have improved with age. 'Like I Never Loved You At All' and 'I'd Wait For Life' were classic Barlow love songs. He was at his best on the opener, 'Reach Out', a track that revealed a more interesting lyrical content – a plea for more tolerance and understanding in the world. Perhaps Gary's lyrical Achilles heel was benefiting from the collaboration with the others.

Quite simply this was an album made by men not boys. Not everyone was impressed. Gavin Martin in the *Daily Mirror* thought 'Shine' was 'truly naff' and added that Gary and co were 'doggedly mediocre talents'. Chris Goodman in the *Sunday Express* found the songs 'formulaic bores'.

Perhaps there was a male–female divide over Take That surfacing among the critics. Julie Broadfoot thought 'Patience' the 'strongest tune' but also loved Gary's ballad 'Like I Never Loved You At All'. Lynsey Hanley in the *Observer* said, 'There isn't a single shoddy or cynical moment on here.' She appreciated Gary's ability to write choruses the size of Wembley. The fans clearly agreed with her views because the album became the second bestseller of the year, behind *Eyes Open* by Snow Patrol, despite being on sale for just a month. It went on to be the fourth biggest-selling album the following year.

Beautiful World is the highest-selling Take That record of all time in the UK, outstripping all of Robbie Williams' solo output. The figure is more than 2.8 million copies (over 4 million worldwide). It was a phenomenal success and Take That could rightly claim the biggest comeback in pop history. Rob's release in 2006, *Rudebox*, was the least well received of his career and sold only 600,000 copies in the UK, although it performed much better abroad.

19

The Summit

The week before Christmas, Leona Lewis strolled onto the stage in a beautiful white dress for the final of *The X Factor* and, accompanied by a piano, performed an exquisite version of 'A Million Love Songs'. After the first verse, she welcomed Take That on stage and Gary took the second verse. Together they sang the big finish and it was blissful. Arguably Gary's greatest song had never sounded better.

Afterwards, Simon Cowell and the judges were on their feet. Gary, who looked dressed for the pub rather than the elegantly suited judge he would become, announced, 'Simon, this is to you, mate. You have a big responsibility. This girl is probably fifty times better than any contestant you have ever had on this show. It's your responsibility to make her the best record you can, so please do that.'

Leona's debut single 'A Moment Like This' knocked 'Patience' off the top of the charts in time for Christmas. Take That got their revenge when they beat her to win the Brit Award for Best British Single in February. They also performed the song and looked like superstars when they did. Gary had been pounding the treadmill at the Holmes Place gym near his home to shift the Christmas pudding and look his best. Even some of the guests at the VIP-laden tables got up to dance and wave their arms in the air. The song had become the anthem of the year.

While all this was going on, there were fears that Rob was losing his battle with depression after an exhausting world tour. On the day Take That were on stage receiving their Brit Award from Alan Carr, he was in The Meadows clinic in the Arizona desert, receiving treatment for addiction to prescription drugs. They didn't mention Rob in their acceptance speech but there was no reason why they should.

When Gary's autobiography was published in paperback in 2007, it gave him the chance to update his success of the previous year. He also now had the confidence to come clean about what he had actually thought of Rob all those years before. The careful restraint of countless interviews cracked to reveal a man monumentally hurt: 'Time may be a great healer, but still, whenever I thought of him, I thought, you absolute fucking c**t. I've never had anyone do so much damage as you've done.'

Their roles were completely reversed. Rob was at one of the weakest points of his life and Gary at his strongest. So Gary did what Rob would have done in the circumstances: he gave the other man a good kicking. This public glimpse of Gary's true feelings probably made him feel a lot better and put him in a position to move on and build bridges. It also made him seem refreshingly human.

When 'Shine' went to number one, Gary turned to Mark and generously told him, 'You must be proud of yourself and you should be.' Mark had suffered for his art as much as his friend. He had spent a fortune on a solo career that never happened; he had even started his own record label. He hadn't suffered public humiliation but privately he needed confirmation of his talent and his contribution. This was it.

Gary acknowledged in *Take That/Take Two* that this was Mark's triumph and a 'massive moment' for him. 'Shine' was the band's tenth number one, making Take That only the seventh act to reach that target in the UK. 'Shine' was co-written by another influential British songwriter, Steve Robson, a contemporary of Gary's, who had also gained his first experience of the music world performing in northern working men's clubs. He would be heavily involved when they sat down to work on the problematic second album of their comeback.

First of all, Take That needed to plan the *Beautiful World* tour. The demand for tickets was again astounding. Every one of the fifty dates in the autumn sold out within forty minutes.

Fittingly, their next big release was a powerful love song called 'Rule The World', which had been specially written for a fantasy movie called *Stardust*, directed by Matthew Vaughn. They composed the song after seeing an early cut of the film and singing some melodies into a mobile phone on the way home. They were booked into Abbey Road Studio One the next day. Like many of the best Take That songs, it took no time at all to finish.

Matthew loved it and decided to use it over the closing credits. It would become one of Take That's best-loved anthems and arguably their most famous song. The song was released to coincide with the tour beginning in Belfast in October and stayed in the charts for its entire two-month duration and beyond. Despite being one of their biggest sellers, it was beaten to number one by Leona Lewis and 'Bleeding Love'. More than fourteen million people have watched the video on YouTube. After some of the rubbish Take That films of the past, this was all the better for being uncomplicated – just the boys singing into microphones at the studio.

Gary had lost another two stone training, knowing the tour would involve the most demanding string of live shows he had ever undertaken. Dawn was again on board and was one of the dancers, dressed in lingerie, who performed a steamy lap dance for the boys during 'It Only Takes A Minute'. Surprisingly, Dawn danced for Howard, but perhaps that was so Gary wouldn't be distracted and forget the words. Her routine had nothing to do with Howard suffering a collapsed lung: that occurred after he had attempted to do the splits on a promotional show in Italy.

The tour was rapturously received. It seemed as if it was now legitimate to like Take That and appreciate the strength of their songs and the power of their live performances. This was a big million-pound show with dazzling special effects, high-tech sets and more costume changes than a Beyoncé extravaganza.

The public and media perception of Gary continued to improve. There were no nasty digs at his weight, his flat Cheshire vowels or the fact that he wasn't in the same league as the other three as a dancer. Instead, Charlotte Heathcote observed in the *Sunday Express*, 'Newly toned Gary Barlow has become the band's hottest property. For a man who admits he's always been hurt by the criticism and abuse he's received over the years, it's heart-warming to hear him getting bigger cheers than his bandmates.' Fiona Shepherd, writing in the *Scotsman* after their performance at the Glasgow SECC, couldn't forget the 'look of sheer enjoyment on Gary's face as Take That's 10,000-strong audience joined in the uplifting chorus of "Never Forget"'. She observed it 'was not something he could have rehearsed'.

Press comments about Robbie Williams reflected how the tables had turned completely, with critics noting that Rob needed the band now more than they needed him. They had to delay their entrance on stage at the Birmingham NEC when one female fan became over-excited at the prospect of seeing her heroes again. Unfortunately, she was seven months' pregnant and went into labour. She missed the concert but gave birth to a healthy baby whom she called Clementine in honour of her favourite Mark Owen song.

The tour was such a success that it was no surprise they received the 2008 Brit for Best British Live Act. 'Shine' also picked up the award for Best British Single. They were disappointed not to win Best British Album, which went to the Arctic Monkeys for *Favourite Worst Nightmare*.

Despite Take That's success, Gary wasn't ignoring his own musical projects. Just after the Brits he received a phone call from the comedian Peter Kay telling him about his new television project, a

Just married . . . Gary and Dawn share a spontaneous kiss after their wedding in Nevis in January 2000.

They are not quite so happy after they realize their private moment was being snapped.

It looks like a wedding but is, in fact, Elton John's sixth White Tie and Tiara Ball at his home in Windsor, June 2004. The host is pictured with David Furnish, Dawn and Gary.

Jason, Gary, Mark and Howard look uncertain announcing the Take That comeback in November 2005. They had been away so long they needed to have their names on the table to remind everyone who they were.

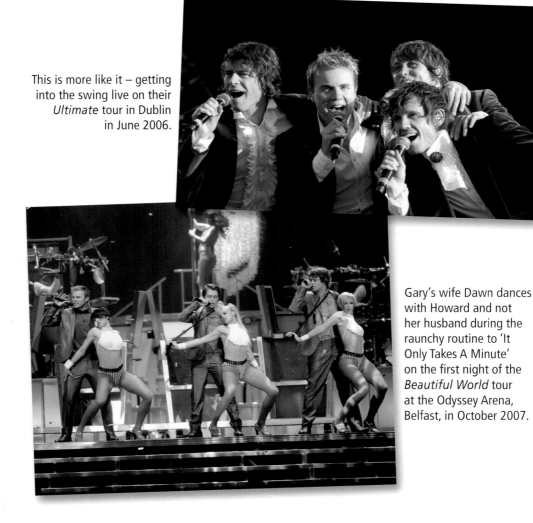

This is more like it – getting into the swing live on their *Ultimate* tour in Dublin in June 2006.

Gary's wife Dawn dances with Howard and not her husband during the raunchy routine to 'It Only Takes A Minute' on the first night of the *Beautiful World* tour at the Odyssey Arena, Belfast, in October 2007.

From boyz to men: Gary had established his new look when Take That were unveiled as the faces of the Marks & Spencer Autograph range in October 2007.

Anyone want my autograph? Gary deserved congratulations when he made it to the top of Mt Kilimanjaro for Comic Relief despite nursing a bad back.

Gary slips through LAX airport with his family on their way to a summer break in Los Angeles in August 2009. During this trip he started writing new songs with Robbie Williams.

After all the years of bad feeling, Robbie and Gary were back on stage together at the Help for Heroes concert at Twickenham in September 2010.

Robbie finally rejoined the band for a reunion tour, which they announced at the Savoy Hotel, London, in October 2010.

Take That perform 'The Flood' at the Millennium Stadium, Cardiff, in June 2011.

The Diamond Jubilee Concert was one of the biggest events of Gary's life. Taking the stage with a queen of pop, Cheryl Cole, to perform 'Need You Now'.

Bowing to The Queen in whose honour he had organized the event. Stars including Sir Paul McCartney and Annie Lennox applaud Her Majesty.

Gary's pride is evident when he plays 'Sing' with The Commonwealth Band conducted by Gareth Malone. Gary's old pal Eliot Kennedy stands between him and the drummer, while Andrew Lloyd Webber, in a pink shirt, shares keyboard duties.

Who better than Elton John to present Gary Barlow OBE with the Music Industry Trusts Award in November 2012 – the crowning achievement of Gary's career as a songwriter.

At the end of 2012, Gary went on his first solo tour for thirteen years. Here he is on stage at his favourite venue, the Royal Albert Hall.

After a momentous year, Gary and his family escape on board a luxury yacht off St Tropez. He playfully threatens to throw Dawn into the Med.

Gary has a moment to himself when he takes to the water on a jet ski.

Travelling in style: Gary joined Chris Evans, James May and Professor Brian Cox on a 'fab' car journey from Land's End to John o' Groats to raise money for Breast Cancer Care in April 2013. It was easier than walking up a mountain!

Time to earn another £1.5 million as head judge on the *X Factor* 2013. Gary poses with the new line-up of Louis Walsh, Sharon Osbourne and Nicole Scherzinger.

Gary Barlow – ready to 'Rule The World'!

spoof of *The X Factor* and other talent shows called *Britain's Got the Pop Factor*. He wanted Gary to help write 'The Winner's Song', which would be sung by Peter in the guise of Geraldine McQueen, the singer-songwriter who wins the show.

Gary loves Peter Kay's humour, especially *Phoenix Nights*, which parodied working men's clubs. Peter grew up in Bolton and, if the cards had fallen differently for him, he might have been performing at the Halton Legion.

He sent some ideas for the lyrics to Gary, who then sat at the piano and worked out the tune. They made the initial demo at his studio in London and spent the whole day laughing. Steve Mac, then producer of Westlife and Leona Lewis, turned it into a record fit for release.

It went to number two in the charts in October 2008. The irony was that it was rather a good song, complete with big Leona Lewis key changes, and might have made number one if it hadn't been sung by Peter Kay in a dress. They wrote a follow-up together, 'Once Upon A Christmas Song', in aid of the NSPCC. It made number five and was both very catchy and very annoying.

Gary enjoyed outside work like this while the band were writing and recording their next album, *The Circus*. He had been approached to write the music for the TV series *Britannia High* and, realizing it was too big a job for one man, decided to hold a winter camp for songwriters. All his friends and collaborators, including Eliot Kennedy, Steve Robson and Steve Mac, descended on Real World Studios in Bath for two weeks. This was part of Gary's other life that he enjoyed just as much as performing. He loved to write and the songwriting world he had created around him was like a secret society in which everyone admired and helped each other – providing they knew how to use the ProTools software. Disappointingly, after all that, the show was a flop and ran for only one series.

Gary was happy to write for any type of artist and embraced all kinds of music: he wrote for Katherine Jenkins, John Barrowman and Lee Mead. It was quite a mix. They weren't all newly written songs but Gary had composed so many over the years that he could dust one off when required. He wrote his song for John Barrowman, 'What About Us?', in half an hour with his friend Chris Braide. Chris was also at the *Britannia High* brainstorming sessions and had won an Ivor Novello Award for 'Anything Is Possible', the 2002 Will Young hit. John sang well but you could be forgiven for wishing Gary had recorded the heartbreaking ballad on one of his solo albums.

The manager of N-Dubz, Jonathan Shalit, got in touch to ask if Gary would be interested in working with them. Jonathan promised him he'd be really impressed by how talented Fazer, Dappy and Tulisa were – and he was. He had heard only one song before he drove down to their Surrey studio in his new Aston Martin. While he had nothing to contribute where the raps were concerned, he did help them find a 'big hook for their track'. The result of their collaboration, during which they spent most of their two days together chatting and eating curry, was probably the most melodious track N-Dubz ever recorded, 'No One Knows'. *Music* magazine called it 'hauntingly beautiful'. Gary was modest about his own contribution, observing on his website that they didn't really need him at all before adding, 'God I'm cool with my kids because of it!' He enthused, 'It was great to discover Tulisa's voice as I think she's a great singer.'

Gary was becoming more in demand, not just as a songwriter but as one of the most recognizable figures in popular culture. His first important involvement with Comic Relief came when Take That sang 'Shine' for Red Nose Day in March 2007. His link to the charity became inevitable when his former manager, Kristina Kyriacou, was appointed its communications director in 2005.

Comic Relief was launched in 1985 by the scriptwriter Richard Curtis and the comedian Lenny Henry. Originally it was intended to raise public awareness of famine in Ethiopia but over the years it has expanded to benefit a huge raft of causes helping to combat poverty and injustice. Kristina did much during her time with the organization to establish Red Nose Day – held every two years – as one of the key fundraising events in the UK.

Richard had become good friends with Gary and approached him in the summer of 2008 to organize a special event to raise money for mosquito nets to help in the charity's ongoing fight against malaria. Over dinner one evening Gary came up with the idea of a group of celebrities climbing the beautiful mountain of Kilimanjaro in the East African country of Tanzania.

Gary set about recruiting eight companions and he phoned each one in person to try to persuade them – nobody said no. He sold it to them by saying it was a chance to see a breathtaking part of Africa and raise money at the same time. He wanted a 'mountain of cash'. It all seemed so easy over a glass or two of expensive red wine. BT came on board as sponsors so all the money raised could be channelled directly into the charity.

Most of the celebrities were already personal friends, like Ronan Keating and Chris Moyles, the DJ who had done much to promote the rebirth of Take That on his Radio 1 show. The others were TV presenters Ben Shephard and Denise Van Outen – she had hosted the *Concert of Hope* in 1997; Fearne Cotton and Alesha Dixon; and, from Girls Aloud, Kimberley Walsh and Cheryl Cole. Gary had never met Cheryl before but she readily agreed to do it when her friend Kimberley was on board. Cheryl had just started as a judge on *The X Factor*. By the time of the climb, the whole nation had fallen in love with her and she was probably the most famous name on British television.

Cheryl had a series of *The X Factor* to complete and Gary was busy finishing the new album, *The Circus*, with John Shanks, so other than making sure they were fit, there was nothing to be done until the new year.

Take That went on *The Chris Moyles Show* to plug the release of their new single, 'Greatest Day', another of Gary's great anthem songs. Jason explained, 'We have to go with a Gary lead track for the first single as it's too risky for us not to.'

It was the right choice. The *Liverpool Post* gushed, 'Gary Barlow is a genius'. The song became the group's eleventh number one. It is an exquisite, uplifting song. They filmed the video while visiting John at his studio in Los Angeles. They kept it simple, arms out-stretched to the heavens, as the sun set over the city, the lights went on and they watched the world come alive. 'Greatest Day' is a song of celebration and has become one of the nation's favourite wedding anthems.

They sang it live on *Children in Need* and donated £250,000 to the appeal. This charity, like Comic Relief, is one Gary particularly likes to support. The song was knocked off the top spot by Leona Lewis (again!) with 'Run', produced by their collaborator Steve Robson, who co-wrote three tracks on their album.

By a weird coincidence, it was released on the day that Britney Spears released an album called *Circus*. The boys won the battle in the UK when it became the most pre-ordered record of all time. It sold 133,000 copies on its first day and passed the two-million mark. Britney had to make do with being number one in the US.

Much of the album had the trademark Barlow rousing chorus and lilting melody. Neil McCormick in the *Daily Telegraph* called it 'pop for sentimental grown-ups'. Jason sang lead on 'How Did It Come To This' and Howard on 'What Is Love' and 'Here'. Their vocal styles were sounding more like Gary's than before. Mark was as individual as ever on the opener, 'The Garden', helped by Gary singing the tricky high bits. Gary sang the lead on only five out of thirteen tracks, although he did sing the title song. The *Scotsman* thought it by far the best one, 'a simple, resonant piano ballad'.

Gary had gone from being the fat one to the fit one and now BBC Music online described him as 'the graceful swan of the group'. He could have been forgiven for thinking he was in a surreal dream.

Bringing him back to reality was his home life. Dawn was expecting their third child; Daniel was now eight and Emily six. Gary observed, 'The reality is that I get home and come through the door to chaos. It's a very normal set-up. It's kids not eating dinners, climbing all over me before I've even got my shoes off. That kind of normality is the key to everything.

'It is a weird environment to be in a pop band but the reality is I go home and carry on my life like everyone else.'

Gary became a father for the third time when Daisy was born on 14 January 2009. He joked that her arrival was the real reason for the climb up Kilimanjaro – he needed some sleep.

Before they left the UK in March, the nine celebrities had to undergo intensive special training. Gary wasn't too worried because he was fit from touring but he was a little concerned about Chris, whose shape resembled that of the old Gary. He was worrying about the wrong person. They all went to the National Olympic Centre in London, where they were tested for their ability to cope with altitude by exercising in a special chamber. It wasn't the real thing but Chris came out on top.

The very name Kilimanjaro conjures up romance and spectacle; the reality is different. You don't need to be a specialist climber to reach the top of Africa's highest mountain, but you require fitness and determination to combat the inevitable reaction, the cold and the high winds. At the summit they would be at nearly 20,000 feet, higher than many planes on long-haul flights. Their trainer warned them of the effects of altitude sickness – headaches, breathlessness and death, which prompted Chris Moyles to ask whether they were always in that order.

This was not a walk in the park and it began badly for Gary when he injured his back ten days before they were due to fly out. It went into spasm while he was training and he hadn't improved things by lifting his new baby. He decided to carry on with the trip because it would have ruined things if the expedition leader had pulled out, but he was in pain for the whole of the climb, downing painkillers continuously. Fortunately, Chris, who is very fond of Gary, kept his spirits up, but even he was astonished at the amount of time Gary spent sleeping.

Chris recalled, 'I think the painkillers made him a bit dopey but he sleeps a lot. Every evening we would arrive at camp and the rest of us would be washing and changing. Gary would go for a little sleep. Two hours later he would emerge and say, "I dozed off for a minute."'

When he did surface, Gary would keep everyone amused with stories of Take That from the old days. Chris's favourite was the time Gary was on tour in Europe and had a shower at 7p.m. before going out to dinner – only he didn't make it. Instead, he fell back onto the bed completely starkers and went to sleep. Seven hours later, when he awoke at 2a.m., the curtains had been drawn, the pillows plumped up and mint chocolates left in a bowl. Gary joked, 'I said to myself, "I must remember to tip that maid."'

The first couple of days of the climb were relatively easy but then most of the girls, Alesha, Cheryl and Fearne, really began to struggle with sickness. By day three Gary was starving and eating more than he had done in years. He recorded in his expedition blog, 'I am really missing Dawn and the kids.' On day five, still in pain with his back, he wrote, 'I have just had the coldest, bleakest, most miserable night I've ever had in my life. It was freezing when we arrived, and at dinner, and minus fifteen degrees when we went to bed. I had every item of clothing on and was still cold. I had a nosebleed before I went to bed.'

After six days, it was a bedraggled crew that set off on the final climb. They began by torchlight at midnight and were expected to take six hours to reach the top. It soon became apparent that Alesha was struggling and was going to need much longer than that. Fearne, Cheryl, Denise and Ben arrived first, having battled through gale force winds. Their Comic Relief despatch said, 'At the summit, God knows how. A temperature of minus fifteen and air so thin your lungs positively burn with disappointment every time you take a breath means you can't stop long.'

Soon afterwards Gary arrived 'in agony' alongside Kimberley and Ronan. A weary Gary exclaimed, 'It seemed like a hare-brained plan six months ago but somehow we're here. I can't believe it. Stretcher for Barlow!' Chris trudged in forty minutes later but there was no sign of Alesha. Two hours after the rest, she gingerly strolled into view. When she reached the others, in a clearing above the rainforest, her celebrity companions broke into song. Exhausted, she collapsed on the ground and said, ''Night.'

Afterwards Gary described his feelings at the top: 'The walk was steep, severe and heartbreaking. Seven months of planning, phone calls, emails, training, sweat, tests and sleepless nights had all led to this. The sun started to rise, it was so emotional and for the first time I lost it and couldn't stop crying.'

They hadn't been battling the elements on their own. A team of 140 guides, porters, cooks and medics had accompanied them, but, even so, this was a real challenge and not the made-for-TV hokum of *I'm A Celebrity . . . Get Me Out Of Here!* Their efforts were rewarded when the trek raised close to £3.5 million.

On their return to the UK, the celebrities were invited to a reception at 10 Downing Street, where Prime Minister Gordon Brown pledged another £2 million of government money to help combat malaria in the region. Gary seemed to be as far away from Gordon as possible during the obligatory photos. He is, after all, a Tory supporter.

The only time that Gary's affable persona slipped was when he was asked rather gormlessly on *GMTV* if Robbie would be 'coming back'. Between gritted teeth, he answered, 'I am running out of ways of answering this now. At the moment, no, he is not coming back.'

The crucial words were 'at the moment'.

20

Progress with Robbie

Gary didn't tell anybody what was going on behind the scenes. During Take That's trip to Los Angeles to work with John Shanks in the summer of 2008 they had got in touch with Rob and invited him to their hotel. It was really nothing more than reciprocating his gesture in London the previous year. He didn't fancy it because he had a raging toothache but his new girlfriend, the actress Ayda Field, said he should go. Ayda was to prove the best thing that had happened to Rob in years and her presence, more than anything else, changed his life.

Rob enjoyed seeing the boys but at that stage had yet to make peace with Gary. He recalled, 'There's a guy in the room I can't even look at.' The feeling was mutual. The next day, however, Rob phoned him and suggested they come over to his house in the Hollywood Hills because 'there are things I want to say that'll help us all move forward.' Gary described the following night to Q magazine, 'We had the "you said I was fat in 1991" conversation.'

Both men were so different now but their relationship with each other was trapped in a time warp. The evening proved a momentous one for Rob: 'I went from having a real problem with this person to literally rolling on the floor laughing with him ten minutes later. We were genuinely sorry we had upset each other.' There was some idle chat about everybody making a one-off single together but they didn't hear from one another for the rest of the year.

The band flew home to promote *The Circus* and prepare for what would be their biggest-ever tour. *Take That Present: The Circus Live* was the fastest-selling tour of all time, with 600,000 tickets for the original eight stadium dates selling out in under five hours. They sold 82,000 tickets for a show at Croke Park in Dublin in under an hour. After extra dates were added, more than one million people would end up seeing them put on clown make-up, lark about on unicycles and strut the stage on a giant hydraulic elephant. The idea was to make it two hours of escapism just like a real circus would be. Gary's back was still a bit dodgy so he rode a toddler's bike with stabilizers instead of a unicycle.

The start alone was worth the admission – an elaborate piece of theatre entitled 'The Adventures Of A Lonely Balloon'. At the end of the specially devised instrumental, the boys emerge from a hot-air balloon to sing a triumphant version of 'Greatest Day'. This was even more Vegas than the *Beautiful World* gigs and the cost of staging the tour was estimated at £10 million, as fifty-eight trucks rumbled from venue to venue. One interesting aspect was that the fans seemed not to mind whether a song was old or new. They cheered and sang along to 'Patience' as enthusiastically as they did to 'Relight My Fire'. The two-hour show ended with fireworks as Gary sang 'We're lighting up the sky for you' from 'Rule The World'.

After the Croke Park concert, Paul Martin wrote in the *Daily Mirror*, 'I have never witnessed a show as spectacular as Take That's night of glory on Saturday. It was . . . quite simply majestic in every way.' Most of the critics, while impressed with the spectacle of the show and Gary's singing, drew attention to the genuine feeling of gratitude the band exuded. Jade Wright said in the *Liverpool Echo*, 'It's hard not to be moved by a band of men in their thirties clearly so grateful to have been given a second chance to play the music they love.' The tour was so prestigious that among the support acts at

Wembley Stadium were The Script and James Morrison. For the last two nights, it was Lady Gaga.

After the four shows there had completed the tour in July, Gary needed to get away from it all and rented a house in the Beachwood Canyon area of Los Angeles for two months for Dawn and their three children. Gary enjoyed his annual visits to California. He and Dawn had carved out a good social life for themselves of family barbecues and trips to Disneyworld. The house was below the 'Hollywood' sign and close to hiking trails and picnic areas that reminded him of walks in Delamere Forest – except it was a lot warmer. A friend explained, 'They don't go schmoozing with Hollywood stars. Occasionally you see them out to dinner but that's it.'

They liked Cecconi's, an Italian restaurant in West Hollywood, but usually they drifted over to their friends' homes. Gary caught up with his music pals, like John Shanks and Chris Braide, who had moved permanently to California. He couldn't spend a summer without working and so joined John to write and record a track with Alesha Dixon. He had first spoken to her about working together halfway up Kilimanjaro. The song 'To Love Again' was one of Gary's melodic ballads but he loved Alesha's lyric about a girl who had been hurt in love. He called it 'very real'.

One of Gary's best mates is the Scottish TV presenter Ross King, the LA correspondent for *Lorraine*, *GMTV* and, subsequently, its replacement show *Daybreak*. He had been the original presenter of the *8.15 from Manchester* programme that had featured Take That all those years ago. Gary would also catch up with both Simon Cowell and Nigel Lythgoe, the millionaire producer of *Pop Idol* and *American Idol*. Nigel had been brought up in the Wirral, not far from Frodsham.

Rob had settled permanently in LA in December 2001. He was not yet part of Gary's social circle but after *not* bumping into each other for six weeks, Gary decided to get in touch. He emailed Rob, inviting him over, and heard nothing for a week. He told *Q*, 'I'm thinking, "fucking hell, I'm going home soon". Out of the blue I get an email saying, "I'm coming over tomorrow". Shit, here we go. So I got a little tune going in the studio . . .' Rob didn't show.

The next day he rolled up at 5p.m. with Ayda, a couple of friends and his pack of dogs. Everyone sat round the pool chatting happily, when Gary announced, 'Hey, Rob, come and listen to this.' And that was pretty much it.

He hadn't appreciated how quick Rob was with lyrics. Gary would agonize for hours hunched over a thesaurus, whereas Rob would have a cup of coffee and get on with it. They sketched out the idea for a song then and there but by the time Gary went to bed Rob had finished the lyrics perfectly. Gary went straight down to the studio and sang them into a computer, emailed them back to Rob, who loved the song and replied, 'Shall we do it again tomorrow?'

The song was called 'Shame'.

The next day Gary went over to Rob's with a stack of recording gear and they worked late into the night on three or four possible songs. 'I sat down and said to him, "I'm going home next week – what is this? What are we doing here" And he said, "That's it now, we've done it – I want to work with the lads."' They then settled down to watch the new DVD of *The Circus Live* tour together.

One of the more surprising things about their new understanding was that both men were able to keep it a secret. Rob agreed to fly to New York in September to work with all four members of Take That on their new album. Gary, as organized as ever, came prepared with ten backing tracks and Rob joined in crafting the songs that would eventually become *Progress*. Rob still suffered doubts about the future and at one point told the others he was leaving again. Mark was able to talk him round – something nobody had tried to do properly fifteen years before.

Gary flew home to work on material and sign artists for his new record label, Future Records. He also needed to prepare for BBC's

Children in Need. He had decided to organize a fundraising concert at the Royal Albert Hall and had suggested that this might be the right occasion for him and Rob to appear together.

His plans were thrown into disarray at the end of October when his father Colin died suddenly at the age of seventy-one. Gary rushed back to Frodsham to comfort his mum and asked for privacy at a sad time. The Barlows are a very close family and everyone was in shock. The old cliché of people never having a bad word to say about somebody was true of Colin. He was a gentle man who had worked hard for his loved ones and had finally achieved his ambition of living in a farmhouse when he and his wife moved to a village a few miles from Frodsham. Gary immediately cancelled his appearance at the BBC *Children in Need* launch. Howard left a message on his answer phone every day for three weeks: 'Just checking on you. No need to ring me back, just making sure you're OK.'

The concert went ahead as planned and raised more than £2 million. Paul McCartney, Cheryl Cole, Leona Lewis and Shirley Bassey, for whom Gary had written a new song, were on the bill of *Children in Need Rocks the Royal Albert Hall*, as well as Take That, of course. Rob was there too. If you blinked, you missed the 'reunion'. They performed separately.

Gary had to choke back the tears as he spoke movingly of his dad: 'It's one of those nights when he would have been here. I'd have loved to have him here tonight . . . This song is dedicated to everybody who's lost somebody they love. Dad, this one's for you.' He then started singing 'Rule The World'.

Paul McCartney and Take That began the encore, 'Hey Jude', and then Rob strode on stage amid 'crazy applause', put his arm around Gary and gave him a peck on the cheek. It was theatrical but perfect.

Almost immediately, it was revealed that Take That had recorded some tracks in New York as a five-piece again. Rob was the source of the leak when he blurted it out during a Radio 2 interview: 'Gaz is an amazing, amazing singer-songwriter. I'm honoured to be in the same studio as him, erm, when we do, in the future. Oh sod it, we've been in and the songs are absolutely amazing.' Graciously, he conceded that Gary was the captain of the ship and he had no problem playing 'second or third fiddle in that band'.

Gary, meanwhile, went ahead with his plans to hold a lavish tenth anniversary party for Dawn, who he felt had missed out on a big wedding. Kristina Kyriacou organized the event for them at the Mandarin Oriental Hotel in Knightsbridge. It was splashed over twenty-six pages of *OK!* magazine which was, ironically, exactly what Gary had been determined to avoid when they had married in Nevis in 2000. Gary loves being the centre of attention but Dawn overcame her natural shyness on this occasion because the proceeds from the event were going to Barnardo's. They also topped the amount up with a personal donation on behalf of all their celebrity guests.

Dawn looked fabulous in a strapless ivory ball gown and Gary buffed up well in a dark suit and chequered shirt and tie. They were like Hollywood stars. The magazine carried more than seventy pictures of the couple's A-list guests, who represented a cross section of the most important people in Gary's life: they included Howard and Mark, Jonathan Wild, Eliot Kennedy, Chris Moyles, Cheryl Cole, Mikey Graham, Ronan Keating, Alesha Dixon, Denise Van Outen, Kimberley Walsh, Richard Curtis, Lulu, Peter Kay, Fearne Cotton, Nicki Chapman, Tim Rice and Jason Donovan, who had become one of Gary's best pals in recent years. They drank Bellinis and ate fish and chips wrapped in a spoof front page of *The Kop*, the fanzine of Liverpool FC.

Dawn and Gary seemed to be beaming in every photograph. He began the entertainment with some rounds of 'Barlow's Bingo' just as he had done twenty-five years before down the Halton Legion. Gary introduced comedian Michael McIntyre, explaining that the latter's DVD was always playing at his house. He then returned to the stage to sing 'Fly Me To The Moon' and sit at the piano to join

Take That's tour band backing the celebrity performers, Ronan, Jason Donovan and Peter Kay. The biggest laugh of the night was reserved for Alesha Dixon singing her hit 'The Boy Does Nothing' and pointing at Gary when she sang, 'Does he clean up?'

Mark sang 'Shine' and Gary 'Back For Good' while Dawn was led backstage to prepare for her surprise moment – a reunion with Timmy Mallett. She had no idea that she would be reunited with her original dancing partner for Timmy's rendition of 'Itsy Bitsy Teeny Weeny Yellow Polka Dot Bikini'.

Marj was there, accompanied by Ian and his wife Lisa. Colin was sadly missed in the pictures of a smiling family group. Gary remained positive and said, 'It would have been great for him to have been able to share our special day but he saw the best of our lives.'

The party was Gary's way of thanking his wife for being there for him. They had never had an argument, reflecting the long and happy marriages of their own parents. Married life gives Gary an escape from the madness of fame. On a normal day he feeds the children and takes them to school. He likes to take his son to football and his eldest daughter to the theatre because she is a performer in the making.

Once a week is date night and he takes Dawn out to dinner so they can talk without the children interrupting. Over a meal he likes to spring the latest news on his wife, like 'We're off on a European tour next week.' She takes it in her stride. Her desire to keep out of the limelight is one of the things that keeps their marriage strong. Gary, who admits he can be a bit of a diva, explained to *OK!*, 'I can go and do a big tour and she's not in competition with that side of my life. That's where people start having problems, when they start fighting for attention.'

Gary's love for his wife and his pleasure at showing her off shone through the evening. If this party had been their actual big day, it would have been the wedding of the year. It's often amusingly observed that there is a curse on couples who sell their wedding day to *Hello!* or *OK!* That's not true of Gary and Dawn but the same could not be said of some of the celebrity couples who were their guests. Cheryl and Ashley Cole, Ronan and Yvonne Keating, Chris Moyles and his long-term girlfriend Sophie Waite have all been hit by the curse since they smiled happily on the night. Mark Owen and his wife Emma survived a rocky patch after he confessed to infidelity and she took him back for the sake of their children.

Rob wasn't at the party. The next time he and Gary got together was in Los Angeles as part of the group of celebrities, Helping Haiti, that sang on 'Everybody Hurts', a fundraising record organized by Simon Cowell for victims of the Haiti earthquake. It was the fastest-selling charity record of the twenty-first century and went straight to number one in February 2010.

The first media backlash against Gary for years came unexpect-edly. He joined David Cameron on the General Election campaign trail when they appeared together at the Brine Leas High School in Nantwich. Where Gary sang 'Greatest Day' with the school orches-tra and then introduced the future prime minister with the immortal words, 'There is no one more with it than Dave.'

In fairness to Gary, he was there to back a Tory initiative called School Stars, a sort of *X Factor* to discover talented young musicians in the classroom. But he did confirm that he would be supporting the Tories at the election, an intention he shared with Simon Cowell, who had told *Sun* readers that Mr Cameron had 'the substance and the stomach to navigate us through difficult times'.

Gary's political outing predictably went down badly with the *Daily Mirror*. The columnist Polly Hudson commented, 'I was more upset about Gary Barlow getting into bed with David Cameron than I was about Mark Owen doing the same with women who weren't his wife.' The problem for Gary was that celebrity and politics don't really mix in this country, whereas it's commonplace in the US.

He was on safer ground when it was announced that he and Rob were going to release 'Shame'. The track would be the single from a Robbie Williams greatest hits compilation, *In and Out of Consciousness*.

Rob's return to Take That was officially announced on 15 July 2010. The subsequent new album and tour would net all five an estimated £15 million each. The official announcement confirmed that Rob would be part of Take That for a year. Even the normally reticent Jason said the news was 'flippin' brilliant'.

It was a good summer for Rob, who married Ayda Field at his LA home in August. Gary didn't go to the wedding but he was a big fan of Rob's new wife, calling her 'Rob's rock'. He observed, 'He's got a diamond there.' Gary thought Ayda was exactly what Rob needed. It was true – he was more settled with her by his side.

Less than three weeks after the wedding, Gary and Rob launched their duet on *The Chris Moyles Show* on Radio 1. They both described their 'big chat', when they had put their animosity to bed and said sorry to each other. Gary observed, 'We just needed to sit opposite each other and talk.' Rob said, 'It's lifted so much off our shoulders.' They made it all sound very cosy, as if they were two old soldiers meeting up in the Legion for the first time in twenty years.

For such a landmark in their lives, 'Shame' was an understated song, an unfussy country tune reflecting on their troubled relationship. Rob's lyric described how it was a shame that they never listened to one another and the emotional upset it caused him. Instead of talking it through, Rob confesses that he had talked in public or, as he says, through the television. It is a basic but true observation that people can spend a lifetime not talking or listening to one another.

The video was much talked about. Some got the fact that it was a light-hearted pastiche of the Oscar-winning film *Brokeback Mountain* – complete with manly bare chests – and others didn't. It's not that easy for two men to sing a duet to each other with a straight face.

They managed to do so in public for the first time when they performed at *A Concert for Heroes* in aid of the Help for Heroes charity at Twickenham in September. Rob had already sung 'Feel' when he announced to the crowd, 'Have I got a treat for you. This is one of the most amazing moments in my professional career so far. It has been fifteen years in the making. My wife calls him my boyfriend, I call him my captain, you call him Gary Barlow.'

It's a pity that 'Shame' wasn't a more powerful song for such a landmark occasion. It had mixed reviews: the *Daily Mirror* called it 'sappy', while the BBC Online thought it a 'really sweet song' and Hannah Fernando of *heat* magazine said, 'It's pretty catchy.' The fans liked it enough to propel it to number two in the charts, only kept off the top spot by Cee Lo Green's 'Forget You'. Fortunately, *In and Out of Consciousness* went straight to number one a week later. 'Shame' was the first track.

Their collaboration was the perfect way to advertise the following May's *Progress Live* tour. Websites crashed after two minutes when the tickets went on sale a few weeks later. By the end of the day, more than 1.3 million tickets had been sold.

Everything was moving so fast that you barely had time to blink before Take That, including Rob, were appearing on *The X Factor* performing their comeback single, 'The Flood', together. You could almost touch the excitement in the studio when the boys, dressed in black, strode onto the stage.

Rob sang the first verse and Gary, barely able to keep the smile off his face, sang the second. Nobody sells a song like Robbie Williams and no one has a more perfect pop voice than Gary Barlow. Afterwards he told host Dermot O'Leary that being back together was 'great'. Rob said it was 'magical'.

The song could not have been more different from 'Shame'. Perhaps that was deliberate. This was nothing like the old Take That – or the new one for that matter. Everyone had been so fascinated by the human story of Rob's reconciliation with Gary that few considered what the music would be like when their two very distinctive styles were fused together.

The journalists had been unable to get their heads around the point of the reunion, veering between suggesting that it provided closure after the bitter split of fifteen years before and speculating that Rob's career had needed a boost. Neither was exactly true. It was a combination of reasons. There was a financial sweetener – all five were expected to earn £7.5 million from the tour alone – but there was also an emotional element for them all, particularly Rob, who said he was envious of the joy the others were having.

For Gary it represented a musical challenge – something fresh to try. The two Take That albums *Beautiful World* and *The Circus* had been phenomenally successful but they were cut from the same cloth. They could have done another of those but there would have been some critical carping that it was the same old Gary material – climactic choruses and calming chords.

'The Flood' was completely different. It was a dark and powerful song with a strident, almost marching rhythm that demanded your attention. It still sounded like a Gary song but one that had been hit over the head with a mallet. The *News of the World* described it as a 'mammoth anthem', while Gary's old mate Elton John called it 'brilliant'.

Disappointingly, despite intense promotion over the next few weeks, it missed being a twelfth number one for Take That, kept off the top by Rihanna's hit 'Only Girl (In The World)'. Most people were clearly waiting for the album because, on its first week of release in November 2010, *Progress* sold 520,000 copies – the second fastest sales of all time in the UK – and it would prove to be the biggest-selling album of the year despite its late release.

The band had found the perfect producer for the sound they developed on this album. The Grammy-winning Stuart Price had produced the Madonna album *Confessions on a Dance Floor* and Kylie's acclaimed *Aphrodite*. He was a master of a modern electronic sound that acknowledged the great days of the eighties and nineties, when Gary was listening to Depeche Mode and the Pet Shop Boys and building his home studio crammed with keyboards and the latest computer gadgetry.

Take That, it seemed, had absorbed all the influences of their youth and forged a mature new sound. Andy Gill of the *Independent* summed it up: 'Those who imagined Take That's reunion album would be a predictable blending of forces will be shocked to hear *Progress*. Rather than pop balladry, the album leans heavily on electronic beats and textures, and reflects misgivings about science and humanity.' The *NME* more succinctly observed that it was a 'triumphant and quite crudely banging stadium synthpop record'.

The nearest thing to a classic Gary song was the ballad 'Eight Letters', which closed the album, as if to remind fans that it was still a Take That record. The hidden track was, for once, one of the best on the album: the lyrical 'Flowerbed' sung by Jason.

They were going to perform their follow-up single 'Kidz' on *The X Factor* final but the rumour was that it was a little edgy for Saturday night viewing. Instead, they sang 'The Flood' again and 'Never Forget' with the three finalists, One Direction, Rebecca Ferguson and the eventual winner, Matt Cardle. It looked like they had been allowed out to perform with the grown-ups as a special treat.

It was easy to see why Simon Cowell feared Take That might eclipse the whole show when they finally performed 'Kidz' at the revamped Brits at the O2 in February 2011. They opened the event with a barnstorming version, complete with dancers dressed as police in riot gear. It was more military rally than singalong and the *Guardian* described it as 'the campest, and possibly the most spectacular, opening to any Brit Awards'.

There was better to come. Take That were crowned Best British Group for the first time, twenty-one years after an ambitious young musician from Frodsham had walked into the offices of Nigel Martin-Smith in Manchester.

21

Head Judge

When Gary was approached by producers from *The X Factor* in March 2011 with the offer of the job of taking Simon Cowell's place, he told them he would need to go and ask the real head judge at home to see what she thought. From a business point of view it wouldn't do any harm to make them wait, but in this case Gary genuinely wanted to know Dawn's reaction and ask his children what they thought.

He was very keen to accept but explained to *Esquire* magazine that his son Daniel had just gone to big school and they were worried that he was at the point where 'people take the piss out of him because his dad's on *The X Factor*'. They realized the children came first. 'When we told them, they thought it was the best thing that had ever happened.'

Gary's involvement in the show was announced a few weeks before the *Progress Live* tour began at Sunderland's Stadium of Light on 27 May. He had been approached to be a contestant on many big reality shows in the past but would never go near them. *I'm A Celebrity . . . Get Me Out of Here!*, *Big Brother*, *Dancing on Ice* and *Strictly Come Dancing* had all been in touch. He observed, 'There must be a list of desperate celebrities and my name must have been at the top because I used to get sent all of them. But I've never been tempted.'

He had known Simon for some twenty years, from the days when the former A & R man had decided not to sign Take That. Their paths had crossed intermittently during Gary's solo career and when the band reunited for the documentary *Take That: For the Record*.

On the surface the two men could not be more different – a soft southerner and a blunt northerner – but they are both driven by a fierce ambition and single-minded desire to succeed. Simon was privately educated and brought up in the genteel surroundings of Elstree in Hertfordshire. As a boy he would watch glamorous Hollywood stars like Elizabeth Taylor and Bette Davis arrive for parties at his next-door neighbour's house. It made a big impression on him: 'I'd love to live in a house like that.'

Like Gary, Simon had to recover from a demoralizing slump when his record label ran into difficulties in the early nineties and he had to move back home with his parents. He turned it around thanks to 'Unchained Melody' by Robson and Jerome, the stars of the TV series *Soldier Soldier*, which became the biggest-selling record of 1995 – the year Rob left Take That.

Simon is not especially witty or clever in his famous putdowns of *X Factor* wannabes. He prefaces his rudeness with 'I don't want to be rude . . .' or 'I have to be honest with you . . .' The television audience loves the predictability of it all and are genuinely pleased when he is offensive. Kevin O'Sullivan, television critic of the *Sunday Mirror*, observes, 'People like this circus show and they love the ringmaster who brings it to them.'

The X Factor is first and foremost a television show and not a talent contest with a serious musical purpose, but Simon has always wanted it to have credibility. So when he decided to leave to pursue his dream of making the programme the biggest in the US, he needed a musical heavyweight to take over. Kevin explains, 'All these shows need a headmaster. They needed someone with *gravitas* to step into Cowell's shoes. Clearly the great composer of all the Take That smash hits is going to fit the bill.'

Rumours suggested Simon wanted to sign Rob but that's not the case. He would, no doubt, have been wonderfully entertaining but he doesn't fit Simon's view of how a judge should act. Kevin agrees with him that a judge should walk a fine line between putting on a great act and entertaining the crowd but not dominating proceedings: 'You just know with Robbie that it would have turned into the Robbie Williams Show. He *is* showbiz. I think Cowell thought Gary would gain the respect of the viewers. I suspect he hired him because he thought, "This guy knows what he is talking about" and not because he thought he was going to be great on television.'

Gary had always had a strong association with *The X Factor*. He was mentioned as a possible judge as long ago as December 2005, when Simon first thought the show needed freshening up with the introduction of an extra category and a fourth judge. That was the year Shayne Ward sang 'A Million Love Songs' on his way to winning the second series. Nothing changed with the format the following season when Leona Lewis sang the same number in the final alongside Take That.

In 2008 there was a special Take That night with all the contestants singing one of Gary's songs. This time JLS sang 'A Million Love Songs' and had to survive being in the bottom two. The eventual winner, Alexandra Burke, performed 'Relight My Fire'. There was one of those mock *X Factor* controversies that week when both Louis Walsh and new judge Dannii Minogue wanted their acts to sing 'Rule The World'. The boys themselves performed 'Greatest Day'. They had realized early on that an appearance on *The X Factor* was the best way of promoting a record or a tour.

They didn't appear in 2009 but there was still a Take That night in which series heart-throb Lloyd Daniels sang 'A Million Love Songs' before being eliminated and Olly Murs chose 'Love Ain't Here Anymore'.

The following year the band appeared on two of the shows. Gary went on to write and produce the lead single 'Run For Your Life' for the winner Matt Cardle's first solo album. By the time that was released in October 2011, Gary was beginning to adjust to his new role on *The X Factor* and could look back with satisfaction on the biggest UK stadium tour of all time.

The tour had been very demanding. The anticipation of seeing the group as a five-piece for the first time in sixteen years had been immense. There was a big difference between being relaxed in a recording studio and playing eight nights in Manchester and then at Wembley Stadium. The wave of goodwill and oestrogen that followed them around the country meant that they couldn't really fail. 'As comebacks go, they're up there with Lazarus. We feel like we know them,' said Jade Wright of the *Liverpool Echo*.

Parachuting Rob back into the band was perhaps a qualified success. The fans adored it but there was the suspicion that the new, more technical material sat uneasily amid the parade of classic hits that everyone could sing along with. Jade wrote, 'The added dynamic of Robbie was a mixed blessing – at times he was on great form, but he remained distant from the rest of the band.'

The concerts were arranged so that Take That would begin the show as a four-piece, then Rob would come on and perform some of his most famous songs, including 'Feel' and 'Angels', before all five would come together for the third part. They played five songs from *Progress*, which meant favourites like 'Babe', 'A Million Love Songs' and 'Everything Changes' were relegated to a medley. David Bennun of the *Mail on Sunday* admired the 'conjuring trick' of putting Robbie back in the Take That box: 'By the time we reach "Pray", Gary Barlow's supreme achievement and a truly great pop song, any lingering sense of awkwardness has vanished. The five are one.'

Gary said they were treating every gig as a football manager might – one game at a time. The scale of the £15 million tour was breathtaking – 287 people were on the road with a further 160 local crew drafted in at each venue. It took forty-eight hours to build the stage. More than 1.76 million fans shouted and cheered them on twenty-seven dates.

Jan Moir in the *Daily Mail* described the audience at Manchester City's Etihad Stadium as 'Doolally Thatters'. Jan had first seen them at Wembley in 1993 and had followed them through good times and bad. She particularly noted that Gary had matured like a fine wine. She wrote, '"Mark used to be my favourite" lots of Take That fans will tell you. "But now it's Gary."'

So why did Gary choose to join *The X Factor* instead of putting his feet up in the south of France or spending the summer at his new country home in Oxfordshire? First, it's the easiest £1 million you can earn on TV. He never mentioned the money in interviews, of course. Secondly, he thought he could make a difference and is genuinely interested in promoting young and talented artists. On his first day, outside the Birmingham auditions, he explained, 'I fancied just taking a back-seat for a while and helping other people develop their careers.' It's no coincidence that his own label was optimistically called Future Records. And thirdly, he knew from watching the progress of his friend Cheryl Cole – not to mention Simon Cowell himself – that you could become a national institution through the power and popularity of the show. He joked, 'It's time Simon went anyway, don't you think? He's been in it too much. Move over!'

Gary attended all twelve *X Factor* auditions, even though it sometimes meant putting in a double shift with a concert in the evening. It might seem a lot to cope with but not considering the crazy early days spent promoting Take That on the road. He seemed genuinely pleased with the reaction as he signed autographs and waved to excited fans. He was asked who would have won if Take That had entered *The X Factor* individually. He didn't draw breath before responding, 'Me', which was a flash of the old no-nonsense Gary that some might think arrogant. He was almost certainly right though.

The contestants had nothing to do with Gary directly until Judges'

Houses. The public have no idea what a laborious and painful process it is for the contestants to reach that stage. James Michael, who made it on to Gary's team in 2011, went to his first audition in Liverpool. 'It was packed. There were thousands and thousands waiting to get in. Eventually I had to sing in front of a researcher in a sort of makeshift booth. I sang "Man In The Mirror" by Michael Jackson. So then I went through to the next stage and had to sing for three producers, all ladies. I sang "Man In The Mirror" again and played my guitar. The cameraman asked me some questions about my music and a little bit of my story. Then I sang a James Morrison song and everyone was smiling and said, "Thank you very much". When I got home, a researcher rang and said, "Will you come back again tomorrow at 5.30a.m.?"'

There were still about a thousand hopefuls on the second day. James recalls, 'It was mostly interviews – just squeezing every story out of you, everything you have got out of you. Then I sang "Man In The Mirror" again and that was it.' After all that, James was contacted by a member of the production team asking him to perform at the *first* audition in front of thousands of people at the Echo Arena in Liverpool. He had to give a list of five songs he could perform to one of the girls working on the show and she came back and told him which one they wanted – Adele's version of 'Make You Feel My Love' by Bob Dylan.

The audition day began with filming. They took shots of James chatting to other contestants and strolling moodily along the river with his guitar: 'They did really in-depth interviews with me before the actual audition.' He met Olly Murs and Caroline Flack, the hosts of the spin off show, *The Xtra Factor*, and was asked where he would take Caroline out for a date – he said they would go for an Italian meal. By the side of the stage he chatted to Dermot O'Leary, who was a 'really nice guy'. The host put him at ease by asking him where he had got his tan. 'I just said I'd been sat in the garden.'

Then it was time to go out on stage and see the judges for the first time. He remembers being surprised at how far away they were – maybe twenty feet. After he sang, Gary said, 'James, you are a recording artist just waiting to be recorded.' It made his day because the observation was from 'one of the best songwriters to come out of the UK'. That's an important point about Gary being on the show: the musicians and performers would rather have praise from someone of his stature than Louis Walsh telling them they had 'nailed it'.

The next time he saw Gary was at Boot Camp, when the judges greeted the contestants on the big lawn outside their hotel in Croydon. They were all assembled in what at first appeared to be four long random lines with about fifty people in each, all cheering wildly when Tulisa, Louis, Kelly Rowland and Gary appeared. Then they gave them some bombshell news and sent one of the lines home without even listening to them sing. Fellow contestant Max Vickers recalls, 'I didn't think that was on, really. We had all made friends on the coach down and then one group had to go straight home. They were fuming about it.'

Both James and Max went through to the next stage, when a group of four had to sing a song together. James didn't impress Gary when they sang 'Breakeven' by The Script: 'I was dead nervous and didn't realize I had my hand in my pocket all the way through. At the end of the song, Gary said, "James, were you bored?" I said I was just trying to feel the song, so he said, "OK, thank you." I thought I was definitely going home.'

To his surprise, they gave him another chance. He went on stage at Wembley Arena and sang 'The First Cut Is The Deepest' by Rod Stewart. He said 'Thank you, Wembley' to the crowd in case he never got the chance to sing in front of 20,000 people again. The next day he was back there to be given the news that he had been chosen for Judges' Houses. Max would be there too.

Afterwards Gary made his way on to the stage, where the lucky ones were laughing and hugging each other, and declared, 'This is one for you.' He proceeded to play them 'Greatest Day', accompanying himself on the piano. This is not something you are ever going to see Simon Cowell doing.

Coincidentally, both Max and James were local as far as Gary was concerned. The former is from Warrington and the latter from Widnes, literally about ten minutes up the road from Frodsham. Both boys hoped that they would get Gary as a mentor.

The contestants genuinely don't know who their mentor is going to be until the door opens and he or she walks in. The producers want to record real surprise when they find out. When the boys realized it was Gary, they ran over and started jumping on him. It must have seemed like the old days when Take That played 'pile-on', where they all leapt on each other and Gary always ended up at the bottom of the pile.

His Judges' Houses segment was going to be in Los Angeles, which was perfect for Gary. He needed a break after touring. A holiday in LA with the family, including Marj, was the best way to start earning his million pounds. The eight contenders didn't see Gary on their journey there. They were filmed all over Heathrow, going up and down escalators and looking excited. They had a glass of champagne in the first-class lounge. Then the cameras were switched off and they were given their economy tickets.

The boys were checked into the L'Ermitage hotel in Beverly Hills, the most lavish hotel they had ever seen. James shared a room with Max. On the first day, they were filmed around Venice Beach getting in and out of limos and playing volleyball with Caroline and Olly – it was all for the cameras. They were given some shopping time on the way back to the hotel. In the evening they chatted to *The Xtra Factor* hosts, as well as Dermot, in the bar but there was still no sign of Gary.

They didn't see him until the next day at the Judges' House, which wasn't Gary's home at all. It belonged to a movie producer and was a palatial mansion high up in the Hollywood Hills, complete with an infinity pool in the grounds. They had no idea who Gary's guest judge would be and feared they might end up with Sinitta, while secretly hoping it would be Pixie Lott or even Simon Cowell himself. James recalls, 'We were standing by the pool and Robbie walked out. He had no clothes on. Naked! He had big massive leaves covering his bits. And we were just laughing our heads off. And he was like, "All right, guys. How are you?" – all upbeat and shouty. And we were made up it was him as well as Gary.'

The eight remaining boys had to sing two songs for Gary and Rob. They were told that Gary had chosen them but suspected it was the producers. After they had all performed, Rob invited them back to his house for a drink. James loved it. 'I was like, "No way!" It was about 11.30 when all the interviews and performances had finished. We got to this enormous house and it was like something out of *The Godfather*. We were all just speechless but he was like, "Do you want a beer?" And Gary was there with his mum and his wife who was really lovely.

'Robbie was just chatting on the lounger next to the pool. He was saying how he loved his wife. And they were saying how they wanted to have kids and stuff. Gary came over and sat down and said I had done great and I was like, "Thanks a lot." It was a down-to-earth chat – telling it how it is. He's got the same accent as me. And I was talking to his mum as well and told her that my nan had seen Gary in the United Services Club when he was fifteen. I had played there as well.'

Gary was sociable but kept a professional veneer because the next day he would have to tell four of them they weren't going through to the live rounds. He had been coached by the producers on how to build the suspense for the television audience. It was a crucial moment for the contestants because this is the most critical decision of the whole series. To be sent packing now when they were so close was the worst possible scenario because selection for the live finals gave everyone the chance to become a star.

This time there was no Rob to lighten the mood. Instead, Gary told James solemnly that it would be a gamble to put him through, before eventually announcing, 'I am going to take a gamble and a risk.' James was then taken to the 'yes' room along with Marcus Collins, Craig Colton and Frankie Cocozza. Max was in the 'no' room. He never saw Gary again after he received the bad news.

Gary was good at this. Sitting by the pool in the blazing sun, he was sincere and sympathetic. He had, after all, suffered enough rejections in his own professional life to know what acute disappointment felt like. At the same time, however, he played *The X Factor* game by using the programme's familiar words: 'I have made my decision . . .'

At the airport the also-rans were in tears. Max recalled, 'Everyone who wasn't through was upset. I was better than the others because I knew I was going to uni anyway and this was only a little adventure.' The journey home was a nightmare, with the four happy boys sitting with the four miserable ones. James was next to one, Joe Cox: 'He never spoke to us the whole way. Just had his head down. I thought, "Oh, my God." I was chuffed really but I didn't want to start jumping around, like, when he was sat next to me. But it was awkward.'

The live finals were a couple of weeks away but the viewing public were already becoming familiar with Gary's judging style thanks to the heavily edited audition rounds. He was very funny, especially when a procession of female hopefuls told him he was 'drop dead gorgeous'. He genuinely seemed to be enjoying himself when the boisterous Goldie Cheung chased him and eventually wrapped her leg around his neck. Tulisa observed, 'Every woman in the country is obsessed with Gary Barlow.'

Some of the banter appeared scripted. His gag writer was reported to be Ben Winston, a personal friend who co-wrote the Smithy Comic Relief sketches with acclaimed comedian James Corden. Kevin O'Sullivan observes, 'You can see where Gary gets his one-liners in. I think he is very careful about what he says. He realizes that when you are on *The X Factor* every step of the way could be good for you or it could be disastrous for you. Gary doesn't go on TV loosely.'

Whether it was Ben or not, Gary's comments at the auditions were very funny. An obvious example was his response to a performer called George who had been on the show before, in 2009, when he had thrown a wobbly. He told the viewers that he had matured, which didn't bode well. Sure enough, he was terrible. Gary told him, 'Things mature nicely like a red wine or a cheese. You've matured like a bad curry.' He told another bad singer, 'If you take singing lessons, make sure they have a refund policy.'

Gary did admit that he struggled at first because 'it's a totally bloody new thing to me'. He appeared more natural and relaxed afterwards on *The Xtra Factor*, larking about with Caroline and Olly, especially when they presented him with a mug with his name on one side and the words 'Head Judge' on the other. He also signed up for Twitter for the first time on the show. His first tweet was the far from inspiring 'Hello everybody' but that didn't stop him gathering 300,000 followers in the first twenty-four hours. He now has nearly three million.

The most controversial contestant in Gary's category was Frankie Cocozza, who was given a bad boy image but was clearly the worst singer of the four in the live finals. He represented the dilemma that Gary would always face on this show: best television versus best music. James Michael recalls, 'We all knew Frankie was going to go through. Even though he didn't have an amazing voice, we knew they weren't going to throw him out. He was like the main attraction, wasn't he?' The reality was that Frankie was a 'dead quiet lad' who used to sit around playing with his mobile phone.

James was surprised that in the week of the first live show he saw Gary, his mentor, for about ten minutes. As Kevin O'Sullivan observes, 'I'll tell you what the judges don't do anywhere near as much as you think and that is mentor. They basically just turn up on Saturdays. They all have a bit of filming to do in the week with their acts but it is easy money.' The only time anyone spotted Gary was when he went jogging with Craig Colton, another Liverpool singer, who needed to lose a few pounds. He was encouraging Craig to eat a more healthy diet.

In the build-up to the live shows, the contestants almost get as much time in make-up as the judges. The stylists try to mould the contestants. They cut James's curly hair really short and shaved the sides. 'Gary came up to the house and said, "What the hell has happened to your hair?" I said the fashion guy had got hold of me and it was supposed to be a little trim. He told me to make the best of it and try and make it look nice. I was gutted.'

At the house, Gary took James through the chords of his first song, The Beatles' number one 'Ticket To Ride'. James thought it was too slow but Gary told him he liked it like that. On the day of the show there is a complete dress rehearsal when every act performs their song but there is no filming. Gary was watching with his pal Eliot Kennedy, who had joined the show in charge of talent development, and told James he really liked his performance and everything should be lovely.

James was very happy with his 'perfect' run-through and pleased that his mum was coming down from Widnes. Gary had offered to put her up in a hotel so she could be there to support her son. Just before James went on stage, however, they showed a video clip of his little sisters and brother. He was completely thrown, 'It choked me up before I went on. I hadn't seen them for two months and it was dead sad. They didn't warn me they were going to do that.'

Each of the judges had to ditch one of their own acts during the first results show and Gary chose to lose James, who observes, 'He sent me home, not the public. You don't know whether it was up to Gary. Nobody knows. It may have been the highest of the high or the producers or someone might have said to put Frankie through. You don't know. I was gutted.

'Afterwards he came up and said, "You've got to realize it's just a

TV show and it's all for entertainment but you are going to be fine. I think you are really talented." I said, "Cheers, Gary."' James tried to contact him on Twitter after the series had finished to speak about some new songs he had written but discovered that he had been unfollowed.

Gary was able to combine his role on the show with other projects. *The X Factor* is one of those British institutions that you can use as a tool to enhance other areas of your life. Gary understood that. He used his new television fame to promote his charity work. He organized the biggest charity concert since Live 8 called *Children in Need Rocks Manchester* at the Manchester Arena in November 2011. It was his second concert for the charity after his Royal Albert Hall event in 2009.

He secured Coldplay – his 'favourite band, lovely guys' – to top a bill that included Lady Gaga, Michael Bublé, JLS and Snow Patrol. Gary sang 'Back For Good' just before Coldplay came on to close the show. The concert raised £2.5 million for the annual BBC appeal.

Not everything he touched turned to gold, however. He co-wrote with John Shanks the final Westlife single 'Lighthouse', which turned out to be their worst-ever performing record, reaching a lowly thirty-two in the charts. That disappointment didn't prevent Gary from winning a special *Q* magazine award as Classic Songwriter – a reward for two decades of hits. He commented, '"Back For Good" would be my personal Classic Song from all those I've written.'

Gary didn't sing one of his own compositions when he duetted with Marcus Collins in the final of *The X Factor*. They sang the Billy Joel standard 'She's Always A Woman'. Gary stayed restrained but his easy, immaculate tone and style contrasted with Marcus's less experienced vocal.

In the end Marcus finished second to the girl group Little Mix, who had been put together by the producers during the show and had built strong momentum. Marcus had been consistently good for the entire series but was overtaken in the home straight.

Perhaps Marcus might have won if he and Gary had chosen a more dramatic duet. In the week of the final show, for instance, Marcus had been sensational performing 'Lately' by Stevie Wonder at Gary's concerts at the Royal Albert Hall. Gary didn't sing but accompanied him on the piano and beamed appreciation at his interpretation.

The two gigs at the Royal Albert Hall were Gary's first important solo shows for twelve years. They raised more than £400,000 for The Prince's Trust. After opening with 'Greatest Day', 'Reach Out' and 'Open Road', he told the audience, 'My second album was so successful, I decided to have seven years off.'

22

Sing

The Queen had only one condition for Gary when she first met him to discuss her *Diamond Jubilee Concert*: 'Don't make it too long,' she instructed her loyal subject. Gary is enthusiastic about the Royal Family and a great believer in traditional values. His audience with the Queen was very brief and to the point. He explained, 'It was a really quick "How do you see this evening?" conversation.' He completely agreed with her about its duration: 'The idea of sitting in a seat for four hours is not fun.'

He had first been approached about organizing the concert in 2009 after *Children in Need Rocks the Royal Albert Hall*. He had readily agreed and promptly put it on the back burner. 'It felt like miles away,' he confessed. At the beginning of 2012, the realization had set in that he was responsible for one of the biggest public celebrations of recent years, possibly outstripped only by the Olympics – and he was due to take part in the Closing Ceremony for the Games as well! To top all that, he was going to be a father for the fourth time at the end of August.

The idea for the royal concert was to present a selection of artists that would span the Queen's reign, or at least most of it. The four knights, Cliff Richard, Tom Jones, Paul McCartney and Elton John, were quickly signed up and joined by Dame Shirley Bassey to form the core of the event. Gary admitted, 'This concert is the biggest thing I have ever done.'

It wasn't as easy as merely acting as a booking agent. He had also been asked to write a special Jubilee song with Andrew Lloyd Webber. It was the second important artistic event of the year for Gary. The first was the West End debut of his daughter, Emily, aged nine. She was a Munchkin in a special performance of *The Wizard of Oz*, produced by Lloyd Webber, to mark stage star Michael Crawford's seventieth birthday.

To prepare for the Jubilee song, Gary asked Prince Charles about the sort of music the Queen liked and the prince had passed him six top-secret CDs from the royal collection. Gary would be sent to the Tower if he revealed what Her Majesty had on her iPod. More importantly, Charles stressed that the Queen took most pride in the Commonwealth and that she wanted as many people from around the world as possible to be involved.

Gary hit upon the idea that after he and Andrew had composed the basic melody and framework of the song he would tour Commonwealth countries to find musicians to take part and he would record them. It would be like a Michael Palin adventure – *Around the World in Eighty Chords*.

Gary travelled over to Andrew's magnificent mansion, Sydmonton Court, in Berkshire in January to work on the song. The two great men of English music sat at separate pianos in the music room. Andrew explained to Radio 2 how it went: 'We got together with embryonic ideas. Gary had an idea for the chorus and I had the idea for the verse. I was thinking "anthem", but we had to involve all the people we could, and it had to be something very simple that people could learn. Working with Gary has been one of the great joys, he is such a fantastic songwriter; it was a completely new experience.'

Gary's portable studio for his Commonwealth adventure was a laptop computer, a microphone and a pair of headphones. He began at Treetops in Kenya, where the then Princess Elizabeth had been staying with Prince Philip when she was given the news in February 1952 that her father had died and she was now Queen. 'I drove there and I wrote the lyrics sat under this lovely tree, which I thought was quite a nice bit of symmetry. She started her reign there and we started our record in that place. That was beautiful.'

The words were simple enough – 'Sing it louder, sing it clearer' – so that the people he met could learn them quickly. The song is all the better for not being a pale imitation of 'God Save The Queen', nor is it overly sentimental. It is an anthem of jubilation for a Jubilee. He had to be careful to make sure the overall effect wasn't too loud or too modern. Prince Charles had warned him that if it was, the Queen was not going to like it.

His travels were filmed by the BBC for a documentary entitled *Gary Barlow: On Her Majesty's Service*, directed by Ben Winston. His adventures were touching and hilarious. Gary bore no relation to James Bond as he looked aghast when his canoe in the Solomon Islands was set upon by spear-brandishing natives. They seemed angry, but it was, in fact, a traditional greeting for the lad from Frodsham. The South Pacific islanders prepared a banquet in his honour: papaya and melon to start, roast pig for main course and delicious coconut milk to drink. Gary's nutritionist would have approved. They also gave him a necklace that meant he could take any of the women and marry them. He observed, 'I didn't tell Dawn about that.'

He recorded slum drummers in Kibera, a deprived suburb of Nairobi, pan pipe players on the Soloman Islands, an indigenous singer in Australia and Rastafarian drummers in the Jamaican Blue Mountains. In all, he recorded 258 people, including Prince Harry, who is very photogenic and good fun on these occasions. Harry was worried he was going to have to sing but Gary reassured him he would only need to play the tambourine.

Despite almost being marooned when a cyclone hit the Pacific,

Gary was back in time to attend the Ivor Novello Awards at the Grosvenor House Hotel when Take That were honoured for their Outstanding Contribution to British Music. It was Gary's sixth Ivor, although he made a point of saying that the songwriting duties were 'a team effort now'.

He needed to go straight back into the studio to finish production on 'Sing' with his old friend Eliot Kennedy and Ryan Carline, the engineer on *The Circus* and *Progress*. Fittingly perhaps for such a patriotic project, the Military Wives sang on the track. Their founder, Gareth Malone, joined Gary and Andrew at the beginning of May to play the finished song for the Queen. It was the most nerve-racking aspect of the whole project.

Gary managed to avoid blurting out the big question 'Did you like it, ma'am?' It was clear from her reaction that she did. Instead, he was delighted that she took such an interest in the work that went into the recording: 'Part of my job was to tell Her Majesty about all the different people from different walks of life who I met along the way. She was clearly touched to see the time and effort people had put into this for her and we were thrilled she enjoyed it so much. It was lovely . . . Despite it being her Diamond Jubilee the last thing she wants is for anyone to put themselves out for her.'

Gary's royal progress hadn't finished. 'Sing' went to number one on the charts after its release at the end of May, just in time for the Jubilee concert itself. A seven-track album, also called *Sing*, which included versions of 'Here Comes The Sun' and 'Land Of Hope And Glory', topped the charts the same week.

At his very first meeting about the Jubilee concert at Buckingham Palace, Gary had looked out of the window, gazed across at the Victoria Memorial and decided that it would be the perfect place for the stage, with the Palace looming behind as a regal backdrop. Not everyone was pleased with that choice. A week before the event he was stuck in a traffic jam nearby and asked the cabbie if there was any way round it. 'Nah,' came the reply. 'Some twat decided to build a stage here.' Gary slumped back in his seat and said, 'Yeah, I can't believe it.'

Seventeen million were watching the television on 4 June when, after a fanfare from the Coldstream Guards, Rob opened the show with his timeless 'Let Me Entertain You'. About 12,000 lucky people were able to watch the concert from an enclosure by the Palace, while a further 500,000 gathered in the Mall and St James's Park. It was a momentous occasion, even if musically a little patchy. Andy Gill in the *Independent* somewhat wearily wrote, 'One old stager after another came on to do a medley of their hits and elicit a whoop or two from the audience, climaxing with Paul McCartney's headlining stint.' He thought Stevie Wonder was the outstanding performer of the night. The American star would surely be knighted by now if he were British.

Gary sang a duet with Cheryl Cole of the plaintive 'Need You Now', the Grammy Award-winning hit from American country music trio Lady Antebellum. Gary can't do 'Back For Good' all the time but perhaps he was being unduly modest in not going solo and giving the enthusiastic crowd one of his own great songs. They both looked a million dollars – Cheryl in a black flamenco dress and Gary in an immaculate dark suit – but he seemed much more comfortable than she did singing to a large crowd. The *Mail on Sunday* said he 'blundered' by joining her on an indifferent song.

Gary was back on stage later for the live premiere of 'Sing'. Andrew joined him to play piano and Gareth Malone conducted the Military Wives, who looked elegant and glamorous for their big day. The slum drummers were there, as well as Australian musician Gurrumul and the African Children's Choir. More than two hundred people crowded onto the stage, with its striking canopy in the shape of a crown, and Gary proudly introduced them as 'The Commonwealth Band'. He said simply, 'We are going to sing "Sing".'

The soloist from the Children's Choir began the verse, while footage from the Queen's reign flickered on a screen behind the stage. The crowd cheered and the overall effect was uplifting, which was exactly the purpose of the whole event. Gary couldn't stop smiling – a mixture of happiness and relief.

At the conclusion of the concert, Prince Charles made the official speech and received a burst of applause as he began, 'Your Majesty, Mummy, I'm sure you would want me to thank on your behalf all the wonderful people who have made tonight possible. All the performers, the artists, the musicians, the comedians who made such jolly good jokes, Gary Barlow for making the whole thing possible.'

Afterwards, Gary escorted the Queen backstage as she was introduced to the many artists who had performed. He then walked her to her car: 'I had a few moments with her, just me and the Queen.' She subsequently sent him a personal letter to say well done. He observed, 'She really enjoyed it.' On 16 June 2012, he was awarded the OBE for 'services to the entertainment industry and to charity'.

It doesn't get much better than this.

Gary was asked by a journalist if in honour of the Jubilee he was going to name his new baby after the Queen. He answered that his daughter Emily already had Elizabeth as her middle name. Instead, they had decided their fourth child would be called Poppy.

On 7 August 2012, he issued a brief and heartbreaking statement: 'Dawn and I are devastated to announce that we've lost our baby. Poppy Barlow was delivered stillborn on 4 August in London. Our focus now is giving her a beautiful funeral and loving our three children with all our hearts. We'd ask at this painful time that our privacy be respected.'

A charity fund was immediately set up by fans to raise money for the stillbirth and neonatal death charity Sands. His friend Andrew Lloyd Webber echoed the thoughts of many when he wrote on Twitter, 'Dearest Dawn & Gary, Madeleine & I are devastated about news of Poppy. Our thoughts & prayers are with you and your family.' Gary responded to the enormous number of condolences, 'Your kind words and lovely messages are overwhelming. Thank you.'

Poppy's death occurred eight days before Take That were due to perform at the Closing Ceremony of the Olympic Games. There was much speculation about whether he would be able to join his bandmates. Nobody knew what he was going to do right up until the moment when his voice rang out into the stadium, 'You light the skies up above me.' The lyrics to 'Rule The World' were unutterably poignant but somehow still joyous.

Gail Walker in the *Belfast Telegraph* described it as a 'moment of raw emotion'. She added, 'It took great courage to perform at all. That he dominated the stage with his sheer professionalism was a tribute to his talent. And dignity.'

Gary will not talk or answer questions about Poppy. It is the line that he will not cross between his private and public life.

Gary's second series of *The X Factor* returned to the television screens six days after the Olympics' Closing Ceremony. Following such an exciting summer for the UK, the launch of the reality show seemed an anticlimax. The public clearly agreed because the ratings of the first programme were the lowest since 2006 and they were consistently disappointing throughout the series, falling well below its BBC rival, *Strictly Come Dancing*.

The early audition rounds and Boot Camp had already been filmed so Gary didn't have to face a live audience until October. The auditions showed him a great deal more relaxed than during his first season, happy to be filmed being grumpy at the lack of talent on display.

When one dire girl group asked, 'Can we do it again?' he responded abruptly, 'No, we don't want to hear *that* again.' Irritated that one boy band looked bored, he told them, 'This is the chance to change your life and it's like you're stood at a bus stop.'

He received the news via a theatrically filmed telephone call from Simon Cowell that he would be mentoring the Over 28s, traditionally the joke category looked after by Louis Walsh. Trying to breathe some life into it would be a challenge to say the least.

The first piece of new filming he needed to do after Poppy's death was Judges' Houses. He called off travelling to Mallorca, preferring to stay closer to home to be with his family. He told producers to find an alternative venue for him, and they chose Boughton House, a splendid country house near Kettering in Northamptonshire. It may not have been the Hollywood Hills but it was a lovely stately home.

Gary asked Cheryl Cole, who had left the show after the 2010 series, to be his guest judge. He told the *Daily Telegraph*, 'I thought, it's probably going to be a no, but I'll ask her anyway, and she came back saying, "I'm not bothered about the show, but if you want me to do it, I'll do it for you." . . . It was a bit like having royalty, even all the crew were going, "Ooh, I can't believe we've got Cheryl."'

The lady herself arrived in superstar fashion by helicopter and her presence diverted attention away from Gary who, in any case, was his usual professional self. They chose Kye Sones, Melanie Masson and the glamorous country singer Carolynne Poole, who had just missed out at Judges' Houses the previous year. He didn't at this stage choose Christopher Maloney but nominated him as his wild-card choice. The public then voted him through to the live shows.

The ninth series of *The X Factor* was quite lacklustre. The ravishing American singer Nicole Scherzinger impressed with her vivacity and good humour but the majority of the controversial moments involved Gary, who gave the show light and shade.

On the very first live show Carolynne was in the final two alongside Rylan Clark from Essex, who had a big personality but a very modest voice. After a sing-off, Louis got himself in a tangle and ended up sending the decision to deadlock. As a result of the public vote, Carolynne was out, much to Gary's disgust. He stood up and stormed off the set, shaking his head. It was TV pantomime but did illustrate Gary's *X Factor* dilemma of credibility versus entertainment.

Kevin O'Sullivan believes Gary's upset was real, 'I don't think there is any doubt that it was a sign of his genuine frustration on increasingly realizing the true nature of the show. Gary thought he would have Rylan in and out within a couple of weeks but Cowell and the gang wanted him to be there forever. And he pretty much was. Musically, it was outrageous that the guy survived more than a week. He just couldn't sing.'

Gary didn't have any personal animosity towards Rylan, whose popularity with the public continued after the show, when he won *Celebrity Big Brother*. Their barbed on-screen banter made such an impression that they were named Comedy Double Act of the Year at *Loaded* magazine's LAFTA Awards. One of their exchanges won Best Joke:

Rylan: I used to be in a Take That tribute band.
Gary: I hope you weren't me.
Rylan: Naa, I was too skinny to be you.

Gary got up from his chair in mock indignation, as if he were going to sort out the upstart. It was good, knockabout fun. In the end Rylan survived until the quarter-finals, so Gary couldn't go on being annoyed by his presence on the show week after week.

Gary's most memorable moment of the series, however, involved a spat with his fellow judge Tulisa in week four. Tulisa, who sat next to Gary, started criticizing his act Christopher Maloney: 'Gary, how many of these eighties' classics are you going to let him keep destroying . . . You do the same thing over and over again with him and it's not working.'

Gary, half smiling, said, 'Tulisa, I don't know what's offended me more: what you've said or the fag ash breath.'

The look of open-mouthed shock on her face was priceless.

Kevin O'Sullivan observes, 'The fag ash thing was a sign he wears his heart on his sleeve. He is not dishing out fakery. But this is his mistake because *The X Factor* is about dishing out fake. It's all deceptive.'

Tulisa did respond, 'Just a note for Gary. Lay off the red wine because I can really smell that as well.' But the damage had been done with his first blow. He later apologized to her on *The Xtra Factor* and admitted he had enjoyed a 'little sip' of wine in his dressing room. The incident certainly livened things up.

Gary had to spend much of the series defending Chris, whom the media hated but the public loved. Despite being labelled bland and boring, he received most votes in each of the first seven shows, and probably surprised Gary by doing so well in comparison to the rest of his category. Gary said, 'He's had the most criticism out of everybody. I only know what I see. For me, he's really easy to work with. Whenever I'm around him, he's the loveliest, sweetest man ever.'

The same week, however, Gary revealed his true musical feeling when he told the brilliant James Arthur after he sang 'Can't Take My Eyes Off You': 'Putting my category aside, and I probably shouldn't say this, I want you to win it.' He added that he loved everything about the artist: 'If I was at home right now, I would be voting for you.' The following week James achieved a higher public vote than Chris for the first time.

In the final, Gary and Chris sang a duet of 'Rule The World' but it didn't have the magic of the Olympics. He didn't win but finished a respectable third, while James beat Jahméne Douglas to the title.

Take That didn't make an appearance in this series but Rob turned up as usual, this time performing a song he had written with Gary, the supremely catchy 'Candy'. They had written it in Los Angeles after the *Progress Live* tour had finished. Rob had come across a piece of Norwegian house music that he liked called 'Eurodans'. Gary loved it, particularly 'the bass line from heaven' and set about reprogramming and reorganizing the track. He took it up to Rob's house, where they finished the melody in about fifteen minutes. So many of Gary's best songs seem to have been written in the time it takes to enjoy a good old-fashioned tea break.

The week after Rob appeared on *The X Factor*, the song became his first number one in eight years and sold more than 500,000 copies, despite not making it on to the Radio 1 playlist. It was one of those songs that sounded like a summer hit despite being released when winter was setting in. Alexis Petridis in the *Guardian* agreed, 'It's so desperate to be a smash hit that it ends up sounding like one of those novelty singles that used to blight the September charts, bought by returning holidaymakers with rosy memories of the hotel disco.'

That may be true but the song seemed to be everywhere for months on end and is arguably Gary's most successful collaboration. It was also his second number one of the year after 'Sing'. Rob's solo album *Take The Crown* went to the top of the charts the same week.

The pair were reunited on stage when Gary was a guest at Rob's O2 concert at the end of November. They sang 'Eight Letters' and 'Different', another track from the album that they had composed together in Los Angeles back in 2010. A few days later Rob returned the favour at the Royal Albert Hall, when they again sang 'Eight Letters' but this time performed 'Candy' together.

Gary's concert was part of his first nationwide solo tour for thirteen years. He played twenty-five gigs, beginning at the Bournemouth International Centre on 13 November and ending at the O2 Apollo in Manchester on 20 January 2013. Originally he had planned just sixteen concerts but the demand had been so high that more dates were added. They sold faster than both the Rolling Stones' London gigs and Rob's solo concerts, which must have given Gary some quiet satisfaction.

It was like a victory parade after a year in which he had achieved so much professionally. Reviewers cheered almost as much as his adoring fans as he performed a selection from two decades of hits. The *Bournemouth Daily Echo* simply said, 'Gary can do no wrong'.

On the day of his concert at the Edinburgh Playhouse, 21 November, he went to Buckingham Palace to receive his OBE from the Queen. He wore a pale grey morning suit, chatted respectfully to Her Majesty and said afterwards that he was 'deeply proud'. Some commentators had suggested that a knighthood would be coming his way after the Jubilee success but he is too young for that accolade.

The OBE is really the start of his progress to becoming Sir Gary. Cliff, Elton, Tom and Macca were all MBE, OBE or CBE before becoming knighted. They were also considerably older. Cliff Richard was the first pop star to be knighted, aged fifty-five, in 1995, and Elton was fifty-one in 1998, so Gary needn't worry it has passed him by for at least another ten years.

The one hiccup to his serene march to that achievement was the controversy about his tax affairs. He was alleged to have joined Howard, Mark and their manager Jonathan Wild in investing at least £26 million in a perfectly legal offshore tax avoidance scheme. A Labour MP called for Gary to hand back his OBE but the Prime Minister, David Cameron, refused to criticize his celebrity supporter.

Taking advantage of loopholes to reduce tax liabilities is a hot political subject and Gary's reported involvement will probably have to be long forgotten before the Queen taps him on the shoulder. Other than that, he couldn't have had a better year. The *Independent on Sunday* said nobody had fared better than Gary from the Jubilee experience. David Thomas concluded, 'To be a National Treasure is to have a sort of invisible knighthood. Gary Barlow is now in definite Treasure territory.'

He can only continue to do what he's been doing: expanding his position as a grand figure of British songwriting and embarking on high-profile charity work. In April 2013 he travelled from Land's End to John o'Groats in a pink Rolls-Royce, alongside Chris Evans, Professor Brian Cox and James May from *Top Gear*, to help raise £1 million to combat breast cancer. Gary was the cook.

He announced that he was closing Future Records to have more time to spend with his family. He explained to the *Daily Telegraph* how crucial his home life was and how he wants his children to grow up in a happy environment: 'I love to be at home. I love to cook. I love to make sure the whole house is pristine. I love to organize the whole sanctuary of our home. And it marks what I've done, what I've achieved.'

Future Records could at least claim to have discovered one potential superstar. The Sierra Leone singer A*M*E was signed and nurtured by Gary, whom she called 'Uncle G'. At the other end of the musical spectrum, he teamed up with Agnetha Fältskog, the legendary singer from Abba, for a duet on her comeback album. He co-wrote the song 'I Should've Followed You Home' and hoped to persuade the notoriously reclusive star to join him to sing it live.

He had spread himself very thinly in 2012 but showed no sign of slowing down in 2013. He announced in June that he was going to help write a stage musical of the hit film *Finding Neverland*, a version of the *Peter Pan* classic. This sort of venture might enable him to become more like an Andrew Lloyd Webber figure in years to come. It could also lead to greater international recognition if, as intended, it ends up on Broadway thanks to the involvement of Hollywood film magnate Harvey Weinstein. Gary could end up cracking America after all, but not as a pop star.

He agreed to return as head judge on *The X Factor*, reportedly earning more than £1.5 million for this tenth series of the show. He doesn't need the money – his current wealth in *The Sunday Times Rich List* is estimated at £60 million – but why turn it down? Kevin O'Sullivan observes, 'I think he is hooked on it and it has taken him to the next level in terms of "star" profile.' Overall the show probably needs a better standard of contestant.

Gary's standing in British music was recognized when he was awarded the MITS Award at a charity dinner for the Brit Trust and Nordoff Robbins at the Grosvenor House Hotel on 5 November 2012.

Elton John made the presentation. Paloma Faith sang 'Back For Good'. Rob was there to sing 'Candy' with Gary perched at the piano. Howard, Mark and Jason came on to perform 'Shine' with him. They all sang 'Never Forget'. It was a relaxed reunion.

A succession of famous names and friends paid tribute to him. Tulisa said he was funnier off screen than on; Caroline Flack observed how laidback he was; and his pal Jason Donovan called him the 'greatest songwriter, musician and band member' in the country. Prince Charles, who was on a Jubilee tour abroad, spoke by video link, 'Over the past twenty-five years, you have become one of the great stars of the British music industry and you are the very embodiment of that rare species, a "National Treasure".'

Elton John was to the point. He described Gary as a wonderful father, an incredible songwriter and a brilliant singer. He added: 'You're a man of your word and a truly great guy. If you were gay, I would marry you. It's my pleasure to present you with the award and, bloody hell, do you deserve it.' Gary didn't know that his great friend was going to be there and the two men kissed and embraced on stage. In his own speech, Gary was typically modest: 'I am so delighted and humbled. I wanted to reminisce about the past thirty years. There are so many highlights – I wanted to pick out one or two but I went blank. Nothing seemed clear. No moment seemed more important than any other because I have loved every minute of it.'

Last Thoughts:
A Million Kisses Later

Royal Albert Hall, London, 27 November 2012

It's not entirely a female audience waiting for Gary; it just feels like it. At least there are some blokes on stage, the musicians in his band. They are playing the intro to one of his most famous songs and you can sense the excitement building. Then the man himself saunters on, cool as you like, and shouts, 'Come on!' The crowd goes nuts and he begins, 'Today this could be . . .' and more than 5,000 women sing back, 'the greatest day of our lives!'

This is going to be one of those concerts where the artist doesn't need to do much – the fans are going to sing every word of every song at the top of their voices. The crowd, as one, is standing up, arms outstretched. Gary thrusts the mic towards them and they respond by singing even louder, 'Stay close to me.'

The second song of the night, 'Reach Out', was the opening track of *Beautiful World*, Take That's comeback album and their most successful of all time. In the ten years they had been away, the boy band had grown up. Now they were men and Gary had become cool. He has always been older than his years and when he returned in triumph he had matured, overcome his professional humiliation and emerged as a family man, approaching middle age, who is comfortable in his own skin.

Gary is the George Clooney of the pop world, better looking and sexier as he grows older. He is probably slimmer now than he has ever been and cuts a dapper and trim figure on stage. If *Smash Hits* were around today, One Direction would probably win all the awards just as Take That had in the nineties, but Gary would give them competition in the Best Haircut, Best Groomed Beard, Sharpest Suit and Best Pressed White Shirt categories. He looks immaculate, a far cry from the teenage fashion disaster that favoured disco outfits and an embarrassing eighties mullet.

The banter with the audience is still there: he announces that the Albert Hall is 'officially my favourite place to play in the world' before retelling the whole Take That story in two minutes, inviting the fans to join him for the briefest hint of 'Take That and Party' and 'Do What U Like'. He asks, 'Anybody here phone the helplines?' and when he hears cries of 'Yes', he adds, 'You should be ashamed of yourselves!'

He doesn't take himself so seriously now, recalling his solo albums – 'the cheering fades' – and, in particular, *Twelve Months, Eleven Days*. 'That album sold fifteen copies worldwide,' he announces as if that is a statistic to be proud of. 'If anybody wants a copy, I've got a garage full.'

It's time to sit down at his Yamaha piano and play 'Open Road', which he wrote while still at school. The next hit is even older. The lush saxophone intro gives it away but Gary can't resist a joke: 'It can only mean one song – yes, "Careless Whisper".' It's 'A Million Love Songs', of course, which he composed at fifteen. He's played it so often through the years but it retains all its beauty and power and his performance remains completely effortless.

He conducts the crowd for a slow build-up to the next song, Take That's first number one, 'Pray'. He shows off a few moves of the band's original dance to the track, which is met by a barrage of cheering. The older Gary doesn't need the boys' harmonies because of the accompanying Barlow choir, which seems to consist of the entire audience. This is like being at a football match where the stands clap their appreciation and sing their team's anthem. 'I've still got it, you know,' he says after one more go at the dance.

Just when it looked like it was going to be a concert entirely of Gary's music, he performs 'Forever Autumn', a song written by Jeff Wayne for *War of the Worlds*. Gary sang it for *The New Generation*, the 2012 version of the classic concept album. The original by Justin Hayward is a treasured song from Gary's childhood and one he rates among his top five favourites.

His support act, the bald Brooklyn singer-songwriter Nell Bryden, joins him for an exquisite version of the melancholy 'Like I Never Loved You At All' from *Beautiful World*. The ballads continue with Gary alone at the piano. It's time for a medley – 'not a mash-up', he declares, but a good old-fashioned medley of the kind he perfected twenty-five years ago at the Halton Legion. This time they're all his songs.

After 'I'd Wait For Life', a squeaky voice from the audience shouts out, 'We love you, Gary!' before he launches into 'Love Ain't Here Anymore', which was his cue for some fun with the audience. He encourages, 'All the ladies sing,' and his adoring fans belt out the chorus. Then, 'All the fellas sing,' and the handful of men realize everyone is snickering at their embarrassment. 'There are fellas here!' chuckles Gary before continuing with 'Lie To Me', the only song he plays from *Twelve Months, Eleven Days*, and 'Why Can't I Wake Up With You'.

'Forever Love' finishes the medley and is a song that seems to be getting better with age. Gary has made it clear how much he was influenced by Elton John, but as he gets older he's sounding more like Billy Joel. The American was less theatrical than Elton but just as melodic and that quality flows through these slow songs – a balladeer accompanying himself on the piano with no frills.

Unexpectedly, Gary decides to sing some swing. His excuse for doing this was that he had realized on stage in 2006 that he loved singing. He had barely sung at all for seven years and during the

Ultimate tour with Take That he finally grasped how much it meant to him. He followed the Sinatra standard 'I've Got You Under My Skin' with the Van Morrison hit 'Moondance'. His versions were flawless and reinforced the view that Gary could sing anything, although most of the audience probably wanted him to stick to old favourites. Afterwards, he jokes that he is releasing an album entitled *Swing When You're Thinning*, rubbing the back of his head.

His version of 'Sing' is crystal clear and sweet, with Gary doing a passable imitation of a choirboy. It possibly lacks the impact of the African Children's Choir and the Military Wives – maybe next time he can get some choral support that isn't from a raucous audience.

There was supposed to be an interval at this point but the concert had started late because of a problem with the mains water supply, so the band plays a long instrumental intro to 'Sunday To Saturday' from the *Nobody Else* album while Gary nips backstage for a couple of minutes. He returns wearing a grey waistcoat, which hints at geography teacher, to sing the song in full, followed by another oldie, 'Wasting My Time' from *Everything Changes*.

The title track from that album is next and signals a walkabout. Exclaiming he needs to get closer to everyone, he disappears into the crowd protected by two very large bodyguards. You can't see his head as he is submerged in a sea of good-natured adulation. Nobody tries to rip his shirt off but half the women in the audience get a kiss that makes their night and probably their year. A million kisses and a few gropes later and Gary reappears smiling and unruffled back on stage with a garland of red tinsel around his neck. It is an inspired piece of showmanship.

After this unexpected audience participation, it is time for an anthem, the type of music that arguably has shaped Gary's success as a songwriter. 'The Flood' has a massive chorus that everyone sings while punching the air. 'Patience', which he describes as 'the song that brought us back after all those years', follows before one of the most poignant moments of the night. It's 'Back For Good', a lovely song that has grown old gracefully. The female audience half sings, half chants every word from start to finish. Curiously, they all sound like they are young teenagers again. Perhaps this was always the genius of the song – it provided instant nostalgia.

How could Gary top that? He announces, 'I love this man from the bottom of my heart. Please welcome on stage Mr Robbie Williams.' The roof nearly comes off the Albert Hall from the screaming as the big man strides on. Gary can't stop grinning with delight as the two former enemies embrace. Rob is wearing one of those jackets that seem to be two sizes too small for him. He is also looking knackered after a series of concerts at the O2. It didn't take a rocket scientist to know he would be here because Gary had been his guest a few nights before.

Rob addresses the audience, 'Good evening, everybody. It's a pleasure and privilege to sing for you tonight.' They perform a slightly ramshackle version of 'Eight Letters' with Rob unsure when it's his turn but the overall effect is transfixing. You can't take your eyes off these men. They are like boxers who have gone fifteen rounds bashing the hell out of one another but hug at the end of the bout and say, 'Good contest, mate, fancy a beer?' They seem to be singing to each other. The difference in their styles on stage hasn't changed much over the years, although Gary has far more charisma now than he did as a younger man: he is still note perfect and sincere while Rob strides around the stage demanding attention.

Gary loves performing live and in the programme notes tonight points out that Rob is the only artist he has ever met who says he hates it. For his part, Rob credits the *Progress Live* tour, when he did twenty-five minutes by himself, as being the turning point that made him realize he could still do it. He is notorious for suffering from nerves but they haven't bothered Gary, from Halton Legion to the Albert Hall: 'I'm a bit of a devil for never being nervous. Maybe it's because I believe in what I'm doing.'

The two friends sing 'Candy'. Rob commands the stage, while Gary stands at a microphone happily singing and banging a tambourine. This song is already Rob's third biggest-selling single in the UK and is going to be popular for years to come. They embrace once more before he leaves the stage to Gary for two more of his classic anthems, 'Shine' and 'Rule The World'.

The encore could only be 'Never Forget' – possibly the most perfect last song ever written, a crescendo of clapping, singing and good feeling. Gary's solo concerts give him the rare opportunity to sing some of his own songs that others in Take That have performed like 'Never Forget', 'Everything Changes' and 'Shine'. It would have been interesting to hear his version of 'Babe' but perhaps that song is now indelibly associated with Mark.

He could have sold out far bigger venues than the Royal Albert Hall if he had wanted to but this was perfect. The fans could literally touch him instead of watching a speck on the horizon. He could certainly return here year after year to sell out a couple of Christmas concerts. The girls in the audience tonight will be there – he makes them forever young at heart. I can see it now . . . Sir Gary Barlow's annual concert, 2032.

He has nothing left to prove as a songwriter or performer. These occupations are his preferred drug of choice and he is not going to give them up. The statistics are overwhelming but perhaps the one that will give him the greatest pleasure is that he has written thirteen number one hits. There will undoubtedly be more in the future. I can't think of another songwriter of the modern era who has written so many songs to sing along to – loudly – as Gary has. So how is he different from the confident eighteen-year-old performing at the Halton Legion? As a performer, he still doesn't make mistakes and knows how to engage the crowd. As a man, perhaps he has learned the importance of a little humility and we like him more for it. He needed to fail to find lasting success.

★

Gary

The Set List

Greatest Day
Reach Out
Open Road
A Million Love Songs
Pray
Forever Autumn   *War of the Worlds*
Like I Never Loved You At All

Medley

I'd Wait For Life
Love Ain't Here Anymore
Lie To Me
Why Can't I Wake Up With You
Forever Love

Swing section

I've Got You Under My Skin   Frank Sinatra
Moondance   Van Morrison

Sing
Sunday To Saturday
Wasting My Time
The Flood
Patience
Back For Good

With Robbie Williams

Eight Letters
Candy

Shine
Rule The World
Never Forget

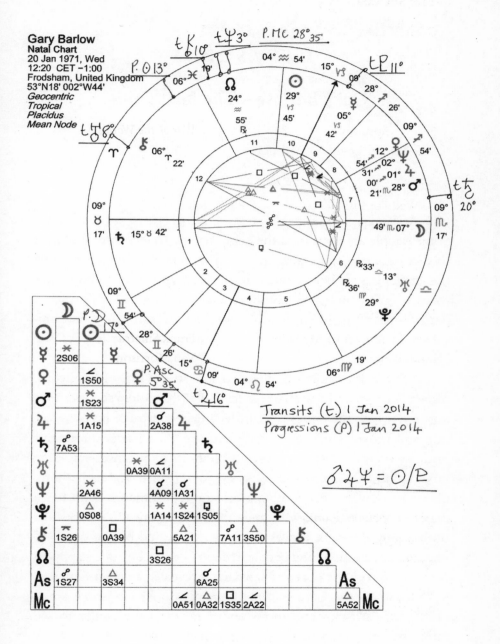

Gary Barlow
Natal Chart
20 Jan 1971, Wed
12:20 CET −1:00
Frodsham, United Kingdom
53°N18' 002°W44'
Geocentric
Tropical
Placidus
Mean Node

Transits (t.) 1 Jan 2014
Progressions (P) 1 Jan 2014

♂ ♃ ♄ = ☉/♇

Gary's Stars

Gary Barlow – The Real Deal

Some people are born with the good fortune to feel comfortable in this world – at ease with the practical aspects of living, enabled by the challenges set before them, inspired by an ideal that motivates them to grow and give to others. Gary has the chart of such a person – a strong, gifted, creative, generous person whose determination is rooted in a sensitivity to limitations and a love of the boundless.

Gary's Sun is in the sober, dignified, industrious sign of Capricorn, placed in an area of the chart associated with worldly success. This position reveals the importance of feeling in control of his own destiny and provides the inner confidence to be a leader. From this promising point, the Sun makes a plethora of positive, sparkling links to other planets, the most eye-watering being with Pluto, planet of power. This combination suggests someone who has a magnetic presence and will rarely treat life lightly. He will instinctively know the right moves to make. Motivated by the desire to understand situations and people in depth, he will be quite happy on occasion to rock the boat and see what is revealed as a consequence.

Thus, so far, there is a picture of an ambitious man who is a natural strategist, with enormous endurance and the ability to see things through. He will do nothing by half measures. As a basis for success, these are important qualities but Gary has greater depths. Between the Sun and Pluto in his chart sits expansionist Jupiter, planet of luck, and imaginative Neptune, planet of all that is boundless. Here is someone who, while prepared to work steadily and honestly towards his goals, needs also to go where angels fear to tread, to hasten to some place where the soul can soar and wisdom is won.

For some this might be risky, but not for Gary. Born with Saturn, planet of discipline and restriction, influencing the area in the chart associated with his home life, he will have been well grounded in reality in his formative years and will remain grounded despite the pull of his artistic drive and creative success. For, while there may have been tests and challenges to overcome in his youth, mostly of a material nature, the planetary picture shows positive influences from both parents.

A Scorpio Moon opposite Saturn suggests an intense, resourceful mother with a strong work ethic. Circumstances may have placed limits on her time so that the young Gary had to grow up quickly. Although she may have found it difficult at times to reach out emotionally, she would have been a communicative parent, combining the ability to think clearly about matters of the world and the heart and encouraging him to embrace the future as well as value the past. Gary would have been very sensitive to her needs, careful not to get under her feet, keen to please. She would have taught him how to squeeze the maximum out of ordinary everyday experiences, to appreciate the importance of material security and permanence and to love his home.

Gary's father embodied many virtues of the traditional family figurehead, accepting his responsibilities to guide and provide with dignity and energy. Large-hearted, he will have enjoyed doing things his own way and would have been good at getting things going. He would have had a positive attitude to authority but would have resisted attempts to be constrained – either in his beliefs or in the home.

Inevitably he would have had periods of frustration, unable to take the steps needed for all his imaginative plans, but his personal charm and kindness would have won him much loyalty.

Gary would have looked up to his older brother in early years, learning from his cautiousness, appreciative of his sense of humour. The family base would have been supportive and steady, enabling the receptive and quietly determined boy to follow his vision – a vision that with four planets at the mid-point between the Sun and Pluto is easy to identify.

The key planet in this 'stellium' is Neptune, planet of transcendence through creativity, of experiences that unite people, of idealism and beauty. It is tightly linked to Jupiter, planet of joy, inspiration and abundance, and this link alone is an indicator of musical talent. Strongly placed in Sagittarius, it is clear that Gary needs to create music that is large, sexy and impressive. It is hard not to emphasize the power of this stellar group placed between the Saturnine Sun and Pluto – planets so involved in the process of creativity, so needed to ground and give concrete form to the abstract ideal of harmonious notes and chords.

A further important observation is that Gary's birth chart is full of positive links and placements, so that the best influence of even so-called 'grim' planets is always called forth. Many challenging links in a birth suggest complexity, personality traits and drives that are at variance and that through the process of integration force maturity and growth. But these negative links, indicative of the 'tortured' soul, waste energy and time. What Gary's flowing chart reveals is a character of profundity and intensity, able to access easily enormous reserves of creativity and thus give form to that which will delight, unite and uplift many people. He will be prolific and he will use his creative and regenerative powers in more ways than one – he is in essence the type who will leave more opportunities than he has found, give more back than he has taken.

But where, for Gary, is the driving force for life and creativity, the arena where wisdom is sought and found? Simply stated – in relationships. Mars, planet of passion, placed in the area of the birth chart associated with partnerships, reveals that Gary will gain intimacy often through confrontational engagement, with closeness won in the ups and downs of battles.

This is partly because, for a person with high levels of self-sufficiency and independence, being close to someone can provoke feelings of anger and insecurity. Yet it is through confrontation that Gary will learn most about himself and for this alone he will invest time and great energy in being with another. He will have learned, quite early on, about his sensitivity to criticism, which he would read as rejection, consequently overreacting. He may also use attack as a form of defence – attack that is subtle but that enables him to remain comfortably in control.

The problem is that while Mars is strong in the sign of Scorpio, it is not well placed in the chart area that demands compromise. Gary could find there are occasions when he has forced issues on the basis of a principle it seems he must uphold at all costs, but the issue may, in reality, be less the point than the winning.

There are other far more positive ways this energy can be deployed and, in the chart of someone born old before his time, someone programmed to learn lessons thoroughly the first time, the likelihood is that Gary will invest in setting joint goals with his partner and attack these with vigour. Huge satisfaction can be gained this way – perhaps establishing a home together, initiating various projects; the more joint activities undertaken, the greater the happiness. Gary will seek someone who is straightforward, bold, who can thrive in a stimulating, lively partnership in which adventures can be sought and journeys made with a degree of personal freedom.

The link between Mars and Neptune throws further light on things. Neptune undermines the drive of Mars and there will have been times when this hard-working man of integrity will have fallen victim to enormous discouragement. There is a clear need here for supportive, committed partnership, which, when met, will allow Gary to give back with great unselfishness, secure and happy to be of service to others. There is also a strong desire to be needed – something that helps build the almost symbolic, and certainly public, image of Gary as a father figure. Whatever way you look at this chart, the picture is one of someone who can carry authority, who can lead, protect, guide, create, teach and bear difficulties with restraint. Gary is an enormously needed role model in a jaded age.

From the playground of relationships, Gary will carry his energy and insights into the workplace, where there is every indication of him being – surprise, surprise – a workaholic. The compulsion to work will be partially driven by the need to establish a solid and successful identity. This will allow him to order his world and from this place of security enable others to feel worthwhile and useful. Here is the man who climbs the ladder and then drops guide-rails down behind him.

Gary is clearly able to communicate well with the world. Given his chosen medium is music, it is evident that this ability will last a long time. Mercury, which rules this aspect of his chart, is in the sign of Capricorn, an indicator that his compositions will ultimately achieve the status of 'standards'. He needs to be emotionally invested in his work and will create a family of colleagues. Power struggles – that he will mostly win – may ensue from that need to lead. Uranus, in the area associated with his work and in the sign of the writer (Virgo), establishes him as someone of original talent, obsessively searching for flaws. This planet makes a challenging link to the chart point associated with career success, warning both of resistance to direction from others – quite a rebellious independence – and of sudden changes.

Looking at the present movement of the planets through the sky and their links with the birth chart, it is clear that since August 2008 Gary has been putting the necessary preparations in place for a future that will now focus more on his external, public world. This was a period of often quite overwhelming responsibility in his working life but the recent progression of Saturn to a position above the horizon in his chart signalled a major shift. Initially there may have been serious problems within close relationships and for the next couple of years he will have to live up to commitments undertaken and promises made. It is in this arena of all official partnerships – not simply that of marriage – that there will be challenges.

One period to note will be April 2014. Gary will experience one of the most important planetary transits, the Uranus opposition, associated with rebellion and the rejection of anything that no longer fits comfortably with the way he see his adult self. Change might be sudden and unexpected and is likely to affect his career and network of friends. There will be a shift in his hopes, dreams and wishes, perhaps, as he decides to detonate his well-respected rise to the top of the pop establishment in favour of some role where he has to please people less. He may also find his involvement with technology becomes greater in some way. What happens in April will affect his professional life in May, when his projects will surprise and please. These following three years are ones of substantial importance for Gary.

All change is loss at some level and at the end of 2014 and continuing into January 2015, the movement of Saturn over Jupiter and Neptune in his chart may dampen his mood. Gary may abandon purely personal ambitions, which might now seem purposeless, in favour of more spiritual objectives. Positively, he will end up with renewed commitment to his goals and this can be a time of decisions that will ultimately prove wise.

In a period of significant transition in terms of life direction and profession, March 2015 is another month that stands out, with Pluto, planet of death and regeneration, reaching the highest point in his chart. During the next two years, the movement of Pluto over this area associated with his public standing will see him questioning the validity of what he has done to date and how he wants to move forward. For someone of such creativity, drive and integrity, and provided his endeavours aren't directed purely for self-gain, there will be opportunities to regenerate and succeed in extraordinary ways.

Can reality be better than a dream? Gary Barlow is the sort to make us think so.

Madeline Moore
June 2013

Life and Times

20 Jan 1971 Gary Barlow is born at 13 Ashton Drive, Frodsham, a large Cheshire village thirty miles south of Manchester. His father, Colin, is a warehouseman at a local fertilizer company and keeps pigeons in the garden.

Sept 1975 Begins at Frodsham Weaver Vale Primary School, a ten-minute walk from home. The highlight of his time there is playing the lead in *Joseph and the Amazing Technicolor Dreamcoat*.

Oct 1981 Watches Depeche Mode perform 'Just Can't Get Enough' on *Top of the Pops* and decides he would prefer a keyboard rather than a BMX bike for Christmas.

Sept 1982 Attends Frodsham High School, where his mother, Marj, is a lab assistant. His friends call him Goose, a nickname given to him by his elder brother Ian, who is already at the school.

Jan 1983 Is in the chorus for Frodsham Panto Group's *Jack and the Beanstalk*. Meets musical director Christopher Greenleaves, who teaches him to play 'A Whiter Shade Of Pale'.

March 1984 Finishes third in his first talent contest at Connah's Quay Labour Club in North Wales. He is hired to be the club organist on Saturday nights for £18.

Sept 1984 Pairs up with Heather Woodall at the Frodsham Carnival and she becomes his teenage girlfriend for four years. Her parents call her Heather Barlow because the young couple are inseparable.

Nov 1984 Takes part in the Schools Prom at the Royal Albert Hall when Frodsham High's Gamelan Orchestra performs. Gary is one of the dancers and wears a sarong. He uses some of his karate moves to appear authentic.

May 1985 Heather and Gary enter their first local talent contest, Starmaker '85. They call themselves Karisma and play a medley of Carpenters songs. They don't win but are named Act Showing Greatest Potential.

Dec 1985 Auditions to be resident organist at the Halton Royal British Legion Club. His mum Marj has to tell the social club committee that he is only fourteen but he gets the job anyway and soon earns £120 a night at weekends. When not playing, he helps call bingo.

Dec 1986 Reaches the final of *A Song for Christmas*, held at the Pebble Mill Studios in Birmingham, with 'Let's Pray For Christmas', which his mum thought too sad.

May 1987 Gary and the Legion's drummer, John Tedford, calling themselves Stax, win a £500 first prize as Greenall Whitley / *Weekly News* Club Act of the Year. Gary puts his share towards new equipment for his bedroom studio. Wins National Schools Make Music Competition with his composition 'Now We're Gone' and records the winning song at Abbey Road Studios in London.

July 1987 Leaves school with six O levels including music, which he passed aged fifteen.

June 1989 Performs his farewell concert at the Halton Legion. His last song at the club is 'New York, New York'. Gigs seven nights a week in working men's clubs, driving himself all over the Northwest in his red Ford Orion.

Aug 1990 Attends auditions for a new boy band at La Cage nightclub in Manchester. Gary had already met manager Nigel Martin-Smith, whom he'd impressed with his songwriting ability, and knows he will be one of the five. He meets the other four performers who would become Take That.

Oct 1990 They appear on the Halloween edition of *The Hitman and Her*, performing a Gary composition called 'Girl'.

Nov 1990 Goes on holiday to Biarritz with girlfriend Nicky but leaves early to go to Florida with Nigel.

Dec 1990 First-ever Take That gig at Flicks club in Huddersfield. They wear leather and perform 'Can't Stop The Music' by the Village People. Gary jokes they were watched by twenty people and a dog.

June 1991 Take That make the notorious video for their first single 'Do What U Like', in which they strip off and roll around in jelly. Gary shows off his new peroxide blond hairstyle.

July 1991 'Do What U Like' is released on Nigel's own Dance UK label and reaches a disappointing eighty-two in the charts.

Sept 1991 Take That feature in a magazine – *My Guy* – for the first time. Sign to RCA Records for a £75,000 fee. Gary is given a £150,000 publishing advance by Virgin Music.

Nov 1991 'Promises', their first RCA release, makes number thirty-eight but stays in the charts for only two weeks, despite extensive nationwide publicity, including *Wogan* and *Going Live!*

May 1992 The band appear at the Children's Royal Variety Performance, where they are presented to Princess Margaret. Gary meets Dawn Andrews for the second time. She had been one of the dancers two years earlier when he made a video as Kurtis Rush performing 'Love Is In The Air'. Take That make their debut on *Top of the Pops* performing 'It Only Takes A Minute'. A week later it becomes their first top ten single.

Sept 1992 Their first album, *Take That & Party*, is released.

Oct 1992 'A Million Love Songs' becomes the first of Gary's songs to make the top ten. He had written it in his bedroom, aged fifteen. Celebrates by buying a bungalow in Bexton Road, Knutsford, and leaves Frodsham.

Feb 1993 Take That win the Brit for Best British Single for 'Could It Be Magic', a cover of an old Barry Manilow song. Go on a promotional tour to New York, where they are photographed larking about in Central Park and Times Square. It was the first of many attempts to make an impact in the US.

July 1993 'Pray' becomes the first of Take That's eleven number ones when it debuts in the top spot. The boys meet Elton John after their gig at Wembley Arena; he gives them a strong warning about the perils of drugs.

Oct 1993 'Relight My Fire' becomes their second UK number one and the first for featured artist Lulu. They top the album charts with *Everything Changes*.

Dec 1993 Take That sweep the board of the *Smash Hits* Readers Poll, winning eight awards, beating their seven of the year before. 'Babe' is their third consecutive single to debut at the top of the chart but hopes of it being the Christmas number one are dashed by Mr Blobby. Gary buys Moorside, a £300,000 house in the village of Plumley, Cheshire.

Feb 1994 Take That perform their now famous Beatles medley at the Brits at Alexandra Palace. 'Pray' wins Best British Single and Best British Video.

May 1994 Gary collects his first Ivor Novello Award as Songwriter of the Year and for Best Contemporary Song for 'Pray'. He takes his mum to the ceremony at the Savoy and is presented with his award by Elton John. 'I was made up,' says Gary.

Nov 1994 Meets Princess Diana when she asks Take That for drinks at Kensington Palace. The next day they appear at her *Concert of Hope* at Wembley Arena.

April 1995 'Back For Good' becomes the band's sixth number one and their biggest-selling single in the UK with sales to date of more than one million. It is also their only top ten hit in the US. Gary decides to buy Delamere Manor in Cuddington, Cheshire.

July 1995 Robbie leaves the band just before the *Nobody Else* tour begins at Manchester NYNEX Arena. The other four carry on regardless. Gary rips off his shirt and sings Nirvana's 'Smells Like Teen Spirit'. *Smash Hits* says the crowd went 'mental'. Dawn is one of the dancers on the tour and they finally get together.

Feb 1996 The *Sun* breaks the story that Take That are splitting and the boys confirm it at a press conference the next day. Helplines are set up to take calls from distraught fans.

March 1996 Gary and Dawn are photographed walking in the King's Road, Chelsea, and are described by the *Daily Mirror* as sharing a 'deep love'. They are already living together. Take That's farewell single, 'How Deep Is Your Love', is number one.

April 1996 Take That perform together for the last time on a TV show in Amsterdam and drop their trousers during rehearsals. Their *Greatest Hits* album goes to number one. Gary has made an estimated £7 million from Take That.

May 1996 'Back For Good' wins Gary two Ivor Novello Awards at the Grosvenor. The day after, he flies to Los Angeles to perform a private gig for his American record bosses. His plane is stranded in Northern Canada.

July 1996 His first solo single, 'Forever Love', reaches number one but is knocked off the top by the Spice Girls 'Wannabe' after just a week.

Aug 1996 Moves into Delamere Manor with Dawn. His parents and brother both have houses on the 60-acre estate. Robbie gives an interview to *Attitude* magazine in which he refers to Gary as a 'clueless wanker'.

Nov 1996 Fires Nigel as his manager by fax and subsequently hires Simon Fuller, the man in charge of the Spice Girls.

May 1997 Meets Prince Charles at a Prince's Trust concert at Manchester Opera House. His debut album, *Open Road*, finally appears and reaches number one but doesn't chart in the US when it is released in October. 'So Help Me Girl' also fails to make an American breakthrough, peaking at number forty-four. Splits with Fuller.

Dec 1997 Shares the stage with Robbie at the *Concert of Hope* in memory of Princess Diana at Battersea Power Station. They don't speak again for nearly eight and a half years. He is named men's Rear of the Year.

Nov 1998 Postpones UK tour because of work on the next album. Performs 'Sacrifice' on stage with Elton John in Manchester.

Feb 1999 Proposes to Dawn over a Chinese takeaway at their London flat. They buy a diamond engagement ring at Tiffany in New York. Plans to marry at Delamere Manor in July are ditched.

June 1999 'Stronger', the first single from the new album, fails to make the top ten. The follow-up, 'For All That You Want', doesn't even make the top twenty despite an appearance on the National Lottery live television show.

Sept 1999 Fulfils a childhood ambition when he switches on the Blackpool Illuminations.

Oct 1999 Eventually his album *Twelve Months, Eleven Days* is released – the title representing the time he spent in the studio recording it. The result is a flop, peaking at number thirty-five.

Jan 2000 Marries Dawn in a private ceremony on the Caribbean island of Nevis. Throws a surprise party for her at Delamere for all their friends and family.

March 2000 Guest stars in the 150th episode of popular TV series *Heartbeat*, playing a hitchhiker, and sings 'All That I've Given Away' in the Aidensfield Arms. Is dropped by his record label, BMG.

Aug 2000 Dawn gives birth to Gary's first child, a son they name Daniel.

Aug 2001 Returns from summer in LA refreshed. Starts working with Eliot Kennedy as True North Music, and subsequently produces and writes for Blue, Delta Goodrem and Atomic Kitten.

Nov 2001 Gary's fan club is closed amid reports he has no future plans for albums or tours – or to do any singing. He is told by his doctor that he is clinically obese.

May 2002 Daughter Emily is born.

Feb 2003 Buys a house in Nice that becomes his young family's retreat. It has three bedrooms, a swimming pool and inspiring ocean views.

Aug 2003 Is back working at Delamere Manor with Mark Owen, who is making a new solo album following his success in *Celebrity Big Brother*. The single, 'Four Minute Warning', is a top ten hit.

April 2004 Talks publicly about the possibility of a Take That reunion while attending a Simon Fuller party at the Royal Albert Hall. Ant and Dec say he would be their dream contestant on *I'm A Celebrity . . . Get Me Out Of Here!*

Aug 2004 Makes a rare public appearance when he and Dawn attend the wedding of friend Mikey Graham of Boyzone in Dublin.

Oct 2004 Co-writes 'Breeze On By', Donny Osmond's first top ten UK hit for more than thirty years.

July 2005 Is caught up in the atrocity known as 7/7 when the Tube train he is on is next to one hit by a bomb near Edgware Road station.

Oct 2005 Meets Jason, Howard and Mark at Cliveden for the last part of a TV special about Take That. They wait to see if Robbie turns up. He doesn't. Puts Delamere Manor on the market for £6.5 million and moves family to fashionable Holland Park, London.

Nov 2005 Premiere of *Take That: For the Record* at the Coronet Cinema in Notting Hill. It is the first time the band has appeared in public together for almost ten years. Nearly six million watch the documentary on television. *Never Forget: The Ultimate Collection* is released and sells 90,000 copies in its first week. The band announces they are re-forming to go on tour. They decide to go forward without Nigel.

Dec 2005 Tickets for the *Ultimate Tour Live* sell out in minutes. Dawn and Gary attend Elton John's hen party in London and Gary sings 'Relight My Fire' with Lulu.

May 2006 Meets Robbie again in a hotel in Chelsea Harbour after Take That play Wembley Arena. It is an awkward meeting but a start.

Oct 2006 Gary's autobiography *My Take* is published by Bloomsbury. His advance is reportedly £1 million but the figure is nearer £600,000.

Nov 2006 'Patience', Take That's first original single for eleven years, tops the charts. The album *Beautiful World* also goes to number one and has since sold nearly three million copies – the most successful of all their albums.

Dec 2006 Sings 'A Million Love Songs' with eventual winner Leona Lewis during the final of *The X Factor*. Her first single 'A Moment Like This' beats 'Patience' to be the Christmas number one.

Feb 2007 'Patience' wins the Brit Award for Best British Single. Follow-up 'Shine' is released and becomes the group's tenth number one.

March 2007 Each of the fifty dates for the *Beautiful World* tour is sold out in under forty minutes. Take That perform 'Shine' for Red Nose Day supporting Comic Relief.

Oct 2007 'Rule The World', written specifically for the movie *Stardust*, is released and becomes the fifth biggest-selling single of the year despite not reaching number one. The *Beautiful World* tour opens at the Odyssey Arena in Belfast.

Feb 2008 Take That are named Best British Live Act at the Brits. 'Shine' wins Best British Single.

Oct 2008 Co-writes 'The Winner's Song' with Peter Kay as part of the comedian's parody of *The X Factor*, *Britain's Got the Pop Factor*. It reaches number two in the charts.

Nov 2008 'Greatest Day' becomes Take That's eleventh number one and last to date. The following week *The Circus* album sells 133,000 copies on its first day of release.

Jan 2009 Becomes a father for the third time when daughter Daisy is born.

March 2009 Despite a bad back, reaches the summit of Mt Kilimanjaro with eight other celebrities. Gary had organized the Comic Relief fundraiser.

July 2009 Lady Gaga is the opening act when *Take That Present: The Circus Live* reaches Wembley Stadium. More than one million people see the tour. Starts his own label, Future Records, to find and sign new talent.

Aug 2009 Meets up with Robbie during a summer holiday in LA and they write 'Shame' together. Robbie agrees to record new songs with the whole band.

Oct 2009 Colin Barlow dies suddenly from a suspected heart attack at home near Frodsham. Gary cancels an appearance on *Children in Need* to support his mum.

Nov 2009 Organizes the BBC *Children in Needs Rocks the Royal Albert Hall* concert, which raises £2 million for the charity. Reunited on stage with Robbie, although they don't perform together. Dedicates 'Rule The World' to his dad.

Jan 2010 Throws a lavish tenth anniversary party for Dawn at the Mandarin Oriental Hotel in Knightsbridge. Guests including

Alesha Dixon, Cheryl Cole and Jason Donovan are treated to several rounds of 'Barlow's Bingo'.

April 2010 Supports David Cameron's School Stars initiative when he joins the Tory leader at a school in Nantwich.

July 2010 It's official: Take That will be a five-piece again for a new album and tour.

Sept 2010 Gary and Robbie perform their duet 'Shame' at the Help for Heroes concert at Twickenham. It reaches number two in the charts the following month.

Nov 2010 The reunion album *Progress* is released and is the fastest-selling album of the century. They intended to rename the band The English for the record but abandoned the idea because it would upset fans.

Dec 2010 Reads a bedtime story about Elmer the Patchwork Elephant as part of the festive programme on CBeebies. Joins Coldplay on stage to sing 'Back For Good' with Chris Martin at a concert in Liverpool in aid of the homeless charity Crisis.

Feb 2011 Take That finally win Best British Group at the Brits. They perform their new single 'Kidz' supported by fifty riot-clad dancers wielding shields.

April 2011 Confirms he is replacing Simon Cowell as head judge on the next series of *The X Factor*.

May 2011 The *Progress Live* tour begins in Sunderland and is seen by 1.76 million people at twenty-seven concerts, including eight at Wembley Stadium. Gary combines concert duties with attending *X Factor* auditions during the day.

Oct 2011 Signs up for Twitter live on *The Xtra Factor* and gathers 300,000 followers in twenty-four hours. Reveals he now weighs less than twelve stone – a weight loss of almost five stone from his heaviest. Wins *Q* magazine Classic Songwriter Award.

Nov 2011 Organizes second *Children in Need* concert, this time at the Manchester Arena. Coldplay top the bill at the event, which raises £2.5 million.

Dec 2011 Plays two concerts at the Royal Albert Hall in aid of The Prince's Trust, his first solo gigs for more than ten years. His *X Factor* act Marcus Collins finishes runner-up to Little Mix.

Jan 2012 Watches daughter Emily play a Munchkin in a West End production of *The Wizard of Oz* to mark Michael Crawford's seventieth birthday.

April 2012 Joins Andrew Lloyd Webber to sing 'Happy Birthday' to the Queen at a drinks reception following Newbury Races.

May 2012 Take That win an Ivor Novello Award for their Outstanding Contribution to British Music. It is Gary's sixth Ivor. Travels around the Commonwealth recording musicians to feature on the Jubilee single 'Sing'.

June 2012 'Sing' reaches number one in the charts. Organizes the Queen's *Diamond Jubilee Concert* outside Buckingham Palace. Gary sings 'Need You Now' with Cheryl Cole. Prince Charles thanks him for 'making the whole thing possible'.

Aug 2012 His daughter Poppy is stillborn. Performs 'Rule The World' with Mark, Jason and Howard at the Closing Ceremony of the Olympics.

Nov 2012 Begins his first solo tour of the UK for thirteen years. Co-writes Robbie's number one single 'Candy' and they are guest performers at each other's London concerts. Receives his OBE for services to the entertainment industry and to charity from the Queen at Buckingham Palace. Wins the prestigious MITS lifetime achievement award.

Jan 2013 Makes a cameo appearance on award-winning comedy show *Miranda* and is snogged by the star, Miranda Hart.

March 2013 Fulfils wish of terminally ill cancer patient by having tea with her in her Hampshire home. Sings 'Back For Good' in the lounge.

April 2013 Joins Chris Evans, Professor Brian Cox and James May, to drive a pink Rolls-Royce from Land's End to John o' Groats to raise money for Breast Cancer Care. The annual *Sunday Times Rich List* estimates Gary's fortune at £60 million, making him the forty-ninth richest man in UK music.

June 2013 Begins his third season of *The X Factor* auditions.

Acknowledgements

One of the best things about starting a new book is not knowing where the story will take me. That's how I ended up in the small Cheshire town of Frodsham on a snowy December morning. It's a great place and proof that you can travel all over the world but still enjoy a welcome much closer to home. Thanks to everyone who helped me in Gary's home town, including Giselle Cropper, Christopher Greenleaves, Glyn Haslam, Dave Mort, Martin Smiddy, Andrew Stanley and Emma Stokes. I wish I'd had teachers like Dave and Martin when I was at school. By the way, Martin is the UK's leading authority on Tarzan and knows everything there is to know about the loinclothed hero – sorry, he won't be my next book!

I want to give a special mention to the Halton Royal British Legion Club, where I spent a brilliant evening. Many thanks to my host, Chris Harrison, for sharing his memories of when Gary was the resident organist there. I managed to track down John Tedford, Gary's drummer from that time. John is now enjoying life in Spain but well remembers his gigs with Gary, especially when they were named Club Act of the Year.

Further thanks are due to Duncan Bridgeman, Max Vickers and James Michael. Since his days as a Take That producer, Duncan has gone on to great things with the concept band 1 Giant Leap –

291

in many ways a prototype for Gary's project 'Sing' with The Commonwealth Band. Watch out for his new movie *Made in Mexico*. He filmed there for two years to illustrate the beauty of that country. Both Max and James have moved on from their *X Factor* experiences and are writing and performing their own music. James is also involved with a terrific Blackpool-based charity called Donna's Dream House, which provides holidays for young people with life-threatening illnesses.

My old friends were as helpful as ever: Kevin O'Sullivan provided thoughtful and amusing insight into the world of *The X Factor*, while Cliff Renfrew was again my guide in Los Angeles.

At Simon & Schuster my thanks to Carly Cook, who commissioned this book and has been so enthusiastic throughout the project; editor Briony Gowlett has offered expert advice and her team of Abigail Bergstrom and Alice Thompson have helped everything run smoothly; Matt Johnson for his cover design; Jo Edgecombe for overseeing production; Kathryn Robinson for publicity; Alice Murphy for marketing; and Rumana Haider, Dominic Brendon and Gill Richardson for looking after the all-important sales.

My agent, Gordon Wise, continues to steer this ship wisely, ably supported by his assistant at Curtis Brown, Richard Pike. I am grateful as always to Arianne Burnette for her stellar copy-editing skills and to Jen Westaway for transcribing my interview tapes. Thanks also to my terrific research team of Emily Jane Swanson and Catherine Marcus; and to Madeleine Moore for another fascinating birth chart.

You can read more about my books at seansmithceleb.com or follow me on Twitter @seansmithceleb.

Finally, thank you to Jo Westaway for her research, her motivation and her cheerfulness – and for getting the beers in after a long day at the computer.

Select Bibliography

Gary Barlow, *My Take* (Bloomsbury, 2006)

Chris Heath, *Feel: Robbie Williams* (Ebury Press, 2004)

Alex Kadis and Philip Ollerenshaw, *Take That In Private* (Virgin Books, 1994)

Piers Morgan, *Take That: Our Story* (Boxtree, 1993)

Martin Roach, *Take That: Now and Then* (Harper Collins, 2009)

Take That, *Take One* (Penguin, 2009)

Take That, *Take Two* (Penguin, 2009)

Robbie Williams with Chris Heath, *You Know Me* (Ebury Press, 2010)

Picture Credits

Sean Smith is the UK's leading celebrity biographer and the author of the number one bestseller *Cheryl*, the definitive biography of Cheryl Cole, as well as bestselling books about Robbie Williams, Tulisa Contostavlos and Kate Middleton. His books about the most famous people of our times have been translated throughout the world. His subjects include Kylie Minogue, Alesha Dixon, Justin Timberlake, Britney Spears, Victoria Beckham, Jennifer Aniston and J. K. Rowling. The film *Magic Beyond Words: The J. K. Rowling Story* was based on his biography of the *Harry Potter* author. Described by the *Independent* as a 'fearless chronicler', he specializes in meticulous research, going 'on the road' to find the real person behind the star image.

www.seansmithceleb.com

Twitter: @SeanSmithCeleb

facebook.com/seansmithceleb

Index

Index

Index

Index

Index

Index

Index

Index